Wrong Place-Right Time; Peacekeeping in Afghanistan, Sudan, Iraq and Somalia

A first hand account of surviving warlords, the U.N. and other hazards

R. Quejas-Risdon

AuthorHouse™
1663 Liberty Drive
Bloomington, IN 47403
www.authorhouse.com
Phone: 1-800-839-8640

© 2011 R. Quejas-Risdon. All rights reserved.

No part of this book may be reproduced, stored in a retrieval system, or transmitted by any means without the written permission of the author.

First published by AuthorHouse   3/14/2011

ISBN: 978-1-4567-1657-8 (sc)
ISBN: 978-1-4567-1658-5 (hc)
ISBN: 978-1-4567-1656-1 (e)

Library of Congress Control Number: 2010918915

Printed in the United States of America

Any people depicted in stock imagery provided by Thinkstock are models, and such images are being used for illustrative purposes only. Certain stock imagery © Thinkstock.

This book is printed on acid-free paper.

Because of the dynamic nature of the Internet, any Web addresses or links contained in this book may have changed since publication and may no longer be valid. The views expressed in this work are solely those of the author and do not necessarily reflect the views of the publisher, and the publisher hereby disclaims any responsibility for them.

Dedication:

This book is dedicated to my family and friends who were so supportive over the years; and to the 1800 plus UN Peacekeepers, both civilian and military, who have lost their lives in the line of duty as of this time.

Contents

Introduction: Grenades With Lunch

Part: 1 The Early Days – Somalia

Chapter 1: First Steps	3
Chapter 2: I meet Mad Max	9
Chapter 3: Life Settles Into a Pattern	15
Chapter 4: Day of the Blackhawk	23
Chapter 5: Road Trip to Nairobi:	29
Chapter 6: A Christmas R&R	39
Chapter 7: Negotiating Under Fire	45
Chapter 8: A Residence With a View	57
Chapter 9: Leaving Somalia	65

Part: 2 Hard Lessons – Iraq, Kuwait and New York City

Chapter 10: Rwanda	71
Chapter 11: The Good Life in the Gulf	75
Chapter 12: Learning the System	81
Chapter 13: Keep Friends Close, Enemies Closer	87
Chapter 14: On the Border	91
Chapter 15: Family Life	97
Chapter 16: Under the Bus	101
Chapter 17: New York New York	107
Chapter 18: September 11, 2001	111
Chapter 19: I pull off Afghanistan	117

Part: 3 Mission Impossible – Afghanistan

Chapter 20: Three Decades to Kabul	133
Chapter 21: Life in the Wild West	141
Chapter 22: Jimmy's House	145
Chapter 23: On to Gardez	151
Chapter 24: Mission Impossible	157
Chapter 25: Peshawar and a Visit to Ali's Arms Emporium	167
Chapter 26: The Ramadan Riot	175
Chapter 27: The Ancient Silk Road to Bamyian	179
Chapter 28: Scorpion House, the beginning of the end	189

Chapter 29: The Last Christmas in Kabul   197
Chapter 30: Out of Afghanistan   205

Part: 4 It Comes Together – Sudan
Chapter 31: Last Tango in New York   211
Chapter 32: An Eventful Stopover in Khartoum   217
Chapter 33: Arrival in Abyei   223
Chapter 34: The Lord Helps Those Who Help Themselves   229
Chapter 35: Duties of the Head of Office   235
Chapter 36: The Show Must Go On   241
Chapter 37: Grass Roots Diplomacy   247
Chapter 38: The White House Special Envoy   255
Chapter 39: A Few Days Off   259
Chapter 40: Building A Retirement Tuko   265

Part: 5 The Case For UN Peacekeeping: Must all good things end?
Chapter 41: My Own Bias   273
Chapter 42: Unique Challenges   277
Chapter 43: The Benefits, Why it is worth it   283
Chapter 44: The Day the Music Died   289

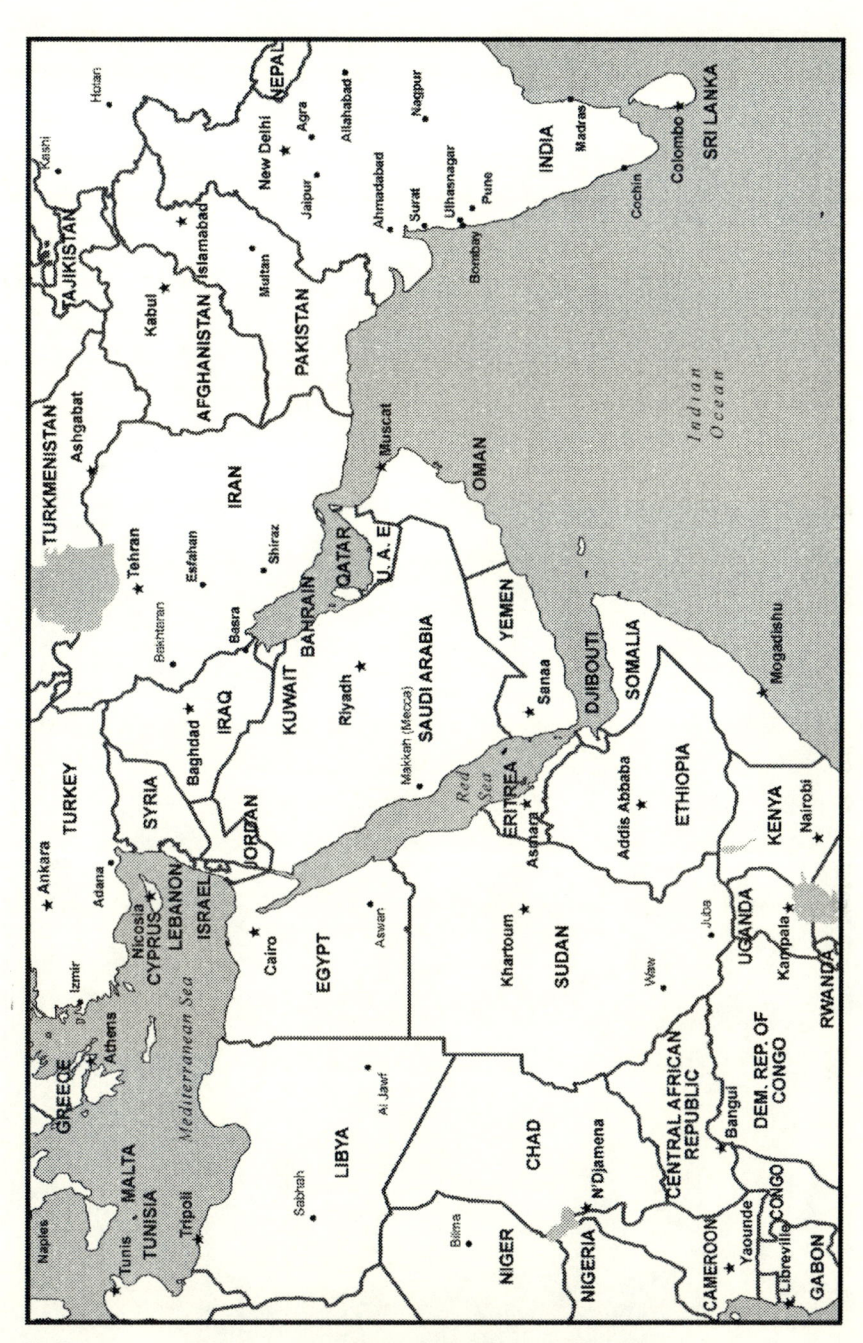

General Orientation Map for North Africa, the Middle East and Afghanistan

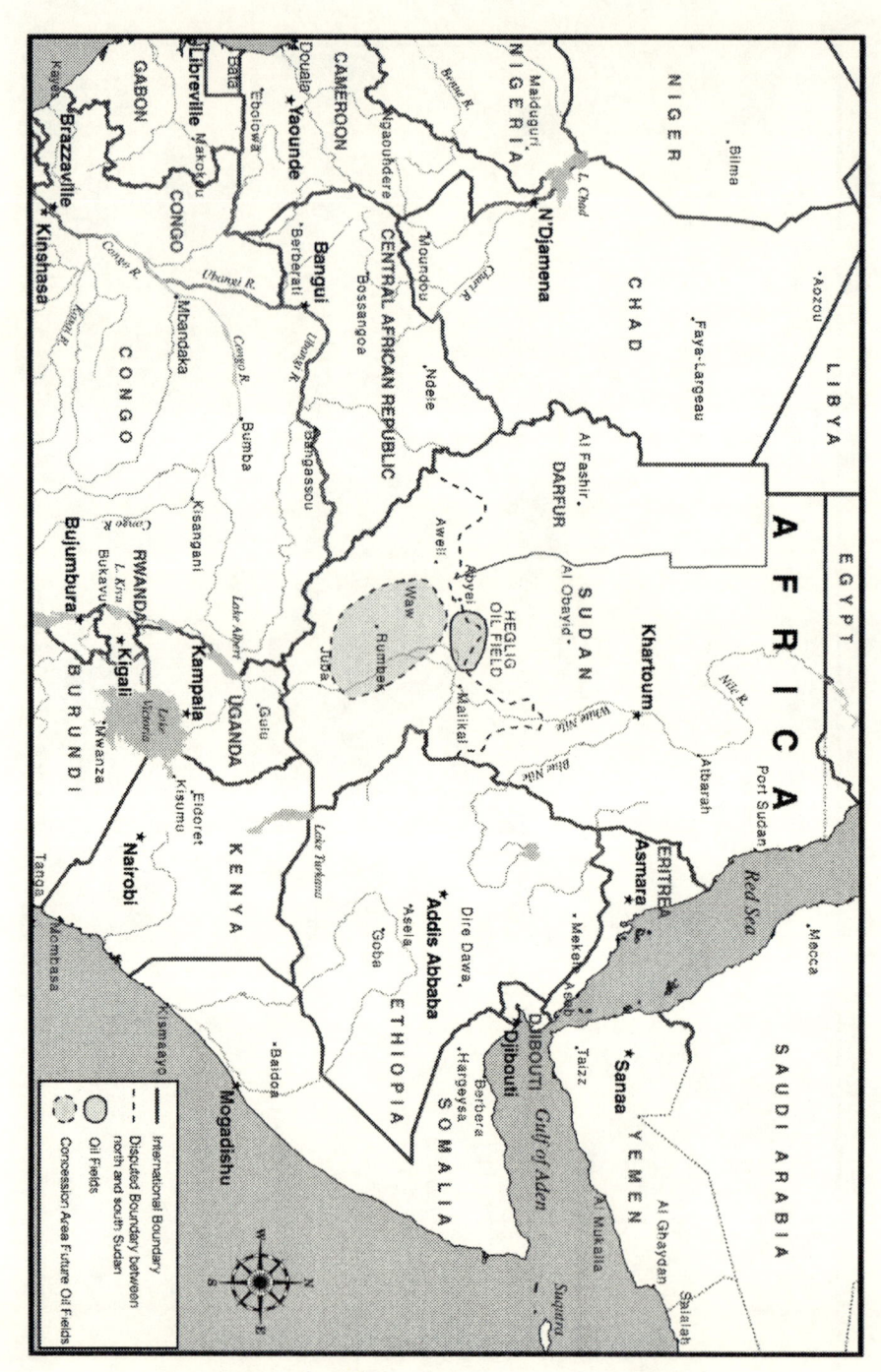

Detail Map for Africa showing Somalia and Sudan

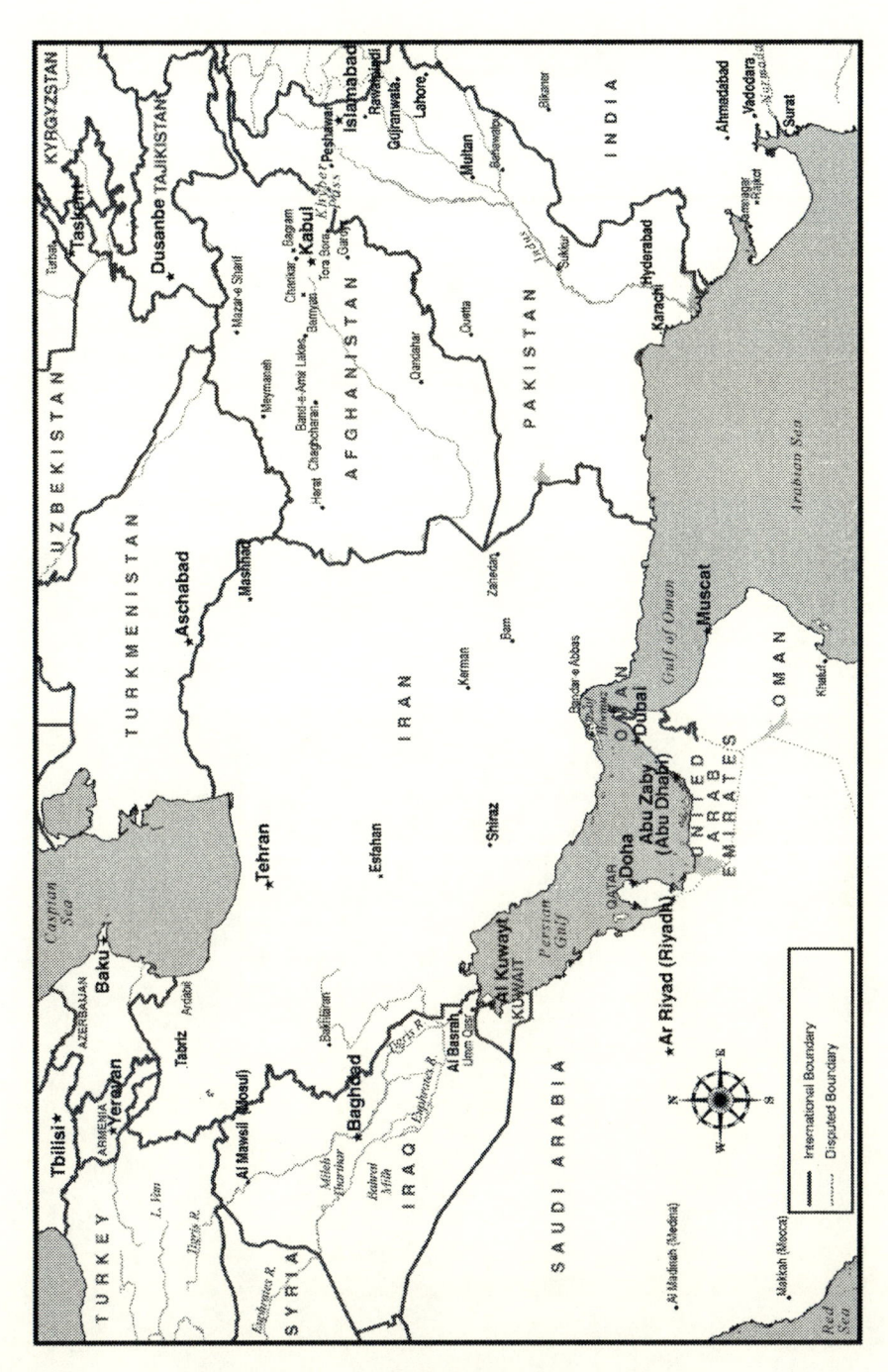

*Detail Map for the Gulf and Central Asia showing
Iraq, Kuwait, and Afghanistan*

Glossary of Acronyms and Terms commonly used in this book:

DPKO- Department of Peacekeeping Operations

UNHQ- United Nations Head Quarters (for DPKO it is part of the Secretariat in New York)

HoO- Head of Office, the highest ranking UN Officer and Chief in a given area. In large missions it may be for a region in smaller missions it may be for the entire operations.

OIC- Officer in Charge. Person appointed on a temporary basis to act as the chief of a section or HoO, or as the most senior officer.

R&R- Rest and Recuperation. Additional leave above and beyond that provided by the regular leave policy, given to staff assigned to dangerous and stressful duty locations.

SPA- Special Post Allowance. A field appointment to a more senior rank, with full authority to act in that capacity. The SPA can be for a short duration or for a period of years, and the individual gets paid at the higher level.

SRSG- Special Representative of the Secretary-General (S-G). Person appointed directly by the S-G to act on his behalf, usually as the head of a large mission or a special delegation.

Force Commander- Chief military officer for a given mission and the person in charge of all military personnel and operations.

CAO- Chief Administrative Officer. As the name implies, this is the officer in charge of all the administrative sections in a given mission. A senior position of considerable power and influence which usually reports directly to the SRSG or other Head of Mission.

DOA- Director of Administration. Essentially the same as the CAO but in a larger mission and at a higher rank.

Section Head or Section Chief. The officer who is in command of a particular function, or section. In the field or mission setting they can be substantive such as Political Affairs, Humanitarian Affairs, Civil Affairs; or administrative such as Finance, Personnel, Communications, Transportation and so on.

UNOSOM- United Nations Operation in Somalia

UNAMIR- United Nations Assistance Mission for Rwanda

UNIKOM- United Nations Iraq Kuwait Observation Mission

UNAMA- United Nations Assistance Mission in Afghanistan

UNMIS- United Nations Mission in the Sudan

Introduction

Grenades With Lunch

Grenades with lunch

Thursday, 23 September, 1993. The UN plane, a Fokker twin engine prop jet dropped down from the Kenya highlands in the cool morning air, executed a slow wide circle over the blue and green waters of the Indian Ocean and followed the shore line north on it's approach to the Mogadishu airport. Finally after ten days impatiently spent in the Imperial Palace hotel in Nairobi (a misnomer for sure) waiting for the final clearance to proceed, five other new recruits and I were about to take up our duties as UN Peacekeepers in what was probably the most dangerous place on earth. Also on the plane were some twenty UN staff members returning from R&R. They were mostly silent, some with looks of grim resolution, some just sleeping. We had been up since O-dark thirty (about 4:30 AM) in order to get to the Nairobi airport at 6:00 AM, in order to wait until 9:00 AM for the delayed flight.

Finally, we were almost there. As the plane descended, we could clearly make out tall stately palm trees scattered along a lovely white sandy beach with gentle waves lapping the shore, along with the remains of utterly destroyed mud and adobe houses pocked with shell holes. Here and there lay the bloated corpses of dead animals. This was to become a familiar sight throughout the Horn of Africa in places like Somalia, Ethiopia, Eritrea and into Sudan. But the first time you see the aftermath of war, especially the effects on the civilians who are caught up in it all, it grabs you in the stomach.

We flew over several miles of this strange landscape before making our final approach. It was as if the scene below us was composed of equal parts advertisements for vacation beaches with palms trees, and posters crying out for humanitarian aid assistance. The last half mile was the weirdest of all. On each side of the runway lay the decaying hulks of planes and helicopters. Some looked like they had been abandoned right after landing, as if the pilot just ran away from it, some like they had crashed, but all of them shot up and cannibalized for parts. Goats and donkeys scampered between the piles of debris and people peered out of a couple of the wrecks as we passed overhead. My God I thought as I realized there were people living in them.

As we taxied to the airport terminal we began to take in the full enormity of this place, and there was a lot to take in. A voice came from the speaker of the plane and said in a slight Spanish accent "Welcome to Mogadishu. New staff members, please remain on the plane for UN Security check." As the door opened the rush of heat was like a pizza oven. It was only a little after 10:30 AM and already it was hot. Two Security Guards in blue uniforms came into the plane, one stocky and about six two, the other thin but tough looking. They each had side arms and an intense look on their face. They advised us to follow them directly to the hanger, don't wander around the airport. Your luggage will be brought into the hanger, where you will be processed and go by convoy to the main UN compound. If they were trying to get our attention, it was working.

The hanger reminded me of a movie set from Mad Max or maybe Apocalypse Now. Rusted sheets of corrugated metal which had pulled loose from wooden beams gently flapping in the breeze, sun blazing through large holes blasted by random rockets and gun fire, backed up toilets and the faint smell of urine wafting through the doors. Somali local staff members dressed in everything from total rags to new t-shirts with "I love NY" logos on them, pushed carts loaded with luggage and boxes from the plane to the check in area. As we retrieved our bags, two international staff members looked at our laissez passer (blue colored UN issued passports) after which we were ushered directly into a waiting convoy.

The convoy consisted of a UN security vehicle with several armed guards at the lead. Next were several Nissan Patrols for passengers, each with a wild eyed young Somalia driver and an armed guard in the front seat. Completing the convoy was a Toyota pickup loaded with our luggage and finally another UN Security vehicle brought up the rear.

As I got into the third vehicle I saw that our Somali guard was armed with an automatic rifle. At a glance I could see it was an old AK-47, one of the most indestructible weapons ever made. Not the most accurate but noisy and effective. The Russians abandoned so many of them when they were thrown out of the horn that it was commonly said there was one weapon for every man woman and child in Somalia. Sitting next to an armed Somali was a bit disconcerting at first, but we soon learned that all of the guards in our housing compounds were members of local tribes that were friendly, or at least indifferent to the UN. Besides, if someone really wanted to kill you in this environment it would be easy. You also learn to trust your gut instincts, not everyone wants to kill you. Admittedly this is a balancing act, but one that successful peacekeepers either have or quickly learn.

*

We roared out of the airport kicking up a long trail of fine sand dust, past two large UN guard posts filled with Pakistani Army guards glaring out from double rows of sand bags. One thing about Somalia, we never lacked for sand to fill the bags. Poking out from slits in the sand bag walls were the barrels of small caliber machine guns and automatic rifles which followed us as we passed. We continued, going far too fast I thought through narrow, rutted dirt streets for about a mile. We caught glimpses of skinny kids, goats and dogs scattering or just staring blankly as we sped by. With a lurch we suddenly ended up on one of the few paved streets in Mogadishu and were pinned back in the seats as we immediately picked up speed. I'm sure the local drivers enjoyed this run, especially with new international staff on board whom they could impress and scare.

Finally after about twenty minutes we reached a secured area where we saw small white street tanks with black UN letters painted on the side (armored vehicles small enough to go between houses and up alleys, have rubber tires and at first glance look like prehistoric animals with pointed snouts). These were provided by the South African troop contingents, and I would guess they perfected them during apartheid. However, we were happy to see them now, as our drivers immediately slowed down. As I later learned, if a vehicle was speeding in this area it was considered a possible attack vehicle and it would likely be fired on, so just as good that we slowed down.

The main UN compound, which was also the former US Embassy compound, was nearly forty acres in size. It was huge, with several permanent holes in the eight to ten foot high fence which ringed the entire area. The locals cut the holes back in each time they were repaired so they could pilferer things, mostly food and water from the warehouses and storage sheds which set near the back of the compound. It was also back in this area that the Canadian Troops would eventually get into trouble for patrolling with a bit too much enthusiasm. The compound was too large to be really secure even though the American Mountain Division and other contingents stationed within the compound tried their best. It was an impossible task and I did not envy anyone for taking on this assignment.

The Turkish Army guards stationed at the compound entrance inspected our vehicles, our luggage and our passes after which we proceeded to the personnel office for in processing. Like most of the other offices, the Personnel office was composed of several of the large prefabricated units commonly used by the UN, that remind one of upgraded white trash trailers. They are usually connected directly to one another or with walkways and set up on blocks or concrete columns to keep out water during the rainy season as well as the many critters that live in such places. At least they have doors, windows and air conditioning, and as time goes by they begin to acquire a lived in look which softens the institutional aspects a bit. Like personnel offices everywhere this one appeared busy and confused. Finally, since it was now almost noon they suggested we go to lunch first. Good idea, I was hungry since breakfast had only been coffee and some kind of bread product.

*

Roberto, a new Logistics Officer recruited from Guatemala and I had gotten to be friends while cooling our heels in Nairobi. My Spanish was better than his English so we spoke Spanglish and got along just fine. He was a street wise, good looking guy and the ladies liked him. We proceeded to the nearest food tent which was run by the Norwegian Army Contingent. Now I have a lot of respect for things Scandinavian (which loosely speaking takes in Norway) and I know they did not have IKEA to work with, but this was a shock.

The tent, at one point in time had screened in walls and screened doors, all of which now had numerous large holes and in places the screen had finally pulled loose. People passing in and out meant the doors were mostly open so the flies had no problem getting inside and helping themselves. And they did. In the middle of the tent, surrounded by a moving cloud of flies was the food table. As a youth I lived on a farm and cleaned many barns, but I have never seen such healthy flies and in such large numbers. However, I was hungry and I did not want to appear to be a sissy.

Roberto grabbed some food and immediately headed for a loud and rather rowdy table of ladies as I took a slice of bread from the middle of the pile. The flies were big but I figured they could not move the bread to get at the pieces underneath. Forgetting my initial hesitation, I grabbed for one of the last slices of cheese (flies be damned). Now, the last thing was to get a bowl of soup. I took a bowl from the table and wiped it out as best I could with a shirt tail and without looking too closely dipped out whatever was in one of the vats and put some in my bowl. Grabbing a bottle of water I proceeded with my tray to an empty table near the door. With the tune and words to "Food Wonderful Food" running through my mind, I opened the water and took a long drink.

As I was about to try the bread and cheese I heard a muffled but distinct explosion off to my right, near the compound wall as I reckoned and only about a hundred meters away. I guessed it was a grenade. About five seconds later another explosion, this time about seventy five meters away, and coming in a direct line toward the tent. Everyone stopped eating and talking, so I assumed it was important. The next one hit about thirty meters away. This time I could clearly feel the shock wave and smell the dust. It was time to leave.

Tearing myself away from the brie and gazpacho, I joined the stampede out the door and didn't stop until I was half way back to the personnel office where I found a bunker and dived into it. The bunker was a large concrete culvert with sand bags pilled up at each end to provide additional cover. Inside there were about ten people huddled near the center. After ten minutes the all clear was sounded and we went on our way.

As it turns out, there was an abandoned hospital located near the compound and some of the disgruntled locals would use the top floors to occasionally lob grenades into the compound. It was a perfect launching pad. Usually, after a few return shots from our guards they would go back to drinking their tea, content that they were keeping us on our toes. This routine was played out several times during my stay and only once did they manage to hit one of the portable units where staff slept. The young lady who occupied the unit had just left for her office. She lost most of her belongings, but if it had been a few minutes earlier she might well have died.

*

As I finally settled into my new quarters that evening, still hungry, I thought back on my first eventful day in Somalia. As time would show, it was the first day of nearly two decades of astounding events. I would go from being a raw recruit to an experienced senior officer in charge of a vital border area of Sudan. During my assignments to Somalia, Iraq, Kuwait, Afghanistan and Sudan I would meet some truly selfless and dedicated people and also encounter some with pure evil. In New York, from the UN Building we would watch the twin towers burn and witness first-hand the reactions of a stunned but resilient city to the tragedy of September 11, and be among the first peacekeepers into Afghanistan afterwards. But most importantly, through all this my family would grow together, and my wife and I would learn the depths of our dedication to each other. I am a lucky man, and this is my story.

While it is all based on true incidents, I have changed the names and some details of the individuals to protect their privacy.

Part One

The Early Days – Somalia

Chapter 1: First Steps

I am told that my recruitment as a UN Peacekeeper took place at a fast pace, and based on my experience with the UN since then, that is so. I applied to an advertisement in the Economist for administrative officers for UN missions in various countries. That was in early May of 1993 and in mid June a former boss whom I had listed as a reference, called me. He said he had just gotten a call from the UN, and was I really dumb or desperate enough to go to Somalia. After we laughed, I gave him an evasive answer about wanting to return to international work, testing the waters and so on. A few days later I got a call from a UN recruiter who asked me a few questions about my background and confirmed my contact details. Still, I did not get too excited as I assumed they were just clearing a list of names for a roster of future candidates.

However, less than two weeks later my wife came in from the mail box carrying a thick letter from the UN Department of Peacekeeping Operations or DPKO. As we read the cover letter, which was an offer of an appointment as Administrative Officer to Somalia, we did not realize how this would completely change the direction of our lives. She was naturally apprehensive but excited. Somalia was a very dangerous place but she had encouraged me to apply for the UN. We both have international backgrounds, I had lived and worked in Latin America before we were married and we had discussed returning to international work at some point. Additionally, we were both strong supporters of the UN and knew how difficult it was to get into this organization.

Lastly, our family was now at a point where I could again accept overseas assignments with minimal disruption. After thinking it over for a couple of days (the salary was excellent), I accepted. From that day on things got hectic as I started getting the necessary vaccinations, buying the recommended field clothes and getting ready to leave. It was an initial appointment of six months. My employer was quite liberal and gave me a leave of absence so we kept assuring each other that if it didn't work out I would return.

Finally, the day arrived and in August I departed for two weeks of orientation before I was to ship out immediately for Somalia. I arrived at UN Headquarters on the East River in New York so proud and excited I felt like I had just won the Nobel Prize. I was told to report to the 24th floor, to a Ms. Kid.

Kid looked up from a pile of files and papers so overflowing that at first I didn't realize there was a desk beneath them. She was a small attractive Asian lady and I could not help but notice her blue shoes impeccably matched her short blue mini skirt. Staring at me and with little expression, she asked who I was looking for. I showed her my letter. She muttered something like "oh shit" and called Becky, one of the many trusted assistants who as I was to learn actually run the UN. Kid said I could sit with Becky and go over the Somalia files, since she dealt with that mission on a daily basis.

Becky's desk sat in the middle of a large open room, along with some twenty other desks and assistants all working on various peacekeeping mission located around the world. There were so many files and folders laying around that they spilled off desks, into piles that filled almost every vacant space. Meanwhile, Becky found a vacant chair and wedged it next to her desk, and using a small space cleared on the window sill as my desk, that was where I was supposed to spend the next two weeks. Several years later when I was brought back to HQ on a temporary assignment, things had not really changed, that was just the way it was.

In addition to the daily faxes we received from the mission (there were very few e-mails in those days) over the next week I read all the policy and operations manuals I could get my hands on. Gradually it dawned on me that I was actually in charge of organizing my own orientation program. So, on Monday morning of the second week, I went for coffee and did not return. Instead I found a UN phone directory and looked up the names of other Administrative Officers and began just dropping in on them. I would explain who I was and that I was leaving for Somalia at the end of the week, and asked them what I needed to know before I left.

Fortunately, one of the first people I encountered was an elderly Indian gentleman with years of UN experience who has remained one of my friends to this day. He is also one of the people that have reached the status of being a legend of sorts in the UN; if I said his name most everybody would know him and have a tale of how he helped them at sometime. I will call him Gupta. Gupta and I spent the next few days reviewing cases from the field, both simple and complex, as he explained how the administrative policies actually work. Policy is very much like law. There is the formal written form and then there is how it is interpreted and applied. The second is the most important to the administrator.

I returned to DPKO on Friday morning and checked out. I don't think they realized that I had been gone but in all fairness, once Kid accepted the fact that I was not simply going away, we developed a good working relationship and I learned to trust her policy interpretations and overlook the indifference attitude.

*

We did not fly directly into Mogadishu, rather to Nairobi, Kenya. There is a large UN compound in Nairobi in which UNISOM maintained logistic and administrative offices. We checked into the Personnel office there and were told we should come back every morning to see if we were scheduled to go on to Mogadishu the next day. We needed to be ready to leave on very short notice, but other than that we were free to go as long as we remained in Nairobi. After seeing the local sights it was boring as we could not really go far. At any one time there were about twenty staff members waiting to go into the mission area and some of us were anxious to get going. Some staff on the other hand, made a career of staying in Nairobi.

One Croatian guy whom I would get to know in later missions, decided to take advantage of this time for a trip to Mombasa where he enjoyed himself for a week on the beach, followed by a safari to Mount Kilimanjaro for another week. When he finally returned they did not seem to know he had been gone. Later, when he finally did report to Mogadishu he became notorious for becoming lost in the compound for hours and on more than one occasion, days at a time. Problem was he was a damned good air operations office when he did work and his skills were in demand. I found him interesting and we became somewhat friendly. I could tell he had been around and I never saw him get very excited about people in authority. He never challenged them, he just worked around them. I learned his tricks and could usually find him drinking a beer at one of several of his favorite places if he was really needed.

At any rate, I finally got my orders to report to Mogadishu and in the introduction section, I have described our arrival. After an eventful lunch, I reported to the Chief of my section, a Middle Eastern woman married to an Italian (I'll call her Happy). Like many of us in the UN, the sharp edges of her native culture had been smoothed off by close and extended contact with other cultures. This is a necessary process if one wants to survive in the UN. With some people the result has a good effect in that they pick up interesting or useful aspects of the other cultures; in other cases they just accumulate more ways to be difficult.

Happy seemed like a mixture. Whereas my reception in NY had been indifferent, this time I was met with a cold stare. To be fair Happy was busy. In addition to training a number of new staff, she was cleaning up the administrative mess left by her predecessor and the last thing she wanted or needed was another UN neophyte to shepherd. As an experienced officer I would find myself in much the same shoes in future assignments.

I tried to explain that while I may not be up to speed on UN policy, I was very professional in my field and could learn the UN spin quickly. That apparently was the wrong thing to say. I think she felt that I was implying she was unprofessional and her stare got a few degrees colder. She suggested that maybe I could be used as a Civil Affairs Officer in Kismayo (out of her way both professionally and actually).

*

In retrospect, this was one of the best opportunities that God handed me and I blew it. If I had agreed then and there to be assigned to Civil Affairs, with that experience I could have arrived much sooner to a destination in my career that instead took me years to reach. My last assignment in Sudan was as the Head of Office for one of the key regions, a position in which I was able to make real contributions and found more satisfaction than in any other assignment in the UN. With the experience I could have gained as a Civil Affairs Officer I would have reached that point much sooner than I did going through the Administrative Officer path.

Happy went back to her work and said I should ask her assistant Alex to help me settle in. Alex was friendly, bright and personable. We quickly became friends and although he is no longer in peacekeeping (but still in the UN) we keep in contact. The only office we could find for me was a converted broom closet, but at least I had a desk, a chair and a computer, and perhaps most importantly I had some privacy.

Alex introduced me around to the other staff in our section, about 30 in all. Most of the staff seemed friendly, but some of them seemed to have the perpetual look of a deer caught by surprise; eyes wide open and apprehensive. As I would find out, they had good reason to be that way. Within a few weeks three of them would be in a vehicle that was shot up on the way home, and one would be evacuated with arm and shoulder wounds that never would heal well.

*

One morning I came in and there was a pile of about thirty resumes on my desk along with a note from Happy. They were resumes for pre-screened certified candidates for senior positions as Political Affairs Officers, and she wanted them summarized and put in some order so they could be presented to the office of the Special Representative of the Secretary General (SRSG) later that week. This was similar to work I had previously performed while reviewing candidates for Police and Fire departments, using a table which made it easier to compare candidates qualifications and experience. Alex had strong computer skills so I gave him a draft of what I wanted and he knocked out an acceptable product in no time.

I proceeded to enter the data for the candidates and presented it to Happy by Thursday morning, in time for her to review it before her Friday meeting. I did not hear anything more about it but it would play a big role.

Chapter 2: I meet Mad Max

Part of my job as a senior officer in our section was to visit other Section Chiefs to coordinate our activities. One of my first visits was to the Chief Transportation Officer (CTO), which is an important position in any mission. Transportation assigns and controls the assignment of vehicles and can help make things run smoothly if they take an interest in you. They can also assign your section the oldest and dirtiest vehicles and while I did not get into all this, I have seen bitter fights erupt over who has the newest Patrol in the unit. I also recall one lower level transportation officer in Sudan who could never quite coordinate a pick up for me when I flew into the Khartoum airport from my isolated location on the north south border. I would be left to find my way as best I could to my hotel, which is not something one wants to do after 10 PM in Khartoum. Finally I met him at a party and we drank a few beers together, after which the situation improved considerably. Like the army, the UN really operates on face to face contact. Who you know is more important than what you know.

The CTO for Somalia at that time was a product of the Australian Army and a very colorful character. Since his name was Max, of course everyone called him Mad Max, a name he both earned and cultivated. His office was in the Transportation Compound which was located near the airport. When I walked into his office the first thing I noticed was an immaculately clean M-16 leaning against the wall behind his desk. There was no clip in it, but I imagine that one was within easy reach in the top drawer of his desk. At first this seemed a bit over the top but I would come to understand why he did this. Transportation, logistics and air ops seem to attract their share of rough characters, or cowboys as they are commonly known, and one cannot appear to be weak in that environment. I would also learn that the roughest of the cowboys do not come from America.

Max and I hit it off immediately as he regaled me with tales of adventure in the military and the UN. Fortunately I have a fairly good grasp of "Aussie speak", which can be nearly as difficult as learning a foreign language. Our meeting ended with him asking if I cared to accompany him on a visit to the site of a proposed transportation garage and compound in North Mogadishu. They had been trying to set up a meeting with the owner of the property for some time and he had just returned from Nairobi. Max thought my negotiation skills might come in handy, so I agreed. I reported back to his office two days later as agreed but he had been called out on an emergency to Baidoa and was sending another officer in his place. Our convoy was to be lead by the Nepalese Army Contingent who had a reputation for being tough. The convoy consisted of two small four wheel drive vehicles. I rode in the first vehicle and Kwamie, a Kenyan Transport Officer rode in the other.

Everything went smoothly until we drew up to the demarcation line separating Mogadishu and North Mogadishu. The line consisted of a highway with a narrow strip of land on each side. It was only about two hundred meters wide but known as a no man's land. Once you started across you could not stop or your vehicle might be riddled with anything from small arms to medium sized machine gun fire, depending on which group was around that day. As long as you moved quickly they did not tend to bother you, at least that is what I understood from the Nepalese officer in my vehicle.

As we neared the highway, the Captain setting in the front seat told me to get down on the floor of the vehicle and stay there. Even though I had on a Kevlar vest and a helmet I did not feel invincible so I did as told. As we came onto the trail and started over the highway and through no man's land, the driver started muttering in Nepalese. It sounded like an eppatith so I assumed he was either praying or swearing. We maintained a steady pace with no problems until we were across the pavement and nearing the other side of the strip, when we heard the crack of small arms fire. I don't think they were shooting at us but I'm not sure as I was too busy hanging on to whatever I could find, trying to keep from being banged into the doors of the truck as we bolted across the strip to relative safety. Once across, everyone had a good laugh and we continued on to North Mog.

*

As we pulled into the North Mog UN compound, we were met by the Head of Office for that district; a large dark woman from West Africa. Sally greeted us all with a huge smile and hand shake followed up immediately with big hugs. She was happy to see us as she did not receive too many official visits, although I do not understand why. North Mog was in a different universe from the rest of Somalia, and although there was indeed fighting between the various tribes and clans, they did not seem as intent on actually killing each other as in Mogadishu proper. In retrospect I am glad for that. Sally had good relations with the major clans and tribal groups in her district and assured us that as long as we were escorted by one of her staff, we were relatively safe.

Moving us to some wicker chairs under the shade of several large mango trees, she ordered fresh pineapple juice for all of us. The juice was excellent and the breeze from the ocean was fresh. My God I though as we finally began to relax a bit, life in North Mog seemed like parole compared to the virtual prison we endured in Mogadishu. After getting the standard briefing, a mixture of the unique political aspects of the district (which all began to sound quite similar), and the obligatory security warnings, Sally assigned one of the junior Political Affairs Officers and a translator to accompany us on our visit to the proposed new garage site. We bundled into the vehicles and left.

The site was only about fifteen minutes drive through streets that while now abandoned, spoke of a former existence of relative status and wealth. Many of the houses had fabulous views of the Indian Ocean and were large two or three story brick and stone buildings. They sat in walled compounds behind wrought iron gates that while now neglected and desolate looking were no doubt well kept and quite beautiful in the past. With the overthrow of the former Soviet style dictator Said Barre in 1991, and the return to prominence of the tribes and clans in Somalia, the situation rapidly deteriorated. Those with any wealth and connections were the first to leave and their less educated and law abiding relatives and tribal members simply moved into the buildings. They were a rough lot, used to making a meager living herding camels if they were honest, or more likely through raiding and piratecy. The local Somalis referred to them as "Camel Boys' and they were armed and dangerous. Society quickly fell to the lowest common denominator of rule by the gun.

We turned down a side street and pulled up in front of a large brick building. It had the remains of a faded sign that identified it as a warehouse of some sort. It also had a large partially paved lot in front of it, perfect for parking and storing of vehicles. The site looked promising and Kwamie and I chatted as we walked across the open lot toward a pair of large double doors.

I was so engrossed by a crackling whizzing sound overhead that I did not hear the first round of gunfire that preceded it, but I did hear the second round, followed again by the cracking whizzing sound. Our Nepalese guards were shouting at us in a mixture of languages and I quickly noticed they had their guns up and were all behind cover. Several were behind vehicles while the rest were kneeling behind the nearest wall, along with the Somali translator. Kuwami and I were about ten feet in front of the others and totally exposed. We quickly ran back a few steps and both of us dove behind the wall with the others, banging our heads together as we did. I remember Kwamie's helmet flew off and I had the strangest urge to laugh as I saw it spinning around at his feet.

From behind his cover, our Somali translator shouted we are UN, we want to speak with the owner. After some more exchanges, during which we all lay with our faces inches above the sand, the translator spoke to us. He said the people inside had sent the owner back to Nairobi and that this property now belonged to the clan, and the elders did not want to rent it. We should go home.

The translator took it upon himself to try to convince them otherwise, and after a few minutes of shouting back and forth they let go with another burst of gunfire over our heads. Thankfully, the Captain of the guards stepped in and said we should go and Kwaime and I agreed. As luck would have it, the wall we were behind, while less than a meter high did connect to a much higher wall some twenty meters off to our right. We were able to inch along it, crouched over until we reached the higher wall where we were safely out of the line of fire. It was more difficult for those crouched behind the vehicles, but after several tense minutes with no more shouts or gunfire, they managed to scramble into the vehicles and back them up behind the high wall. We immediately got into them and left the area. Again, this was one of those times when if someone had really wanted to shoot us, they could have.

*

Sally clicked sympathetically through a gap in her teeth and shaking her head, said you never know about these people. If we were really interested in the property she could try to contact the clan elders but suggested we wait a few days. Meanwhile, she advised us that lunch had been arranged at a restaurant that had been famous before the war when it was frequented by westerners and sometimes even served lobster. Somalis, like many other Muslim do not eat shell fish which is too bad as the lobsters from that part of the Indian Ocean are large and sweet.

The restaurant was a one story rambling affair with thatched roof and open sides. By this time, nearly 2:00 PM (14:00 hours for the uninitiated) the heat was at its height and even the breeze from the ocean was just hot wind. The owner was a tall elegant looking Somali who dressed western style and spoke fairly good English. He did not have lobster but did have a local fish caught fresh that morning. By way of proof he pointed to the fishing boats that had been beached right beside his restaurant.

The fish, similar to a small red Bonita was served grilled, with rice and a mango salad. It was delicious, and we spent an enjoyable couple of hours eating, drinking tea and laughing about how Kwaime lost his helmet. After awhile, even Kwaime joined in and screwing up his face showed us his scared look. I did not mention how I had nearly relieved myself in the sand.

The return to the main UN compound in Mog late that afternoon was uneventful and we arrived in Max's office well before sunset. We did get a bit of a dressing down the next day from the Chief Security Officer since we had inadvertently left our radios off most of the afternoon and did not do our routine check ins. Still, it was a small price to pay for the excellent fish.

However, I think Max was jealous that he was not able to make it, as it was exactly the sort of thing he liked. Since leaving Somalia I have not met up with Max again. However, I have heard that he left the UN and is now heading up a security firm that does work in Australia and Europe, and doing very well thank you.

Chapter 3: Life Settles Into a Pattern

My first weeks in Somalia had been hectic. I had already survived grenades lobed at the food tent and warning shots fired over my head. After these somewhat unnerving events, it was nice to have life settle into a routine of sorts.

The days all started alike in Mogadishu; fresh in the morning but with a blinding sun and the certainty that it would be hot by noon time. Activity started between 5:00 - 5:30 AM in our house with the first round of cold water showers. The water came from tanks on the roof, which were warmed by the sun so the water was cool, not really cold. There were six to seven of us assigned to this house, sharing two bathrooms. We had worked out a routine of shifts in the bathrooms and as long as everyone followed it, things went more or less fine. Our house consisted of all males, not by choice or design, just the way we were assigned as we arrived. Most houses had a mix but I must say the all male houses were usually slightly less sociable and considerably messier. On the other hand one seldom found unmentionables hanging out to dry in the bathroom, that is of the female variety. Each house had a small staff of Somali staff to clean, cook and do laundry. They tried their best but it was a constant battle to get them up to an acceptable standard.

In addition, we had at least three Somali guards on duty at all times, armed with the ever present AK-47's. The guards had settled in under the shade of a large car port and had beds for sleeping as well as a small fire pit to brew the endless pots of tea they drank along with the Khat they would chew when it was available. Khat is an herb that provides a mild narcotic stimulant, similar to but much stronger than coca leaf. When a lot of Khat is combined with long hours of sleep loss it becomes a potent mix rendering one edgy, aggressive and belligerent. Not the exact combination you want with armed guards, especially our already volatile Somali guards. To add to it, if there was a threat, as many as eight or nine guards would be on duty chewing Khat and drinking tea.

A few staff members were housed in the main UN compound but most of us were located in houses very near the airport. This part of Mog had been the prime residential section before the war and most of the houses were large and obviously had been very nice when maintained. Our house was adequate but the previous owner was clearly not as wealthy as many in that neighborhood. The houses rented by the UN were identified by numbers and we were simply house twelve, a two story faded green block and stucco house. As was common, located on the roof, almost as an afterthought were small rooms for the servants and a laundry room. Concrete water tanks, a large wash basin which drained over the edge of the wall and lines for hanging laundry completed the top level of house twelve. The surrounding houses were essentially the same but larger, with three and even four floors.

The main entrance of our house opened into a living room and adjoining dinning room, furnished with an odd assortment of well worn overstuffed furniture. In the back end of the house was the kitchen, a bathroom and a walk in pantry. One large setting room on the ground floor had been converted into a bedroom and was more like a suite as it had a locking door and its own bathroom. This was already taken by Jim, an older Field Service Officer who had been one of the first UN staff to be assigned to Somalia. Jim was from the Caribbean but nobody knew for sure which island as he spent most of his time in his room and even when he did speak he mumbled so badly no one could understand him. It didn't help much that Jim usually had a strong drink, usually rum in his hand. One of our other housemates was from Jamaica and he could not understand him. When Jim went on R&R he insisted that his private cleaner would stay in his room, and that we were to stay out of it. The cleaner was a local Somali woman who spent many nights apparently cleaning his room, or at least we thought so as she seldom left it.

One afternoon we came home to be met by two UN Security Officers and a delegation of elders from the woman's family. The Security Officers informed us that Jim had been sent to Nairobi and would not be returning. Seems he was supposed to marry his cleaner, or at least that was the arrangement with her family, and that was why she was staying with him. Old Jim had insisted on a trial run but when the time came to pay the bride price he decided he did not like her after all. The family was very put out and had issued a fat- waw on Jim (death threat under which anyone in the family can kill him) so to avoid trouble he was immediately sent out of the mission.

We assured the family elders we were in agreement with them that Jim was a scoundrel but when they suggested that one of us take the lady on as our cleaner, we very politely refused. After several rounds of tea and cookies they left and fortunately that was the last we heard of it.

*

The second floor of our house had four bedrooms and another bathroom. I shared one of the second floor rooms with a young Ethiopian fellow whose name we could not pronounce (not unusual with Ethiopian names), so we just shortened it to BB. He and I got to be quite close and I even met his wife once on an R&R to Addis Ababa. BB had many great stories and a very entertaining way of telling them.

One of my favorites was when his wife (a quite beautiful woman with Nubian features) and their young daughter visited him in Nairobi. They checked into the Palace Hotel with great anticipation. The first night, after the daughter was asleep, as BB described it they "did the damned deed". Apparently they did it with some vigor not to speak of abandon. The next morning the daughter was angry and would not even look at BB over breakfast. The mother asked why she was mad at daddy and with a defiant look she said because daddy was beating you up last night and you were yelling at him. We always looked forward to BB returning from R&R with fresh stories.

The one advantage of our house was that we had an excellent view of the airport and the adjoining sea which were to our east, and most of greater Mogadishu to the north. We sat on the edge of the airport district on a slight rise, and our views to the east and north were unobstructed as it was over the roofs of single story houses and shacks. We spent many evenings on the roof taking advantage of the cool breezes and the fantastic views of the night sky.

*

After a cold shower and shave, we had a breakfast which usually consisted of tea or instant coffee, Tang, cereal with powered milk and occasionally yogurt. My favorite cereal was Wheatabix, an English cereal that is ... well, English. It is whole wheat flakes pressed into large flat pellets that look like horse food, but it is fun to crush them into the milk and they taste good. All food items had to be shipped in and were mostly frozen, canned or dry. The Italian's were active throughout the Horn of Africa up to the Second World War and their influence is still felt in local food. Our cook made a decent pasta sauce and one time he served us a surprisingly good pizza. After that we had pizza at least once a week. On the other hand, as seems to be the case in much of Africa, fresh vegetables are scarce and we tended to get the canned variety especially peas, corn and green beans. I noticed this in Kenya, Ethiopia and Sudan as well, where fresh veggies are usually cooked to death, I suppose because of health considerations or maybe the lingering influence of the English.

At about 7:00 AM a small bus stopped at the front gate and after looking up and down the street to make sure no strangers or non-UN vehicles were around we all filed past our armed guards and hustled into it. The bus then moved on to the next UN house, finishing its route at the main Transportation Compound, where Mad Max had his offices. Inside the compound were ten to twelve large busses and about that many security vehicles that together formed a convoy. Each bus had a number in the front window and we were assigned to a particular vehicle so it was easier to do a head count before we set off. However, the element of surprise was completely lost as this long convoy snaked its way through Mogadishu, ending its bumpy dusty run at the main UN compound.

There were two routes we took from the airport to the main compound. The first and most frequently used route went more or less directly through the south side of Mogadishu. Near the end of the route, we had the option to either continue on the more direct main street, or turn right and take an alternate street into the compound in order to skirt past a neighborhood where some of Mohamed Farrah Aidid's fellow clan members and supporters lived. These were the most common routes and took about thirty minutes.

The second route was much longer and was used only when there was a real dangerous situation in Mogadishu. It took a total of one and one half to two hours, and took us completely south of Mogadishu. Leaving from the main UN compound it followed an isolated dirt road formerly used by truckers taking cows, camels and goats to Nairobi and returning with trade goods. At an abandoned fuel depot southwest of Mogadishu, it turned east toward the coast and took us through a series of low sand dunes, a place I dreaded as I always thought would be perfect for an ambush. After about ten to fifteen kilometers of this, the route turned north and this time took the old costal highway to the airport and our houses where we were again in the "secure area".

I still remember the daily drama our van went through at house eighteen, the last house on our route. There was one guy who lived at that house that was never ready on time. We inevitably had to wait five or more minutes while his house mates yelled at him to hurry up. This was not just inconvenient; it was dangerous to have a bus full of people sitting unprotected in the street.

*

We typically arrived at our offices around 8:00 AM. Slowly Happy became used to me, and assigned me to cover some of the many meetings our section was required to attend. One such meeting was the weekly briefing issued by the office of the Director of Administration (DOA) who was another legend in peacekeeping whom I will call Daniel Munson. He was already nearing retirement in 1993 but as a young soldier had been assigned in his countries contingent to the first UN Mission in the Congo. His incredible career has spanned the history of UN Peacekeeping and I believe he is still active today.

As a testament to his sharp memory, years later in 2005 I was on a temporary assignment in New York and he was on leave from Timor where he was serving with the UN. Quite unexpectedly he poked his head into my office and asked if he could use my UN phone directory. These directories are hard to come by and guarded with a close eye. As I handed it to him he said he remembered my name and commented on how we had worked together somewhere, was it Iraq? When I said it was Somalia he smiled and replied of course, you worked with Happy. After catching up on old times and a short discussion he walked off with my phone book.

When not in meetings I oversaw about half of the staff in our section and occupied myself researching and answering more complex issues concerning application of policy. This was similar to my previous positions before I joined the UN and would provide me with the background and experience necessary to take on future assignments as Chief of Section.

*

One other memorable routine was placing a phone call home. In those days satellite communications and mobile phone technology were still not routine and getting a call through to anywhere was an ordeal that reminded me of movies about soldiers calling home in World War Two. There was a large tent with open side flaps where you would sign up for a call and wait as much as an hour until your name was scribbled on a chalk board with a number after it. That was the booth you were to use. Although there were doors on the booths, it was so hot you left the door open to get any breeze you could.

Besides the noise from the crowd in the tent, you had to contend with the shouting coming from other booths in at least seven different languages, so it was usually difficult to hear. It is rather hard to have a private conversation, let alone an intimate one with thirty plus strangers listening to your every word. We managed to get home calls about every second or third week.

Over the years, perhaps the most dramatic progress I have seen as regards life as a peacekeeper has been in communications. Now, even in the most remote locations all staff have access to private e-mail and direct dial phone calls to anywhere on earth. You pay for the calls but at a very reasonable rate. Still, even the primitive facilities we had in Somalia were far better than my first time as a young Peace Corps Volunteer in rural South America in the seventies. During nearly two years there I called my home once and that was a major undertaking that required two weeks just to set up. The call was so bad that my mother would not believe it was me until I reminded her my birthday was the next week.

One other leap forward in technology that I must mention, at least in my view, was the pressure cooker. In the field you tend to eat a lot of bad food and sometimes none. In this regard Sudan was to be the worst in my experience. However, after enough time a pressure cooker renders even the toughest goat meat chewable.

So, our routine continued as time slowly passed. However, sudden and dramatic events were never far off, as we were constantly reminded.

Chapter 4: Day of the Blackhawk

October 3, 1993 started off like most others with no hint of the long dramatic hours ahead. We took our cool showers as we complained to ourselves about how messy our housemates left the bathroom, ate breakfast, filed into the waiting buss, silently cursed out the lazy bastard in house eighteen who was never ready on time, and peered out the windows with anxiety as the convoy made its way to the UN compound.

However, as the morning stretched on we begin to hear a few rumors from people who came into our office, about activities taking place in the airport, that the military wing of the airport was especially busy. Finally, one of our staff, a young American who himself had recently spent a tour in the Army made a trip to the airport to pick up supplies that had arrived on the morning flight. When he returned just before noon he came to my office where Alex and I were going over some tables on my computer screen and closed the door.

Something was definitely happening he reported. The civilian terminal of the airport was separated from the military hanger but as he entered the airport he could see a lot of extra military personnel hanging around and checking gear. He thought they might be American but could not be certain. Still we were not sure if whatever was happening was in Mog or one of the other major locations and they were using the airport as a staging area. Maybe it was just a normal troop rotation. Anyway, it was now a little after noon so we decided to go to the new cafeteria which thankfully had replaced the nasty food tents. Not only was the food somewhat better, there were far fewer flies and it was air conditioned.

About an hour after we returned from lunch I was getting ready to attend a meeting in the DOA's office when Happy called me on the phone. In a monotone voice she informed me that we had been ordered to prepare for early departure at 14:30 (2:30 PM) and I should notify all staff in our section to prepare immediately.

Alex and I split up the office locations and notified every one of the new orders. Everybody wanted more information but all we had was rumors so we just keep quite. At 14:15 the busses lined up in their usual places along the main street of the compound and we made our way to our assigned ride. Some people were talking nervously, speculating about what was going on, and trying to get the latest rumor from friends. Some people were silent and a bit grim since we were never dismissed early unless it was serious. As I got on the bus I noticed that in addition to the usual Somali Guard on each bus, there was an international staff Security Guard in front with the driver. We also noticed that there were extra security vehicles in the convoy and I pointed that out to BB, who rode the same bus as me.

As the convoy pulled out of the main gate we noticed another strange thing. Normally there would be at least thirty to forty kids who crowded around the busses and either asked for handouts or yelled at us as we pulled out of the compound gate. The young boys especially liked to wave at an attractive Filipina lady on our bus, who had short hair which she had done in tight curls and which stuck out from her head in all directions Betty Boop style. Today there was almost no one there, and it felt rather ominous.

After going a short distance the convoy turned right onto a side road, and continued past a small stand of stunted trees that lined the banks of an old irrigation ditch. This meant we were taking the long route that skirted south of Mog, over to the shoreline and up the coastal highway. I did not like this route. While it did avoid heavy concentrations of population, it also exposed us to isolated areas where it would be easy for snipers to hide or to launch an attack on the convoy. However, we did have a helicopter escort that followed the convoy and acted as an airborne observation post.

At the end of the first leg, the convoy made the left turn that took us through the sand dunes and past the abandoned oil tanks. I felt this would be the area where if anything was going to happen it would be along this stretch. The convoy moved slower than usual to be sure all vehicles kept their proper distance; not too close so it would be easy to hit more than one, but not too far apart so that they could be cut off and isolated like a slow cow out of the herd. Time passed very slowly as we scanned the dunes and scrub brush for any movement, or smoke of a cigarette, or flash of metal or glass in the sunlight. Through the dunes we crept and with what seemed like terminal slowness, past the oil tanks. The sound of the helicopter overhead as it performed its passes was reassuring.

About the largest ordinance the Somalis had were rocket launched grenades and machine guns mounted on the back of an old pickup, usually a Toyota. These battle wagons, or Technicals as they were called were always old but the damned things ran forever. The limited range of this ordinance meant they would have to get fairly close to launch an all out attack. Years later in Afghanistan, we would have to contend with Katyusha rockets, which introduced a new dimension.

As we made another left turn onto the coastal highway, we begin to loosen up a bit. I became aware of a conversation and suddenly realized that the only sound in the bus had been the sporadic exchanges between security guards on their hand held radios. I also realized I had not had a drink since we left the compound and took a long swig from my water bottle. The Indian Ocean, a lovely teal green blue rolled into shore off to our right and I imagined how nice that would feel about now. We were moving a bit faster now as we went past an occasional compound of houses, some abandoned and shot up. I realized this was the same route we had followed on our final approach into the Mog airport.

Suddenly the busses in front of us came to a stop. Ours was the third or fourth vehicle and through the windshield I could clearly see a column of thick black smoke boiling upwards. Our security guard, standing with his rifle in his hands ordered everyone to remain seated and be ready to get on the floor. He informed us there was a road block of burning tires. We could hear the helicopter hovering overhead as it checked for any combatants. Off to our left was a small rolling sand dune with some scrub brush and clumps of sea grass. To our right the road sloped off about six feet and there was a quarter of a mile distance to the sea. There were the remains of several abandoned houses between us and the shoreline. In short there were locations where snipers could easily hide. Whereas the grenades had been blindly lobed over the compound wall, and the shots were warning shots fired over our heads, I felt this was different. For the first time I felt that I might actually be in someone's sights and my first reaction was mild nausea and rapid heartbeat. I had a similar reaction some years earlier when a gun was thrust in my face during a hijacking (thankfully short lived) and it does not get any easier with repetition.

After about ten minutes of this standoff, security staff and the helicopter determined there was no emanate danger in the area and the busses were directed to go around the burning tires and continue. About ten kilometers further on, as the convoy went past the airport and filed into the Transportation Compound, everyone was quite relieved. We were directed to go directly to our houses and remain in lock down status for the rest of the night.

I made a quick pass into Mad Max's office and ask him what was going on. He informed me that several American helicopters were staging a raid on a location in Mog but something had gone wrong. He said either they had run into a lot of fire or maybe one had actually gone down. I remember thinking how unlikely that was. Bringing down a combat helicopter with small arms fire is only done in Rambo movies. Right?

*

Back in our house I immediately changed into comfortable shorts and a t-shirt, put on my helmet and Kevlar vest which were required during lock down, and cautiously went to the roof top for a better view. There were a couple of UN helicopters crisscrossing the area and they would report anyone they saw on a roof top or otherwise exposed, so I made sure to stay under a portion of the roof where it jutted out and provided some cover from their view. Soon I was joined by BB and several other housemates.

Off to the north, in Mog itself we could see a thin column of smoke and dust in the distance. I judged it was about one or two miles away. About the same distance away, but further to the right and closer to the sea port was a second area of mostly dust. We could hear the distant sound of gunfire, but we did not realize at the time the intense fighting that was raging so close to us. Accurate information did not start coming out until later the next morning.

One of the Somali guards, who spoke some English came to the roof and said he had heard that a second Blackhawk had been shot down. We were all in shorts and vests and he started laughing at us, at how funny we looked and why did we not get a vest for him. As the ribbing continued we volunteered to stand guard so he handed me his AK-47. One of the new arrivals had brought a decent camera and he took photos of us. Finally the guard retrieved his rifle and went back down stairs.

As the sun was beginning to edge down in the western sky, we saw a column of armored vehicles and troop carries make its way out of the airport, go past our house at some distance, continue past the area known as K4 which was a junction of several main streets, and slowly push its way into the city towards the areas where the smoke and dust had been. In the column I could make out American, Egyptian, Pakistani, and Malaysian flags along with others. We realized this was probably a reinforcement column and it began to dawn on us how serious this was, that there were people like us fighting with every ounce of their being to survive. No doubt a number of people had died or been wounded that afternoon and it would likely go on late into the night.

I began to feel a bit strange watching this and thought of how citizens of Washington, DC had taken picnic lunches with them as they went to watch a battle between troops of the north and the south fighting just outside the city during the American Civil War. It always sounded a bit ghoulish to me. As it became dark we could no longer make out anything so we retreated downstairs to the dining room where we monitored our radios the rest of the evening.

The full effects of that day would only become known later. In addition to the numerous deaths on all sides, it precipitated the withdrawal of American support and backing for UNISOM in Somalia. UNISOM would wind down in less than a year.

It would also figure large in a decade long debate over "lessons learned" from

Somalia. Mainly that peace-making, which involves military activities, and peace-keeping agendas are incompatible and cannot be done at the same time. Peace-making had failed and there was no peace in Somalia. Furthermore, the efforts to isolate and confront Aidede only fanned the flames making any efforts at peace-keeping impossible. And, to be fair both peace making and peace keeping were nearly impossible since there was no Somali government to give an air of legitimacy to the effort, not even a puppet government.

To make matters worse, to those of us on the ground there seemed to be so little coordination between the efforts of the peacemakers (essentially military) and the peacekeepers that their vastly differing agendas did not take each other into account, let alone support each other. The ability to tightly and successfully coordinate agendas and programs would only slowly and painfully evolve into the Provincial Reconstruction Team (PRT's) and similar programs used in Iraq, and now in Afghanistan.

If only someone in a decision making position had had a better knowledge of history, or had read the works of authors such as Max Boot, in particular "The Savage Wars Of Peace". They would have know that the essential elements of the tightly integrated PRT approach had been worked out and successfully used by American military forces even before World War I. Albeit this was on a limited and less sophisticated scale, and in the Caribbean and Central America. This seems to be a case of those who ignore history are doomed to repeat it.

Chapter 5: Road Trip to Nairobi:

After three short months, which seemed much longer, Alex and I were assigned to go to the town of Baidoa. Baidoa is a Somali oasis town about thirty minutes flight west, towards the boarder with Kenya. The UN presence there consisted of a contingent of India Army troops supporting civilian staff working in Civil Affairs, Humanitarian Affairs and Political Affairs. In addition there were of course a number of administrative staff. We were tasked to visit the administrative staff and while I audited files Andrew would check IT programs.

It was a welcome assignment even if it was only a day trip; fly out early in the morning and return before dark. At least it was a break from the usual routine and we would get a chance to see another side of Somalia, hopefully less violent and chaotic than Mog. We packed one change of clothes just in case the flight was delayed or cancelled. However, we only packed a few crackers and a can of sausages since we would be able to eat in the Indian mess which was another treat, as it would be a change from the bland and predictable food in Mog.

If you have ever eaten authentic Indian food, the kind they fix at home, not the watered down fare you find in many restaurants, it is incredible. I truly believe it is the hottest spiciest food on earth, but if you cut it with enough yogurt you can eat it and the complexity of flavors is still outstanding. You will however feel it for the next few days as it works its way through your entire system.

Once, after a few days diet heavy to Indian food I flew out to met my wife for a romantic R&R. The first day, as we were flying from Nairobi to our beach hotel outside Mombasa she kept asking "What is that smell, are we near a restaurant?"

Finally that evening as I was down to my skives and we were getting into bed she looked at me and asked if I had taken a shower that morning. Then she grabbed my arm and rather loudly and rudely sniffed it. Actually it was more like a snort, but I did not point that out to her. "What is that" she demanded, wrinkling up her nose. She is a strong woman but finicky when it comes to food smells.

After several more snort tests she demanded that either I take a long hot shower or she would sleep in another room. I think it is the cumin; it comes out through the pours in your skin, if you eat enough of it. At any rate, that first night was a bit awkward but she got used to it after that, and we can highly recommend Mombasa.

*

Anyway, Alex and I were looking forward to a break in the routine as well as the food, so early in the morning we reported to the airport, each with a small bag. The plane was a small twin engine bird and we shared it with about ten other civilian staff and Indian soldiers returning to their post. Everyone seemed pleased to be getting out of Mog. Baidoa was relatively small and rural but it was much cleaner and more peaceful than Mog and the staff assigned to that area seemed rather happier than the rest of us.

Since the trip was relatively short we did not get much above 6,000 feet and we could still see quite well. This was very different from the memorable approach to the Mogadishu airport. True, there were the occasional shot up abandoned vehicles and compounds, but for the most part this looked much more like normal rural African countryside.

It was dry season, but life appeared to be quite active around the temporarily dry stream beds and the occasional oasis, where there were scrub trees and some green vegetation. There were small herds of goats, sheep and camels scattered about peacefully munching on bushes and whatever plant they could find. It was actually peaceful and rather pastoral, from the air.

As we approached Baidoa we skimmed over the tops of tall palm trees, so close to the plane that it seemed you could just jump onto them. The town consisted of the classic brown and red adobe houses set inside walls made of stick and mud, forming small compounds of about an acre in size. At the center of town was an open square that served as a meeting place and where a market could be held. The streets were not really streets, more like lanes between the compound walls running more or less in predictable directions. Since it was dry there were no mud holes so it looked relatively clean and I can imagine that after a long hot bumpy trip through the desert by camel back, it would be a welcome sight. The few small stores and street vendors, where one might be able to get a warm Coke or tea, added a since of civilization.

*

We were met by two Tata "jeeps" and several Indian Officers. Let me translate. Jeep has become a universal term describing any vehicle with off road capability, usually a 4 wheel drive. It can be any brand. Tata is the largest Indian national vehicle manufacturer and one sees Tata busses, lorries (trucks for you North Americans) and "jeeps" everywhere outside of Europe, Japan and the west. The Indian Officers greeted us warmly and explained they were there to escort us to the officers mess tent where we would have tea before we got to work.

The UN compound was only about one mile from the landing strip and tin shed that served as the terminal, so we settled into the lead jeep and roared off. Our driver took corners too fast and dramatically swerved to miss a goat which was standing only about ten yards off the path as he smiled and told us how his Tata was "better than American". I was impressed and nodded back, more interested in keeping him on the road than discussing the fine points of engineering. Besides, it did seem like a decent vehicle.

We were met by the second in command, a Major who was typical of the Indian Army, or to be fair of many military personnel I have had the honor to work with during my peacekeeping days. Trim, well groomed, gracious enough, usually intelligent but frequently with an overtone of arrogance towards civilians. He snapped off a salute (I must look ex-military as I get that quite often) and escorting us into the officer's tent, gave us a concise briefing on the area

Even in the extreme heat of the North African desert the tent was surprisingly comfortable, I won't say cool. The ceilings were high and fans were strategically located to keep the air constantly moving. The walls of the tent were adorned with military company insignia, and pictures of the offices and men performing manly acts. I love this variety of military field décor; my favorite one was a Nepalese officer's tent in eastern Sudan which had a mega poster in vivid color of a mountain scene, complete with Sherpa, fixed to the wall just as you entered. It seemed to pull one in as it was such a sharp contrast to the flat brown desert and scrub brush just on the other side of the canvas wall. Back in our tent, after the briefing we were offered tea.

*

Let me explain a bit about the varieties of "Tea". Indian Tea (at least in the field) usually consists of fruit juices, samosas, various hot curry balls, fried crispy spicy noodles, and at least three assorted sweets. Oh yes, and tea with milk. The exact content of a "tea" varies with the culture of the country providing it, for example a Kenyan tea frequently offers small sandwiches and biscuits (which is what cookies are known as outside the US), whereas a good English tea includes scones or biscuits along with Devon clotted cream, which is my favorite.

However, tea is always offered with ceremony and hospitality no matter how simple and I have made a meal of "tea" on many occasions, when that was all we were likely to get that day.

By the time we finished tea we were already running a bit late and would not have much time for our real mission, but I think that may have been part of the plan. Nobody likes an audit. I went straight to the Personnel files (always rife with errors, omissions and just plain screw ups) as Alex pried open some computer files. Actually we did not want to find much as it would require a long report and endless arguments, so we proceeded with some care.

Before we knew it we were summoned to lunch, a summons I seldom turn down, especially in an army mess. I know that may sound strange (who likes army chow) but when you are in locations where there is little or no food the mess is more like a three star diner. Alex (who is Filipino and not especially keen on Indian food) even put me to shame as he loaded up on the dhal and rice, curried chick peas with beans, and chicken.

My plan was to eat some of everything before I went back again for my favorites. A sort of divide and conquer plan I have worked out over the years, beginning when I was the smallest of four boys at our family table, and one I swear by.

After lunch we were stuffed, and the heat made us drossy. This, along with the endless tea and pleasant conversation at the officer's mess, made the time pass quickly. Too quickly, as we heard our plane taking off in the distance. I recalled how that morning the pilot, a surly person of none discernible origin who reminded me of a short Clint Eastwood but with dark oily hair, had told us he did not wait for anyone so we had *%##@ better be there when he landed.

I later found out he had an equally surly lady friend, who reminded me of a short Rosie O'Donnald, with whom he shared quarters back in Mog. Such arrangements are not uncommon and are politely referred to as a "mission marriage". Our Clint did not want to get stuck without Rosie in the Somali hinter lands. Instead, he stuck us in the hinter lands.

Of course we could have bunked with the Indian troops but the next plane was not scheduled for three days and we did not want to face the wrath of Happy when we got back three days late to Mog. As we were pondering what to do, we heard a small plane circling overhead, preparing to land. The Tata driver was only too happy to rush us back to the landing strip where we greeted the pilot of the plane as he stepped down.

*

He was Canadian (which by good fortune I also speak), and explained how he was not really a pilot, rather he was certified as one, but piloting was not his job. Many Canadians have experience as bush pilots and are actually damned good, or perhaps you are so happy to make other than a crash landing that they just appear to be good, but either way. He was a regional administrator for an NGO that worked on water management issues in the Horn of Africa. He was dropping off an engineer and some boxes of supplies and would be glad for the company, if we wanted to go to Nairobi.

Nairobi. That was in the wrong direction, but still it had a couple of things going for it. First was the Imperial Palace where we could sleep in a bed and not a cot, and have a flushing toilet. Second we would not have to share a tent with a bunch of strange men. Finally, the UN had at least one flight a day from Nairobi to Mog and with any luck we could get back the next day without even being missed. The only problem was, as Alex dryly pointed out, this was not a UN plane and if something happened our survivors would not get any insurance payment.

Still, rather than face Happy we risked it and before dark we were checking into a shared double room at the old Imperial. At that time Alex was not married and all the lady staff at the hotel knew him, so we got a nice room. It had small windows that faced a brick wall but it was far away from the smell of the kitchen fans and the noisy elevator.

The next morning which was a Friday, we called the UN airport office and were informed that all flights were full and the earliest we could get back was on Monday. Brilliant, we just went from a two day AWOL to four days and there was now no way we could sneak back unnoticed. Oh well, nothing we could do so we notified the personnel office of our location, and as we prepared for a brief holiday in Nairobi we realized that between the two of us we had just about enough money to pay for the hotel and maybe meals for two days.

As we were pondering what to do, who should walk into the hotel but my Croatian friend who was apparently on another one of his "unauthorized" walkabouts. Over coffee he explained how this was indeed a legitimate R&R and that he was meeting his wife in Greece. He found our situation amusing, but not too unusual for a guy like him who frequently found himself in such situations, and since he was flush agreed to loan us a couple hundred dollars. Great, now as well as eat we could drink a few cold Tuskers.

Tusker is a pretty decent Kenyan beer. It is named after a famous elephant, that in 1923 reportedly charged and killed one of the two British brothers who had founded the brewery early in the last century. In the beast's defense they were trying to shoot him, so in his honor the surviving brother named the beer after him (the elephant) and struggled on as the sole owner of the brewery. Our life was looking up. We would still have to face Happy and maybe get reprimanded but we were out of Mog, drinking Tusker and able to relax a bit.

*

The Imperial Palace sits in the middle of a narrow street which is more like a wide alley which ends in a large open courtyard, which in turn is lined with shops and small restaurants. At that time it was in a more or less safe part of Nairobi, located only a few blocks away from main government offices and a nice shady park.

That particular afternoon I was on that narrow street returning to the Imperial after having lunch at a restaurant in the courtyard, and as usual the narrow street was crowded. I noticed that people ahead of me were skirting around something and my first thought was it was someone sitting in the street begging. Possibly some of the abandoned women and children that flocked to this area as there were usually quite a few westerners and they had money, or at least more than most.

As I got closer I noticed it was a young man setting on a ragged old brown blanket. At first he appeared to be a healthy man in his late teens or twenties and I cynically thought OK, what's his trick. Everybody has a trick.

As I got nearer to his blanket I noticed he was holding up his right arm, only his arm, as he had no hand. The hand had been amputated above the wrist. Thank God, at least it was healed with no signs of blood or infection.

For some reason I immediately flashed back to an old man I saw begging in front of a church in Quito, Ecuador some years before and how strange and distorted his limbs looked as he had elephantitous. Years later it was discovered that elephantitus can be almost completely reversed over time by carefully and gently scrubbing the infected area with plane disinfectant soap and warm water. I'm sure that poor man died as an outcaste before this simple fact was discovered.

Then I noticed that this young man on the dirty brown blanket was holding up his other arm, and it too was a stub. Oh my God, was he involved in some accident, and why is he sitting. I glanced at his feet and it was like something hit me square in the stomach. Both of his feet were missing with only stubs stabbing out from the pant legs.

I was stunned. I was unable to react and just kept walking forward, unable to really understand it all. What kind of fiendish accident or sickness was responsible for this?

Then, as I was a few yards from the hotel it came to me almost like someone had slapped me in the face. This was no accident. I knew that severing limbs, hell, hacking off arms and feet with machetes and axes is practiced by some rebel groups to terrorize and intimidate. This is more commonly found in West Africa than in East Africa, but this was the only thing it could be.

There are a few times when a door seems to open to another dimension, another place and it's as if you can see things that are hidden, that have to be hidden because they simply cannot be lived with. What kind of pure evil would drive anyone to do this to another human being? I can even somewhat understanding outright killing, as it sometimes seems like the only option, but this was so evil and hateful. I cannot even attribute this to someone acting like an animal; animals kill to eat and to protect themselves. Only humans do this. The door was open and for a few seconds I could see what we are all capable of.

I sat down in the lobby to focus myself. I could not go back and give him money; I had to keep the door closed for now. Instead I found one of the cleaners and giving him two five pound notes I asked him if he could give five pounds to the beggar. As he scampered out the door I mumbled thanks and went to my room. The world looked pretty dammed depressing just then.

*

Years later, when I was stationed in New York as an Administrative Officer responsible for a mission on the coast of West Africa, I got a phone call from an organization based in Boston. This small NGO specialized in women's issues and the lady on the other end explained how several years back the mission had commissioned her NGO to do research and compile a report on tactics used by the rebels against civilians in that area, especially against women and youth.

The report was finished on time but the mission had been dragging their feet on paying the NGO, which did not surprise me. The papers probably got lost, and then forgotten. That sort of thing was all too common as anyone who has tried to get their unaccompanied luggage and their final pay settled after a mission assignment, can attest.

The small NGO was getting desperate as it had put much of its limited funds into this project. They were about to be audited and for sure would get a bad report, which would have severe negative effects on their ability to raise funds. To support her claim, she scanned me a copy of a letter from the mission accepting the report and acknowledging the request from the NGO for payment. Still after nearly two years they had received nothing in payment, and now their communications to the mission were mostly being ignored.

With this, I contacted the Finance Office of the mission and after several unsuccessful attempts to get them to move I finally went directly to the office of the United Nations Ombudsman in New York and requested that they look into the matter.

This office can be very helpful as a last resort, and I had taken care to build a good relationship with them by responding quickly whenever they requested information or assistance. One of the staff members I knew in that office took up the issue and with this added pressure the mission began to make payments.

To thank me, the NGO sent a copy of the report in question and I made the mistake of reading it, or at least I started. I stopped in chapter three after reading the notes taken during an interview of two girls barely in their teens who were raped, abducted and finally escaped after being held at a rebel army camp for several months. Before they were abducted, they were forced to watch as child solders were ordered to hack off their fathers arm. Nobody said the world of peacekeeping is all fun. Sometimes it comes at the cost of innocence and even sanity. I filed the report with other mission documents.

*

But for now Alex and I were going to enjoy our long weekend in Nairobi, and on Monday morning we managed to get on a flight, sneak back into Mogadishu and then into the compound. We quickly and quietly went to our office, threw our bags under the desk and pretended like we had been there all along. When we had not been summoned by Happy by that afternoon, we assumed we had pulled off the all time road trip to Nairobi.

Chapter 6: A Christmas R&R

Somalia was classified as a hardship mission because of the bad security situations and difficult living conditions. Like most missions classified as hardship, it had a leave policy that provides for extra break periods. The name used for this has changed over the years but we just called it R&R and everybody looked forward to it.

In Somalia, staff was eligible for an R&R for every eight weeks spent in the mission area. This consisted of five additional work days off which had to be taken outside the mission area, and we were allowed to use the UN flight to Nairobi. This was a highlight and most staff members had their R&R's scheduled and planned out for their entire period of assignment. Not that they we were lazy or only thinking of vacation, rather it took our mind off the realities of where we lived, and you needed to schedule your flights well in advance as they filled up quickly.

At any rate, my wife and I had planned an R&R for early December, the first time we would have seen each other since August. We planned to spend it in and around Kenya since neither of us had been in Africa before. I had to coordinate holiday coverage with Happy so one of us was present at all times, and she pulled rank and took the actual holiday off. Throughout my career I have done quite well however, managing to get about half of the Christmas holidays off.

So on the first day of December I flew to Nairobi and checked into the Imperial Palace. Early the next morning I was at the airport anxiously waiting for the overnight KLM flight from Amsterdam. My wife is Asian, about five feet two, with black hair. I figured she would be easy to spot in an airport full of tall Kenyans and largish European types. However, as her flight began to file out of the arrival gate the first ones out were, of course a Japanese tour group. Needless to say my wife blended in and my plan to spot her did not work so well.

As I was straining to find her I suddenly became aware that someone was standing beside me, also staring intently at the crowd. I turned and it was her, trying to see what I was straining to see, since she was obviously there already.

This seems to happen quite often with my wife, she is trying to figure out what I am doing when it all seems so obvious to her. She wonders how, living and working in the places I have, I could survive without a personal minder watching over me at all times. Perhaps all wives feel that way about their husbands. But now we were together again, after our emotional separation which took place several months ago and so far away.

This was our first R&R and I look back on it with particular fondness. One big advantage of my years spent in peacekeeping has been the opportunities it has given us to travel. We made a point of meeting as often as possible in someplace new, and have been privileged to hit most of the "must see" places as well as many exotic or just off beat ones. But one of the most romantic and memorable was this first R&R and the safari we took to the Masari Mara of Kenya.

I had never been very interested in a safari and only looked into it at my wives' insistence. However, making reservations from Nairobi where it was cheaper, and with the additional discount I got from our travel agent as a UN member, the price was right and it was hard not to go.

So, after spending a few days in Nairobi and Mombasa, getting to know each other again, we went by small plane west to the rolling plains of the Masari Mara. The flight out was enough in itself. The grim city surrounded by sprawling acres of shacks gave way first to scattered farmsteads and then to the endless rolling hills and open plains, occasionally broken by riverbeds and stands of trees.

*

Wrong Place-Right Time

Our plane landed at a small dirt strip about half a mile from the Safari camp. Sitting in the distance, the camp was located next to a ridge of rolling hills, facing an open plain that seemed to lead to the horizon and beyond. As we proceeded by Land Rover towards the camp, the first thing that struck me was the silence, broken only occasionally by the cry of a bird or the low whine of the wind. I personally love the silence of nature and do not mind being completely alone with it and here, in the silence I immediately felt myself relaxing. Other than the few people working in the camp and the other guests, there were no human as far as one could see. After the cramped, crowed and dangerous cities we were forced to live in this was the best thing I could imagine.

The camp, which was spotlessly clean, was composed of tents pitched on raised concrete slabs to keep snakes and insects out. Each tent had a sitting room, a separate bed room, and a bathroom complete with a shower which was fed from an overhead tank. The tank was heated by the sun and the water was always refreshingly cool. The sitting room, furnished with dark stained wood chairs, tables and cushions was comfortable and inviting. The beds were covered by white muslin mosquito nets draped from the ceiling, with oil lamps on small tables set on each side of the bed. It was as if we had just walked into a movie set and I half expected to see Indiana Jones come swaggering in.

We arrived in time for mid morning tea and it was English style with a choice of excellent Kenyan teas. It was served in the main dining area and we had a choice of either sitting inside the large dining tent or on the open veranda under a small grove of Jacaranda trees.

The view was striking. As far as one could see were gently rolling grass lands, populated by scattered herds of animals, either mixed together or seemingly paying little attention to one another as they grazed. What really struck me was the complete absence of anything man made. There were no lamp posts, no roads, no overhead wires. The only thing one could see was what had grown there naturally or had walked or flown in.

This is a striking scene during the day but at night, with an endless sky absolutely filled with stars, it is truly humbling. Much is written about the

African sky, but once you see it, away from city pollution you immediately understand why it inspires people so.

*

I noticed that the camp area was surrounded by a very tall cyclone fence with a tightly closed gate, tended by a guard. The fence was there of course to keep out the wandering herds of gazelles, zebras and elephants, but even more to deter the baboons and monkeys. Monkeys can be funny as they clown around and grab food from the tables, but baboons which are large and unafraid of humans can be dangerous.

However, just enough of the monkeys got over the fence and past the gate to make eating on the veranda an adventure. Once when I left my breakfast unguarded for a minute, one of the rascals grabbed a sausage off my plate, and running up the nearest tree wolfed it down. All I could do was get another sausage.

We were taken on "game drives" by Land Rover in the morning, late afternoon and again after dark when the different species of animals are most active. The most spectacular thing I remember about all of the animals is that they were seemingly unconcerned and usually unaware that we were nearby, even if we were in vehicles.

Some of the species have very unsavory habits (smelly hyenas rolling in mud) or look really comical (baby wart hogs running with their tails standing straight up), but they all share one thing in common when viewed on their own turf and on their own terms. They have dignity. It makes you realize that human beings are just another species, and one that has not survived as long as most of these have. We may make a big impression on ourselves, but not on them. We owe it to them to make sure they can survive, that we do not force them out of existence through our greed, mismanagement and disregard for the environment..

*

After several days on safari we returned relaxed and sun tanned to Nairobi. Before my wife left she wanted to shop for some Christmas gifts, so we went to a well known market area in Nairobi which has a lot of stalls where local artisans exhibit and sell goods.

It is located in a large open area surrounded by block walls on three sides and is roofed over to protect you from the sun and rain. It is a noisy area, filled with folks all anxious to sell their goods and almost kidnapping you into their stalls as you walk past. As is always the case the goods range from nice to quite cheesy and half the fun is finding the good stuff.

Entering the market area I had a vague uneasy feeling of being surrounded as we stepped over piles of blankets and baskets and worked our way down the first aisle looking for wood carvings.

This was the first time I was conscious of a change beginning to take place in me, and one that has not only remained with me but increased in intensity over time. I suppose it is linked to self preservation and is not necessarily bad, but it does sort of rob you of a simpler view of things.

I found myself instinctively checking things out. Where are the exits, which are also places that people can enter; watch them. Look for anything suspicious or any concentration of people; avoid it. Look up, is there anything above you. Stay away from plate glass windows, and keep a solid wall to your back to limit the areas that you need to watch. Look for any person or thing that seems out of place, listen for anything unusual or out of place, what do you hear and smell, and above all, trust your instincts. When there was a loud shout from the stall next to us, without thinking I jumped behind a nearby stack of bags.

As I said, this gut reaction to surroundings has only slightly lessened over the years, and from talking with other peacekeepers I know it is a phenomena that occurs with many of them as well. It is not some macho affectation, it is an unconscious reaction. At times it seems inappropriate and you begin to view all your surroundings with suspicion, or at least with an eye of caution.

Shaking it off I found my wife and we finished our shopping, but after all these years I still find myself reacting almost instinctively at a sudden noise, when a taxi blows it's horn or I'm surprised by someone running towards me or…well you get the idea.

Chapter 7: Negotiating Under Fire

Flying back from R&R, the talk in the airplane was all about the raising level of tensions in Mogadishu, particularly in the area around the airport. The increase in security in and around the airport was noticeable when we landed.

The situation got worse daily and near the end of the week fighting finally broke out between two of the major clans, which resulted in a complete shut down of the airport. The factions were firing at each other across one end of the airstrip and no flights could get in or out. In addition to the usual AK's they had brought up "technicals" and apparently had shot up a small plane sitting on the ground. This presented a serious situation since all personnel and much of our supplies went through the airport and we depended on these flights.

Happy called me into her office and asked if it was true that I had been a labor negotiator before I joined the UN. When I confirmed it she said the DOA, Daniel Munson wanted to see me in his office immediately. She also said to take him the latest table of candidates we had reviewed and prepared. I knew better than to ask what was up, so I just proceeded to his office.

Munson's assistant showed me in and after an exchange of greetings I handed him the list of candidates. The only other person in the office was Nat, the Chief Security Officer, who was the only slim Fijian I have ever met. As a group Fijians are not overly tall but tend to be built like a Humvee, and I have always been glad to find a few of them as Security

Officers in every mission I have been in. They seem to command respect just by their presence. Nat was well built but not your typical rugby running back for the New Zeeland All Blacks. I met him again him several years later in the Geneva office and he had not changed very much at all.

There is a great UN "urban myth" concerning a small Fijian Military contingent in the Gaza Strip some years back, whose members had a few drinks and got slightly out of hand. Suffice it to say it took a number of regular army troops several hours to corral and bring them under control after they nearly destroyed a hotel. It only ended when one of their own senior officers cajoled and shammed them into submission. Even if it is not altogether true, it is a good story.

*

After motioning for me to sit down, the DOA said there would be several others joining us and that we needed to discuss the airport situation. He took a brief minute and glanced at the candidate form I had just given him. Looking up he thanked me and commented what a help this had been over the past weeks. He also said the office of the SRSG appreciated it as well. Happy had never passed this on to me, but maybe in her own way her request to give this to the DOA was a subtle nod of recognition. Such were her ways.

As we spoke the door opened and two men whom I recognized as Political Affairs Officers (PAO's) came in. I had spoken to them before at one of the noisy boozy weekend parties that the mission was becoming known for. I remembered them as they were usually together, they were both Scandinavian, and the shorter and less senior of the two looked like Tim Conway the comedian. However, he was sensitive about the resemblance and to make up for it he did not smile very much. Nor did he have a sense of humor.

Next through the door was a Senior Legal Officer, a tall Nigerian called Sonnie. Working together, he and I got to be somewhat close over the next few weeks and I would see him occasionally over the remainder of my UN career. I never again worked with the PAO team, although I was impressed with their patience in dealing with the situation we were about to get thrown into. We all sat down and introduced ourselves. The DOA put the senior PAO in charge of the team, and then asked Nat to brief us on the situation at the airport.

*

There were members of several rival clans living near and around the airport. Most of them were involved in the dispute but the actual fighting seemed to be between the two largest groups, and was apparently over jobs and hiring at the airport. Since the UN operated the airport and was responsible for the hiring, we were going to get involved whether we wanted to or not. In addition, we could not allow the airport to be closed even one day, and this fighting, once it got started could go on for days or even weeks. Without the daily flights bringing in critical supplies the mission would quickly grind to a halt.

The DOA wanted us to go in as a team and make contact with the parties, find out what the issues were and either settle it or at least get the airport open again. We would go in by helicopter with a close protection team provided by the US Army, which was good news. An Egyptian military contingent was permanently stationed inside the airport so was already there and would provide backup, also good news. He did not ask us if that was OK or if we wanted to do it, so we all nodded in agreement. To be honest, my mind was racing and I was wondering if this was such a good idea, but it had to be done and better me than someone with no negotiations experience.

Nat said in a mater of fact way, that the fighting was not going to stop just because they saw a UN helicopter so we would be going in under fire. With that in mind, and with the memory of the recent Blackhawk incident still very fresh, I was beginning to think this was not such a good idea. I did not have time to consult Alex, but I was quite sure that if something did happen this time, my survivors would at least get the insurance money.

After a bit more discussion, Munson told us to meet back at his office in twenty minutes after we had locked our offices and gotten into our gear. Gear consisted of a helmet and Kevlar flack jacket (a light armored vest) which everyone was issued as soon as they arrived in the mission area. Returning to my office I informed Happy of the DOA's assignment. She glanced up from the file she was busy marking up with red ink, and with a grunt returned to her task. I strapped on the vest, put a bottle of water in the pocket of my cargo pants and with helmet in hand returned to meet up with the other members of the team.

A van was waiting for us and we were driven to the heli pad located near the main gate, where a bird was waiting. I am not real familiar with helicopters and I know this was not a Chinook but it was also not the small kind that takes tourists around the Grand Canyon. It was a large to medium sized Russian built craft, designed to carry both passengers and cargo. The middle area of the craft was open for cargo which was tied down with rope nets, and along the sides were benches for twenty or so passengers. This craft is very common in UN operations and a reliable workhorse. It is not flashy but with a good crew it feels solid beneath you. In my experience the good UN crews are Russian, Canadian and sometimes Indian. I will not comment on the others.

In addition to our negotiations team of four, we were joined by two Somali local staff translators and the close protection team composed of six members of the US Mountain Division, with an Officer who was in charge. I did not see his rank. He informed us that everyone was to remain seated and that no one was to get out of the helicopter until he gave the command. Other than that he did not say much.

The copilot informed us that we would come in slow so as not to surprise or threaten anyone, but we should be ready for a quick departure if we started to draw unnecessary fire. I was going to ask what necessary fire might be, but I learned as a kid to curb my curiosity. Besides, I was not feeling very glib, these idiots were using real bullets. Earlier that morning one of our local Somali staff had been killed when he was caught in crossfire while fueling a plane.

The copilot wished us good luck and with that we put on our ear muffs while the motors started their thundering loud warm up. As we lifted off my stomach was churning with every whoop of the blades but I must admit I was also thinking that we probably would all survive this, and if we were successful what a great story this would make.

From the air, the city actually looked calm as we passed over it and one could easily imagine there really was no problem on that quiet sunny morning. We would land at the airport and all would be normal. This idea was quickly shattered. We started our slow, high approach about half a mile from the landing zone so everyone could see first that we were alone, and second that we were not a Blackhawk.

From the ground, just the sight of a Blackhawk flying can raise the hair on your arms. Not only do they seem to moan and scream, but with all the munitions pods and guns hanging off the sides, they look for all the world like Teridoctiles, or some other primitive winged dinosaur looking for something to kill. They are predators. Our bird, on the other hand, with its round body and fixed landing gear looked like a friendly old pigeon. At least we hoped it did.

As we slowly approached the airport my mind was racing, yet in a way things seemed to be happening in slow motion. I was aware that my heart beat was faster than normal but slower than I would have expected. In hindsight I was concentrating mostly on what was right in front of me. I was alone and quite unaware of anything except what was happening right where I was. I was taking in everything and my senses seemed extremely sharp as the adrenalin raced through my body. This was much the same reaction I recall experiencing years earlier when I was abducted from a bank in Argentina by several men who turned out to be plane clothes police officers, who as they put it were looking for enemies of the state. After holding me for several very tense hours in an unmarked building and playing good cop – bad cop while they banged the table and cleaned their weapons, they decided I was not the profile or type they were looking for. They released me with the warning to get out of the country and even offered to drive me to the airport but I politely refused.

*

As we approached Mogadishu International we could see there were two large groups of armed men facing each other across the tarmac. The main body of men tapered off into smaller groups spread over several hundred meters, forming ragged lines of combatants separated by less than one hundred meters at the narrowest part. All of them seemed to be armed and many were firing, pretty much in the direction of the opposing group. Somehow this struck me as odd, some of them were actually firing in random directions, as if they were in a different battle. There were no technicals or battle wagons visible, which was good. Slowly the helicopter settled toward a spot between the main concentrations of men, but out of the line of direct fire, and finally touched down.

As the engines slowly ground down we could hear the gunfire all around us, but it did not seem to be directed at us. Still it was not reassuring to know that so many bullets were flying around so close to us. All it would take was one stray or one mistake to send them through the relatively thin skin of a helicopter.

The army officer gave the command to slowly open the door, but he also motioned to us to stay seated. After a brief time he nodded at the translators and slowly they looked out the open door. They must have recognized some of the men as they began to waive and even smile. It occurred to me that they were probably used to such situations, or at least much more so then we were.

Then, cautiously they descended the steps and motioned to the nearest group that they wanted to approach. By the time they had advanced about twenty meters they were met by several men who were already talking and pointing at the other group. Soon they were surrounded by a group of older men who were presumably elders and looked like they were in charge. The gunfire began to die down, first from those nearest to us and then from the others.

One of the translators was joined by a couple of the elders who did not have any weapons, and they began to slowly walk across the airfield toward the other side, motioning as they walked for the others to meet in the middle. I remember being very impressed by their courage and was afraid we might see them get shot, but as they advanced, several men began to walk out from the opposing group. We watched intently out the small windows of the helicopter, craning our heads to see. The talk was somewhat animated with arms occasionally lifting and much pointing but we could not hear anything.

When there had been no further escalation after several minutes, the close protection squad began to descend the stairs and took up positions around the helicopter. They had their weapons ready but pointed clearly upwards, not threatening anyone.

As we stepped out of the helicopter, I scanned the area and the first thing I noticed was the small plane that had been shot up earlier that morning. It looked like the plane we had taken to Badoia last week. It was sitting across the field near some barrels of fuel. The dirt around the barrels was dark and I assumed it was spilled fuel. Under one of the wings of the plane lay the body of the worker who was shot along with the plane. It was too far away to see much detail but it was clearly a human body, and since there was so much gunfire no one had even covered it. It lay in the hot sun but there was nothing we could do at that moment.

When we were out of the helicopter we were immediately surrounded by armed men all talking and trying to get our attention. They were not threatening us but I could not help but think that the situation could change very quickly. This was not a disciplined army and it was clear that no one person had command of the people and the situation. It was both volatile and dangerous and the sooner we could get them to agree to talk, the better. One odd thing I did notice was the smell. It occurred to me it was the smell of sweaty bodies all hopped up on adrenalin and I could not be sure if it was them or us.

*

We asked our Somali translator to tell us what he had been able to learn. It was no secret that the UN planned to do extensive repairs to the airport and the fighting was over who would be hired by the UN to work at the airport. Each clan wanted to get their members hired over the others. We had just let a contract which was awarded to an American firm known by many of us as Burn and Loot (which sort of rhymes with their name). The name is a bit unfair since they only do what we ask them to do and no doubt do it faster, cheaper and better than we could. They would need to hire as much as a hundred and fifty to two hundred additional staff to do unskilled labor and since there were very few jobs available it was clearly a matter to fight over.

Finally the other translator returned and confirmed what we had been told. Gradually we got representatives of the two warring factions to agree to meet in the middle of the field and here is where Sonnie, the Nigerian Legal Affairs Officer was very helpful. He was a large man with a quick smile and expansive friendly manner, and since he was also African the Somalis found him more approachable.

Gradually over the next few weeks they would come to accept the rest of us but at this point Sonnie was center stage. With the help of the translators, he explained to all how the UN does not hire based on a clan or tribal basis and that we would no doubt hire from all groups. While this was not what they wanted to hear, it was not a foreign concept to the locals as that was the practice for all hiring we did.

The more he talked the more animated Sonnie became until he had some members from both sides smiling and nodding. He was speaking too fast to have it translated but at this stage we just wanted to get the shooting stopped, get the hell off the tarmac and get the planes flying again. In addition to the shooting, we were standing in the open and I really began to notice how hot it was getting.

One thing I learned from Sonnie which would prove useful in latter assignments in Iraq and Sudan was the importance of personal contact. In the west we give much weight to following policy and process. In much of the world, how you feel about a person and if you trust them can be as important as which side they are on and can mean the difference between failure and success, or sometimes between life and death.

*

One of the officers from the Egyptian military contingent, a Major as I recall, suggested that we continue discussions in the airport maintenance building which was nearby, which gave us the opening we were waiting for. We suggested that the elders and representatives from each side leave their weapons behind and join us where we could continue discussions, in the shade. We made it clear this was only discussions and that ether side was free to leave at anytime. We also asked for their assurance that they would not start firing again while we were meeting. Finally, after mulling this about, and with a lot of reassuring and encouragement from us they agreed and a small contingent of the Egyptian officers lead the group to the building. Reluctantly the elders left their guns with other members of their clan, who remained just outside the doors as we filed into the building.

We tried to set the stage by having our team sit together at one end of the table, and encouraging representatives of each clan to sit on one side or the other. I was pleasantly surprised when they sat down and began to talk among themselves rather than shout at each other. To add to the sudden air of civility the Major had bottles of water passed around. Another lesson learned, a show of hospitality no matter how small goes a long way. It seems to put the receiving party in some sort of obligation to you and defines you as a friend or at least not an enemy.

Each side was anxious to speak and each person had to speak until they were finished. Each speaker usually repeated much of what was said before and maybe added one thing new so that by the time we had worked our way around the room the issues were, at least on the surface quite well laid out. And the issue came down to jobs; how many would there be and who would get them. It was clear this would not be settled quickly or easily.

When he got a chance to speak, our team leader emphasized how this issue could not be settled by fighting and that we were willing to discuss it further. As a show of good faith he suggested that we allow the airport to open again as there would be no need for new jobs if it remained closed. A good point I though. At first this seemed to fall on deaf ears and it seemed like they may resume fighting. But by remaining calm and with a lot of talking and repeating ourselves we finally arrived at the following. Each side would withdraw and allow the airport to reopen. We assured them that in any case the UN was not ready to hire anyone yet so we would meet with their elders over the next days or weeks to discuss the matter, before any hiring was done. Finally, they were not to resume fighting over this issue as long as we were in discussions. I think they agreed in part because it was getting late and they all wanted to get home before dark.

As we left the building we noticed that men from both sides were already leaving, and best of all no one was shooting. That was encouraging. Those who remained, crowded around their elders who began to recall the meeting. I was afraid that some of the hot heads would disagree and want to continue fighting but finally they all began to leave.

As we climbed back into the helicopter I realized how exhausted I was, both mentally and physically. We had been running on full since mid morning and it was now about five in the afternoon. As soon as we arrived at the compound we reported back to the DOA that the airport was opened. We would be meeting on a regular basis to hopefully hammer out an agreement and while it was by no means settled, at least we were talking instead of fighting. He expressed his gratitude that we had succeeded in getting the airport open, and he wished us luck with the rest. As we departed he was phoning the office of the SRSG to give him the good news.

*

Over the next month we met once or twice a week with representatives of the clans and on our insistence we got them to allow some of the smaller clans to send representatives to the meetings. In retrospect this was an error and could have doomed our efforts.

Each meeting was similar to the last; both major clans emphasized how they should be the ones to provide the staff needed for renovation of the airport, we repeated the official UN stand on hiring based on qualifications and the small clans were progressively pushed into the background. Gradually we put forth the idea that the UN would try to hire on a quota basis, with the two main clans providing the majority of the new employees and each smaller clan would also get a share.

The process was helped along by the hospitality of the Egyptian military who provided water, tea and biscuits (the common term for cookies) for all of the meetings. Once, they even pulled out all the stops and provided a lunch, which was quite possibly the best meal I had all the time I was in Somalia.

It started with yellow lentil soup, humus and various salads, then an excellent rice pilaf with pine nuts and raisins, roasted lamb, chicken and other assorted dishes. For desert we had dates, yogurt and tea. I was watching as everyone piled their plates high with food and I could not help but wonder when was the last time many of the people in that room had had all the food they could eat. Again, the Egyptians displayed the hospitality that the Arab culture is so rightly famous for. I would benefit from this hospitality in Iraq, Kuwait and Afghanistan as well, and it is one of my best memories from those hard days.

*

The negotiations ended almost as abruptly as they started. At the meeting that turned out to be the last one we noticed that none of the minor clans were represented, and when we finally got underway the elders of the dominate clan asked to speak first. After thanking us for our hospitality they announced that they would be sending their men to take all of the jobs. As they were making this announcement I expected the members of the other clan to explode or at least to walk out, but there was actually more reaction from us, the UN team than from the others, who just talked quietly among themselves. To the credit of our team leader, he objected and asked why the sudden change after things seemed to be going well, but did not over react.

There was no reason given or even offered, and as the talks continued it occurred to me that they had probably settled this themselves and they were just letting us know what the final arrangement was. They were not used to a formalized negotiation process, at least not to ours and had probably met and settled this in their own way. I really wish I could have been present at that meeting.

We emphasized to them that the UN could never agree to hire from only one group, what if they did not have people who could do the work. They nodded and said they wanted most of the jobs, which signaled to me that we had reached the best agreement we were likely to get. I leaned over to the team leader and said it appeared to me that they had left the door open a bit and we had about the best deal we could expect, and it would keep the airport open. He agreed and after another hour of back and forth, it became obvious that both sides seemed OK with whatever had been worked out. It also began to appear that we were now the one's holding things up.

We told them we needed to discuss this with the DOA and wanted to continue the meetings. They agreed and we all left, but when the time for the next meeting came only our team showed up for the scheduled meeting. Through the translators we eventually learned that indeed the elders from the two main clans had met and agreed what portion of the jobs each would get. However, it worked. A settlement was reached and we moved forward with the work on the airport.

In retrospect I believe we did play a role. We successfully got the two sides to stop shooting at each other. Then by engaging them in a series of negotiation meetings we gave them time to work out whatever agreement they arrived at. This is very similar to the process of mediation, whereby a mediator provides the parties time and space to work after the normal negotiation process has broken down.

During my career before joining the UN I had negotiated nearly thirty labor agreements, handled some difficult strikes and represented clients in labor court. However, this still ranks as perhaps the most memorable, or should I say colorful negotiations I can recall and the one I am still most proud to have been a part of. By way of thanks the members of the team received a call from the office of the SRSG, which was enough for me.

Chapter 8: A Residence With a View

Residence number five was a large four story villa adjacent to the Transportation Compound. Being taller than most surrounding residences it had a commanding view of the airport, the ocean and all the surrounding buildings, as well as the Transportation compound and was rumored to have been the home of a very wealthy commercial magnet in pre-war times. It was a corner building with a clear view of the main street which led from the sea port , past the airport and continued into Mogadishu.

The building also had other interesting features such as a huge fully secured car port large enough for vehicles to turn around in, a unique stone wall running the full length of the first floor, and it had several well furnished bathrooms. It was a perfect party building, but the residents were a bit more mature than most of the other staff and made sure that no loud parties were held there.

Instead, these parties were held in house four next door, which was separated only by a brick wall through which a door of sorts had been cut allowing easy passage from house five to house four. In fact, similar doors had been cut in other walls resulting in what the residents referred to as an "underground railroad" connecting a row of some five residences.

A typical house four party would take place on Thursday or Friday night (the Muslim work week being Sunday through Thursday) and would start after sundown. Sometimes it would be an afternoon party with barbeque and whatever else we could find. The most popular international musical group at the time were the Gypsy Kings which was played at every gathering and I can still hum most of the first album.

At about 22:00 hours (10:00 PM), if we were lucky the local Irish pick up band would appear and after a wee bit of whiskey could be persuaded to play. Actually it took no persuasion, in fact if you tried to stop them it would have been a fight for sure. The strange thing is I never remember seeing any of the band members outside of when they were playing at a party. Someone said most of them were in the Transportation section but I'm not sure.

Anyway, I have never heard a better pick up band at least for Irish music and they were very popular. Over the course of a few months we all got to know their repertoire and people would shout out requests. My favorite was "Whiskey in the Jar" which they usually played last and it always brought the house down. Their version was particularly raucous and ended with some excellent mandolin riffs.

The parties at house four also provided the ugliest incident I can recall between staff members. The booze had been flowing one Friday evening when a group of African staff decided they had had enough Irish music and tried to cut the Rovers off.

It quickly took on racist overtones and punches were thrown along with a chair or two. Luckily there were enough Security staff attending the party and with a flying wedge of some pretty big bodies, they managed to separate them before it got real ugly. It was not too unusual for individual staff members to take a disliking to one another, being in such close quarters and all but I don't recall ever seeing it break out into a fight, other than that one time. That was house four.

*

In addition to the structural aspects of house five, the residents were interesting as well. Mad Max had a large room on the top floor with its own bathroom, and he spent most of his free time up there entertaining various guests. There was Bulldog, a Senior Security Officer from the New York office who with his barrel chest and prominent jowls actually looked very much like the classic carton bulldog. He lived on the third floor. Bulldog had an easy manner and although we never exchanged more than a few words at a time we became friends. I looked him up one time when I was in New York and he was about to retire and go back to his native island to live the good life.

There was a Lebanese lady who was a university lecturer in Sociology and who worked in Humanitarian Affairs. She made great Lebanese food. Also on the third floor was the quiet and unassuming Chief Communications Officer, who in his next assignment would die of burns he suffered in the crash of a UN helicopter in Central America.

Alex lived on the second floor and when a room became vacant in house five, he suggested to his house mates that I move in and I took the opportunity. I had been living with the same group of guys in house twelve in close quarters, and it was time for a change. House twelve was fun but being all guys at times it reminded me of a frat house, but not an Ivy League one.

*

At the time I moved into house five, there was a bit more than a month left on my initial appointment to UNISOM, and when the Personnel Office contacted me to see if I wanted to extend, I was having so much fun I naturally said yes. Actually, I had discussed this with my wife and since I was learning the ropes of the UN, had developed a working relationship with Happy and was getting a bit of a name in the DOA's office, we decided I should extend.

However, within a few days a response came back from HQ and they wanted to transfer me to another mission. It was explained that the number of staff in Somalia would be drawn down and we surmised it was in part a response to the withdrawal of American support for the Somalia mission.

At first I was upset but after a few more faxes, DPKO sent an extension of my contract as an Administrative Officer, in Rwanda. When they heard this, my friends in the Personnel Office got quite excited and explained how it was a plush assignment in comparison to Somalia. There was relative peace. Since it was located on a mountain plateau it was green and cool, and there was fresh food. My wife was also pleased as I would be getting out of Somalia which was clearly dangerous.

So things seemed to be set. I would be returning home in a few weeks for a visit with my family before transferring to Rwanda, where I was told that my new Chief would be much easier to work for than Happy. Although I was sad to be leaving Alex, BB, the DOA, and other friends I had made, things were winding down and I began to sort through my stuff with an eye to packing.

Meanwhile, at least my part of the mission seemed to be moving along rather well. Thanks to the efforts of the negotiations team the airport remained open and hiring for the renovations continued with relatively few problems. The DOA was pleased with my work including the review of candidates that our staff was conducting for his office, and even Happy seemed content. There were some recent demonstrations by a group calling themselves the Somali Student Association but even that did not seem to pose a threat.

*

On a Friday afternoon, just two weeks before I would be safely out of Somalia, I went to the roof top of house five where we had created a small lounge with some plastic chairs and a table under a shaded area, to enjoy one of my last hand rolled cigars (a Punch Rothschild). I took along a cold drink. I also took along some sort of briefing papers and pretended to read them as my mind drifted off to more interesting things.

Earlier that morning the student association had been out, walking from the airport past our residence and continuing through the area where UN residences were located. They carried a banner which I could not read and were chanting slogans but they did not seem too violent so we were not very concerned. I asked our Somali Guards what was written on the banner but they did not understand it so I would have to ask one of the translators next day. At any rate I did not think it had to do with the airport issue.

I lit my Punch and as I was enjoying the first smoke I heard shouting in the street below. Peering cautiously over the wall, being careful not to expose myself I saw that a small group of the demonstrators had returned.

There were three young men walking on the street that ran past one side of our residence and joined up with the main street, which in turn lead down a slight incline to the airport. They were throwing rocks at nothing in particular as they walked.

Around the corner, on the main street I also had a clear view of the entire area including two Nepalese soldiers who had just passed the main entrance gate to the Transport Compound. They were following a route they regularly took, like beat cops on a security patrol. This did not look good, if the young men started throwing stones at the soldiers I knew they would retaliate.

As the three young men rounded the corner, they and the two soldiers were only about twenty meters apart. The soldiers stopped in the middle of the street facing them. It was a tense moment as I expected the rocks to fly, which would have been far better than what happened. To my amazement, one of the Somali men started running straight at the two soldiers waiving his arms and shouting. Without thinking, the other two joined him and within a few seconds they were tight on the soldiers, who stood their ground but did not move at all.

They continued to shout and wave their fists but still the two soldiers did not make a move. Even their faces remained completely still. I remember thinking how they did not appear to be afraid or intimidated, just very stern and determined and I hoped to hell the young men saw the same thing.

As the stand off continued the two soldiers began to slowly back away towards the gate of the Transportation Compound and I thought for a second that cooler heads might prevail. But just as it looked like we might avoid disaster, the man who had lead the charge made the last mistake of his young life. He reached out and grabbed the barrel of the rifle that one of the soldiers held firmly in his hands, and tried to pull it free.

I remember noticing how, in spite of what I thought was extreme provocation, the soldiers still held their weapons pointed upward at about a forty-five degree angle and not towards the demonstrators.

Being pointed upward, the gun barrel required only a short downward jerk and it was pointed directly at the head, and then I heard the single sharp crack of the rifle. At the same time I saw the back of his head just explode as blood shot out, and mixed with shards of bone splattered across the wall; our wall to our house.

Unfortunately I had a perfect view and it seemed as if the blood actually arced as it left the back of the head on its trajectory towards the clean white wall. The young man fell straight down as if someone just flipped a switch and turned him off. He did not twist or turn, he did not fly backward or lurch, as if in a movie. He just fell right where he stood and did not move at all. A large pool of thick very dark blood, almost black in color began to ooze and form in a circle around his head and I expected to see him twitch or jerk, but he never did.

Ducking as if to avoid the blood and bullets, the other two immediately ran off and stood a few meters away. There was no place to run if the soldiers chose to shoot them and they looked scared. The soldiers however, continued to back cautiously towards the Transportation office and within a few seconds disappeared inside as the gate closed behind them.

For several long seconds the two young men looked at the corpse of their friend lying crumpled in the street and finally they began to shout and curse, then run in the direction of the airport, leaving the street silent, very very silent.

I guess it is no exaggeration to say I was stunned and took a deep breath as I had unconsciously stopped breathing for a few seconds. This incident had to be reported immediately and as I reached for my walki talki I heard a Security Guard from the Transportation Compound calling India Base (India Base stands for Information Base. It was part of the operations center and acted as the command center in such situations). He reported a shooting but had a limited view and could not report much more than that there were no UN staff shot. I came on and identified my call letters, Hotel 5 and informed India Base of my location.

We had all had the required security training and knew we should remain calm and stick to the facts of what actually happened when reporting on an incident, but I had just seen a man killed and it was real. Forcing myself to concentrate, I confirmed that one Somali national had been shot and was almost certainly dead, and I confirmed that no UN staff members were injured.

India Base asked for details and I relayed how the three nationals had approached the UN soldiers (I was on an open radio channel and did not want to use identifying indicators such as nationalities, any more than necessary) and how one civilian had grabbed the rifle and was shot. When asked if the injuries were fatal I blurted out "sure as hell looks like it" which I guess was not too professional but it just slipped out. India Base requested that since I had a view of the area that I stay behind cover but continue to monitor the situation for further incidents.

*

Left alone with my thoughts for the moment, I recalled how many of the UN waki talkis had been stolen and as a result we knew that our communications were being monitored by locals. That is so in all missions and makes it necessary to change the radio channel configurations from time to time. That being the case it was very likely that many people were listening and knew my approximate location, and it was quite possible that one of them was a sniper. I made a point of staying well down behind the low wall running around the perimeter of the roof, only occasionally peeking over to be sure the body was there and it was real.

After about fifteen minutes I heard a vehicle approach from the direction of the airport, and peering cautiously over the wall I saw it was a large older model Ford Crown Victoria, dusty brown and rather beat up. I immediately raised India Base and gave them a running commentary as the car stopped and two men and the driver jumped out and stood around the body for a moment before they picked it up and rather unceremoniously pushed it into the back seat.

The car made a U turn and sped back in the direction of the airport. All that was left was a large stain of blood and brains on the street, and a smear on the wall that I thought looked much like a Picasso sketch. It's strange the connections and observations your mind makes in such situations, almost as if you have no control over it.

Shaking my head I signed off from India Base and after staring out at the Indian Ocean for several minutes I prepared to leave. I could not help but think that that young man was someone's son, or worse yet, someone's husband and the father of a child who would never see him again. He had made a hot headed mistake and while I did not blame the solider, he did not deserve to die for that. If death were so easily caused by careless thoughtless errors, than I would be dead several times over.

As I walked past the white plastic table to go downstairs I noticed a cigar butt in the ash tray. It was a Punch Rothschild and I had unconsciously continued smoking during this entire time. As I descended the stairs to my room, I thought how accustomed we (or at least I) had become to death and fighting over the past few months. How my mind took it all in but had no choice but to tuck it all away somewhere, only to have it resurface perhaps years later, like a body thrown into a lake, which surfaces at an inconvenient time, demanding to be dealt with. That is the way most of us reacted, pushing the worst things down somewhere inside our mind. Those who could not do that did not extend their contracts.

Chapter 9: Leaving Somalia

Perhaps seeing this man loose his life so quickly and unexpectedly affected me more deeply than I was aware of, but I was now ready to leave Somalia. I could see how easy it would be to get killed, if not intentionally by some camel boy or a sniper, then by a stray bullet which God knows there were enough of in Mog.

The thought of my skull exploding against a wall was something I could not let myself dwell on. I began to get what friends of mine who had been in Viet Nam called short timers syndrome; when you have only a short time left and you are just sure you are going to get killed before you can get out.

At any rate, I became extra cautious and even avoided being in the open or going up to the roof top any more than I had to. I know it did not make much sense, but maybe I had just been lucky up to then and the odds could turn against me at any time. Something that was beyond my control, and that was the part that scared me. It was not something that made me unable to function, just a nagging thought that would not go away.

I threw myself into packing, writing my handover notes and attending a couple of parties. In missions there is frequently an official farewell party or function for staff members who are leaving, where the person is roasted a bit, a few tears flow along with the wine or beer, and maybe a plaque, or photo signed by all is given to the guest. In Somalia I don't recall this happening. Maybe it was because the mission was so large in comparison to many that had taken place before UNISOM, or maybe it was because the turn over rate was so high it was impossible to keep track of the comings and goings.

I had a few drinks with some friends in one of the canteens scattered around the compound, gave my notes to Happy and the night before I was to leave I spent extra time going over all the departure details in my mind until I finally fell asleep.

*

Checking out of any mission is one of the most trying things you will ever undergo. As would be expected you have to account for and turn in every piece of equipment issued to you, but that is the easy part. The tough part is walking around the compound trying to find the office, and then the only person in that office who is authorized to sign off on your checkout form. The procedure is excessive and most of it could be handled with one e-mail from the Personnel Section.

This procedure is especially difficult for an administrative officer or anyone who has fiscal responsibilities, procurement responsibilities, a vehicle checked out to them, or communications equipment. In Somalia I had three of the four and walking from one end of the forty plus acre compound to the other, under the beastly Somali sun was exasperating, but in hindsight it was good training for all the future checkouts I would have to endure.

The most trying check out I had to do was in Sudan where we also had to close out our local bank account which due to the medieval banking procedures took a full day, unless you could find someone to stand in line for you. I finally resorted to bribing a local security guard to "push" my documents in front of others in the line, and I returned later that afternoon to pick them up. Not setting a good example I know but I did have a plane to catch the next morning.

When we completed the first phase of the checkout in Mog, we had to catch the UN plane to Nairobi and once we arrived there, we had to check out of the regional UN office in Nairobi.

*

On the morning I was to leave I took my bags with me to the office and since I had turned over all my equipment and files and could not do any work, I went to the cafeteria for coffee where I felt I would be out of Happy's sight. She had given me a good performance evaluation and I wanted to leave it at that.

At eleven, as instructed I took my two bags to the Transport Office to catch the shuttle bus to the airport. There were five of us leaving that day and we were anxious to get going, but we were told there was an indefinite delay as there was fighting near the airport.

My first thought was that fighting had started again over jobs at the airport which meant I would definitely not be going anywhere. However, it was only some street fighting that had closed the main route to the airport, but did not involve the UN. The flight could leave as late as 15:00 hours (3:00 PM), any later than that and it could not get landing space in Nairobi. So we waited. With every hour that passed our tension rose until the five of us were not being very civil. We were ready to leave.

Finally at about 14:30 a Security Officer explained that there was a lull in the fighting. It could start again at any minute but this was our last chance to make the flight that day. We threw our bags into the bus and with an armed security vehicle in front and another one behind us, we roared out of the compound. Our luck held and we pulled into the terminal at 14:45. The plane was already warming up as our bags were tossed into the luggage compartment, the door was shut and before we could fasten our belts the plane was moving.

*

As the plane gained altitude we passed by the same silent sentinels that left such an impression on my first flight into Mog. The crashed and abandoned aircraft still stood on each side of the landing strip as a testament to the endless war, as did the shell pocked houses and heaps of empty plastic water bottles. Finally, almost mercifully we were too high to see details and ahead the mountains rose abruptly to the Kenya plateau.

As we finally began to relax I drifted into a sort of sleep state and recalled a conversation I had with a Somali kitchen worker at one of the afternoon parties. His name was Ahmad and his English was good enough for me to understand.

We were discussing how the war had gotten started when with sad eyes he explained that he had recently lost his wife. She had contracted what would normally be a routine sickness, but as there was no medical help available she died leaving two small children. I was devastated for him as I imagined how I would react if I lost my wife. After a few moments of silence I told him I was so sorry to hear it, and asked him what he would do now. He responded "Oh, my other wife will take care of them" and excusing himself went back to work in the kitchen.

This was one of the lesions I learned from Somalia. It would be easy to think he was being callous, that this heathen had several wives so he didn't care if he lost one, that not being a westerner he just does not value human life like we do and so on. I have heard them all. And maybe some of these judgmental observations do apply in some cases, but certainly not all.

In many places people grow up with death happening all around them. In Somalia hundreds of thousands of people had died of starvation, more hundreds of thousands had died from sickness and diseases, and God knows how many died from war and violence. And this had gone on for years with no end in sight. Under those circumstances if one allowed themselves to be affected by every death they would not be able to function. They simply could not survive the psychological trauma. I know that within the short span of a few months I had developed the ability to simply push such things under, and go on. So much depends on circumstances and on the human imperative to survive.

Part Two

Hard Lessons – Iraq, Kuwait and New York City

Chapter 10: Rwanda

After nearly eight months away, I arrived home during a spring snow storm. It was actually a light one by northern standards, but after the heat of Somalia the large fat flakes of snow and temperatures hovering only a bit above freezing were more than enough. My wife was busy planning an early graduation celebration for our son who was in his senior year and already anxious to start university. Our daughter, as precocious as ever was busy with girl scouts, band and perfecting her entry in the upcoming science fair.

After the initial hectic round of parties and visits with friends I just slept for a few days and began sorting through my stuff preparing for Rwanda where I would be starting my next assignment in less than two weeks. I also spent some time in the local library researching Rwanda, which in the days of paper based knowledge is how it was done. I did not find much beyond a few brief US government reports.

After a few days of this routine I was feeling somewhat at a loss so I visited my old office, since I was on leave and still technically an employee. Everyone seemed happy to see me but I felt like a visitor. They stopped to talk to me but it was obvious that they were preoccupied with their own work and their own world, which I understood completely. My former director was fascinated with my experiences in Somalia and spent a considerable time talking with me, after which I made one more pass around the office and left.

I had made the change and I think at that time I was aware that for better or worse I would stay with peacekeeping. I was already getting anxious to get back to "the field", something that really gets into your blood. I missed the thought that at any minute something unexpected, rather wild and yes, dangerous could happen. The next, and last time I would go back to my old office would be four years, at which time I was a complete stranger to most of the staff.

*

On the morning of April 7, 1994 I was in the bedroom busy laying out things to be packed, when my wife shouted from downstairs asking if I had seen the news. We did not have a TV upstairs so I walked downstairs where she was watching a CNN report on the death of Rwandan President Habyarimana. His plane had been shot down under questionable circumstances as it attempted to land in Kigali, the capital city. Key moderate members of the government had been assassinated by units of the military and extremist members of the Hutu tribe. Within a few hours these same groups began to attack the other main tribal group, the Tutsi as well as moderate members of the Hutu.

"You can't go there" my wife said, "they are already pulling the UN out". That seemed reasonable but I had not heard anything from DPKO and I did have a visa and ticket to fly to Rwanda at the end of that week which was only about three days away.

We followed the news closely and the situation continued to get worse, so when I had not heard anything by the next afternoon I phoned Kid at the DPKO office in New York. Once she confirmed that I was not in Rwanda she seemed relieved and said "stay where you are, we'll get back to you". My first reaction was that this was sloppy on the part of DPKO, but as I would learn first hand in later missions when I was responsible for such matters, evacuations are seldom neat and clean. In addition to staff in remote locations which have to be extracted, there are always those on leave and on official business outside the mission area which have to be accounted for.

Then there is always the unexpected to be dealt with. For example when the UN compound was bombed in Baghdad in August 2003 killing the UN Special Envoy Sergio DeMello and twenty one other UN staff, one person was officially announced as dead only to be found in a hospital several days later, covered in bandages. It can get messy.

On the up side this gave me more time to spend with my family and we made the most of it. My wife arranged another party complete with a poster made from the photo of me standing on the roof in Mog with helmet, flack jacket and rifle. This entertained our friends immensely. I had time to attend the local school science fair where our daughter entered her exhibit, and we took a long weekend and visited the university campus where our son would attend starting in September. I was enjoying the break but after four weeks I was starting to get anxious that I might somehow get lost in the shuffle and not get another assignment.

Finally I got a call from DPKO telling me I would be assigned as the Officer in Charge of my section in the United Nations Iraq/Kuwait Observation Mission. UNIKOM was established in April 1991 after the first gulf war, to monitor the fifteen kilometer wide demilitarized zone that ran the length of the border between Kuwait and Iraq. I would be stationed in the main UN compound in Um Qsar, Iraq which is located on the Arabian Gulf and is the only true salt water port in Iraq. While it was a much smaller mission than Somalia, I was the OIC which was a definite promotion. Saddam Hussein was still in power but the war was over and the gulf was relatively quiet in comparison to Somalia and Rwanda, and with the promotion to OIC my wife was pleased, as was I.

I now had five days to get ready for Kuwait and Iraq, which was actually quite similar to packing for Somalia. I was also pleased to learn that I did not need any additional vaccinations or shots but that should not be a surprise since I had had just come from one of the most unhealthy environments around.

The day before I left we were looking at a map of the gulf and decided that our next R&R would be in Dubai. With this plan in mind, and the realization that I was not going into a live war zone, our separation this time was easier.

Chapter 11: The Good Life in the Gulf

After Somalia life in the Gulf was going to be quite easy. This was evident as soon as I landed at the airport in Kuwait City in May of 1994. Instead of an armed escort I was met by one of the local staff who whisked me through customs and had my bags before I even had a chance to look around. The Kuwait airport was essentially a large open building without much in the way of signs or directions. Most people who used it were just familiar with the facility and knew where to go. It was getting a bit old but it was clean, which is true of Kuwait in general. Kuwait is a clean place and I have never gotten sick eating at even small cheap restaurants, which is more than I can say for the US.

The airport has since been thourhly modernized and now looks much like a typical European airport. It is modern, clean and efficient, although it is constantly clogged by all the expat workers leaving and returning for visits to the Philippines, India and Pakistan.

The UN had an office in Kuwait City located in a three story villa on the southern edge of the city between the first and second ring roads, and it was modest by Kuwaiti standards. By most any other standards it was just shy of being a palace with circular stairways, a small indoor garden and pool, and plenty of air conditioning. After filling out a few forms and performing other routine processing in tasks, I was loaded into a Toyota Hiace van along with two other new staff members and we left for Un Qsar, a little over an hour to the north west, on the border with Iraq.

I noticed immediately that we did not have an armed escort nor did we have an armed guard in the vehicle which made me a bit nervous at first but it quickly became obvious that the most dangerous things in Kuwait were the Kuwaiti drivers. They were totally outrageous, and it is still one of the most dangerous places to drive outside of the Washington beltway. Every vehicle was large, driven as fast as it would go with scant regard for lanes, and with no consideration for pedestrians, animals or other vehicles. The only smaller sized vehicles on the street seemed to be the UN cars which were Toyotas and Mazdas and when they came up against a full sized Mercedes, BMW or Cadillac traveling just under the speed of sound, they usually lost out. Things have improved a bit over the years but Kuwait is still a dangerous place in which to drive.

*

Driving through Kuwait City there were still scattered signs of the damage and destruction left by the Iraqi invasion but things seemed to be back to normal and in fact quite well cleaned up. It was hard to tell looking at some buildings if they were just old and showing the signs of neglect, or if the discolored and chipped walls were the result of shelling and fires. But as we got to the edge of town and turned northwest to take the now famous highway to Um Qsar, the driver who was Lebanese and spoke Arabic, French and English explained that we were passing through the area where the American planes had caught up with the retreating Iraqi army and knocked out tanks and trucks by the hundreds. The locals had various names for this junction such as the fish tank and the shooting gallery since the planes and rockets just pounded the hapless souls Saddam had sent into Kuwait, as they tried too late to retreat. He said it took weeks to clean up the deserted and destroyed vehicles, and the bodies.

*

Driving north, the paved two lane highway skirted around the bay and past a large stand of pine trees, each about fifteen feet tall. The trees were all dead, whether from lack of water or effects of the war I never did determine, but they were a ghostly shade of grey and one of the strangest sights I remember from Kuwait. With the long strands of moss which grew on the branches trailing in the breeze, and being planted in rows they looked like phantoms, marching out of the sea behind them. I once stopped and spent some time walking through the area. It was once apparently a park as there were still a few scattered groups with blankets spread out enjoying picnic lunches of falafel, olives, flat bread and babakanush. It felt rather sad and depressing, almost as if it were a national grave site but in a strange way I enjoyed it.

Several times we were forced to slow to go around large pot holes which were in fact bomb craters. Once when we stopped for a few minutes to let a large herd of camels and sheep cross, our driver advised us not to walk in the desert or off the side of the road as there were still unexploded ordinance and land mines, and while most of the un-cleared areas were marked there was always the possibility of stumbling upon one.

Sometime later, when I was traveling with a patrol near the Saudi border a land mine was pointed out to me by one of our demining crew. Even though we were less than two meters away, I had to concentrate to see it. It is no wonder that unsuspecting people, usually simple farmers, women collecting firewood and children are frequent victims of these ghastly things, not to mention the many farm animals and flocks that get blown up around the world every year.

*

It was technically spring and still relatively mild by Gulf standards but it felt hot to me. The sun was strong and tended to burn exposed skin in a matter of minutes so the air-con was already in full use. I would eventually become quite accustomed to the Gulf weather and look forward to the winter months when we would go camping in the high desert and enjoy the Meditterarian like climate. One other indication of just how hot it was is that the security guards all had gloves in their pockets which they used to open the metal gates, which got so hot in the sun that they burned bare skin. I took to keeping gloves in my car after I got a small second degree burn from the seat belt buckle one particularly hot afternoon.

After about an hour we arrived at the border between Kuwait and Iraq, which was well marked by UN signs pointing to the main compound in one direction and the military camp where the troop contingents were stationed, in the other. The main troop contingent was from Bangladesh with smaller contingents from other countries including Argentina, India, the US, Scandinavian and several African countries. The Russians also had several officers stationed in Um Qsar but the main Russian contingent was in Baghdad.

Since we were now inside of Iraqi territory, several Iraqi guards were also stationed just outside the compound gates. We could tell the mood in Baghdad by the deminer of these guards. We had local staff from both Iraq and Kuwait and they were brought in daily by UN busses. At least once a week the Iraqi guards would find some reason to hold the busses up for an hour or more while they pretended to search for something, or just to confiscate bottles of water and snacks from the staff.

However, this time we passed without problem and found ourselves inside the compound which was somewhat like being inside a prisoner of war camp. The compound was about ten acres in size and surrounded by double walls of barbed wire, each about ten feet high. Along one side of the compound the town of Um Qsar encroached to within twenty yards and the local Iraqi population would keep a weary eye on us from their shacks. The children would alternately throw rocks at us or beg for water and food, but mostly they just ignored us.

The compound consisted of a hospital building built and donated to the Iraqi people by the European Union years ago, but which had since been abandoned by the Iraqi government. It had suffered some damage during the gulf war but repairs had been made by the UN. The main building held the offices of the Force Commander who was also serving as the head of the mission, the Chief Administrative Officer, the substantive offices (Political Affairs, Humanitarian Affairs, Legal Affairs) and the Military Affairs offices. The other administrative offices were located in a separate wing about fifty meters away.

At least the office buildings were permanent structures and not the white trash trailers we had in Somalia. Our living quarters however were in trailers, but I had my own trailer with private bathroom to myself since I was now a section chief. Our compound was fairly well kept and had a surprising number of trees and shrubs planted back when it was a hospital, which provided shade and made the hot dusty environment a bit more bearable.

I was introduced to my new CAO, who was a short slightly stocky Irishman who had spent a good part of his career with the UN in the border area of Israel, Jordan, Syria and Lebanon. Tom was classically educated, soft spoken but with the streetwise toughness of a priest from a poor perish. He had a noticeable Irish lilt which hid the fact that he could be one tough guy, in a nice sort of way. We hit it off quite well and would work together for over two years until he was transferred back to his former post.

I settled in, determined to make my career with UN peacekeeping, but as I would find out there were many landmines along the way.

Chapter 12: Learning the System

On my first day in the UNIKOM office I was visited by the Chief Transport Officer and the Chief of Security, who after introducing themselves told me they had a problem. One of the local staff Drivers had been a problem since he was hired but to get rid of him was proving to be a bureaucratic nightmare, or at least more work than either of them was willing to do. His most recent and most serious incident occurred at a staff party about four months earlier. The party was given in the military camp on the Kuwaiti side of the demilitarized zone, and the driver (Porto was his nickname) was supposed to be on duty that evening so he could drive one of the vans transporting staff back to Kuwait City after the party. There was some alcohol served at the party and Porto managed to get quite drunk and belligerent. Violation number one, drinking while on duty.

A Security Guard took the van keys away from him and arranged for another driver to take his duty, but Porto took this as a personal affront and when the Security Guard was not looking he took the keys out of the guard shack and got into the van, intent on driving back to the city. Certainly that has to be violation two. As he approached the security gate one of the guards stepped forward and instructed Porto to halt. Instead, he gunned the engine and although the guard managed to dive out of the way, the van still hit his leg as it sped past, causing a severe strain.

After about a hundred meters of unsteady driving, the van careened into a ditch and Porto was dragged out and locked up in the Security Office for the night. The van was extensively damaged and had to be written off. In accordance with the regulations, a Transportation Committee was convened to hear the case and recommended that he be placed on leave immediately, with a further recommendation that he be terminated. All terminations must be approved by Human Resources in head quarters. The recommendation had been sent to New York as required, but for over three months there had been no response. Meanwhile Porto was enjoying fully paid leave. I was surprised that this case had lingered on for months, but I would learn that it is not uncommon for disciplinary and dismissal cases to essentially slip into a black hole waiting for some committee or tribunal that never seems to convene.

We had three immediate problems. First was the message this sent to all staff, that there were no consequences for even a serious violation of rules. Second, we were down by one driver in the rotation roster and it was causing scheduling problems for the Transportation Section. Finally, the Security Guards were quite upset and things were getting tense between them and the Drivers.

Fortunately, Porto's contract was now up for extension at the end of the month so we had a short time to work. I quickly convened the Transportation Committee and presented the case that they might recommend that Porto's UN issued driver's license be revoked for drunk driving and attempting to hit the Security Guard. They were only too happy to present the recommendation to the CAO who signed off on it. With that in hand I informed Porto that since he did not have a valid UN issued license he could not perform his duties, and therefore his contract would not be extended. I also advised him of his right to appeal, which he did.

A few days later I got a rather terse call from the Personnel Section in New York, asking in effect who the hell I thought I was to be terminating a staff member without going through the proper protocol with HQ. I recognized the name of the person on the other end of the call and knew that while she was HQ staff she was the same rank as me, and I felt confident we could make the case that he had been terminated for good case. Luckily I also had Porto's file on my desk so I reviewed the various faxes and letters sent by my predecessor and made it clear that the mission had not heard one word in response. In light of the lack of guidance from HQ the mission had taken the steps it felt were appropriate. After several long seconds of silence she asked if I would fax all of the relevant documents for review which indicated to me they had either lost them, ignored them, or could not find them.

The reaction from the staff in the mission however, was good. The Section Chiefs were pleased that someone was able to get rid of Porto. The local staff, for the most part were also pleased as they felt that Porto had really stepped over the line and had it coming. Even the CAO was pleased.

So much for my colleagues in the mission, but HQ was another matter. While I did not hear anything back and they let the matter stand, some time later I learned that this issue had come up when I was being considered for a promotion and it may have played a part in my being passed over.

*

The case of the drunk driver only served to focus attention on the problem with alcohol in general; there was too much of it and it appeared that it was finding it's way into the city. It was perfectly legal for the UN to sell liquor in the PX (which was located on UN territory in the compound) and it caused no problems with either host government. Sales were carefully controlled and only International staff could purchase it. However, when I arrived there was no limit on the amount any one individual could purchase and we were selling a lot of booze.

The head of the PX Board, who was also a Security Officer brought to my attention that certain individuals were buying several cases of hard liquor, several cases of wine and many cases of beer on a regular basis. They always said they were just giving a party, but even if they gave a party every week it could not account for it. Since a bottle of Johnny Walker Black, the preferred drink on the local black market (and still a good scotch) was going for as much as $80 a bottle and we were paying about one forth that in the PX, it did not take much imagination to see where most of it was probably going. To make matters worse, many of what I termed mass purchases were being made by members of two of the smaller military contingents. The head of the PX was concerned that if this continued, the host governments would get upset and put pressure on us to stop importing alcohol, even for our own staff.

I presented this to the CAO along with a recommendation that we place a limit on the monthly purchases per person to try to bring some control into the situation. He agreed and drew up a limit, which was still liberal enough that if any one person had drank all the booze he was entitled to purchase he would have likely died of alcohol poisoning. The PX Board approved it by a mixed vote and we implemented the plan.

While it would be a bit of an overstatement to say the crap hit the fan, we did get some immediate and less than positive reaction. First, it was no real secret that I had been involved and a few individuals approached me demanding to know why the board had placed these limits on purchases. I explained that the PX was there for the use of individual UN members only, that far more booze was being purchased than could possibly be drunk by all of the UN staff in the mission put together, and the limits being placed were still very reasonable. I also got several calls during the middle of the night from what sounded like drunk angry people but they were rather incoherent so I can't be sure it was about the PX issue. Slowly, over a few weeks the reactions died down, but it really stopped completely only after the current members of the two un-named smaller military contingents finished their tour and were replaced by new contingent members.

A few months later the Legal Affairs Officer, who happened to be the same nationality as one of the contingents hinted to me that this action had cost his countrymen quite a lot of money, but refused to state it in so many words. However, he understood the need for this action and was not upset by it, so we had a good laugh over a beer.

*

After being shot at and having grenades launched at me in Somalia, life in UNIKOM was actually rather quiet. One of the most exciting things to happen occurred in the early spring of one of those undeterminable years. The Iraqi military would occasionally do something to provoke the US and the UN, and this time they started pulling tanks up to within sight of the Um Qsar mission headquarters. This made us tense but none of us believed they would be so reckless as to attack us. Our Russian contingent which was stationed in Baghdad, and who had the best relations with the Iraqi government immediately reassured us they were working on it and after a few days the tanks did indeed pull back to Basra.

A few days later, as I was out jogging one morning in the demilitarized zone I heard a strange sound overhead. It was a combination of a whir and whooshing sound. I looked up and going overhead were two Cruse missiles. They looked like large cigars, dark gunmetal grey in color, and were churning along at what seemed like such a slow speed I was afraid they would just fall to the ground. I guessed they were only a few hundred feet up, well under any radar. A strange sight, I stood and watched them until they disappeared over the horizon.

When I got back to the compound several of our staff confirmed that they had also seen also them so it was not my imagination. It was later confirmed that two Cruse missiles took out a radio and communications center near Basra, one no doubt used by the tanks sent to harass us.

Chapter 13: Keep Friends Close, Enemies Closer

One of my duties in UNIKOM was to apply for work visas for national staff and to renew the visas as they expired. We had an interesting situation in UNIKOM in that all national staff (also known as local staff since they were recruited locally) from the Kuwait side were in fact third country nationals from the Philippines, India, Pakistan and a smattering of African and Middle Eastern countries. They had come to Kuwait to work in the oil economy and since the Kuwaiti government was very supportive of us, they allowed us to recruit from that labor pool. All of the local staff from Iraq were of course Iraqi.

For the Iraqi visas, I dealt with a Captain of the National Police who represented the immigration service. He was a few years younger than me and every time we had business to transact he insisted on coming to my office rather than having me go into Um Qsar to his office. Our first couple of meetings were strictly business like and he seemed a bit weary of me, me being of a nationality that his government officially despised.

He seemed like a decent person and I always met him at the gate to be sure our guards did not give him problems and offered him tea or water before we started discussions. In effect I treated him like we would any official visitor. On his third visit he noticed the photos of my family on my desk and asked about them. After I explained who was who in the photos and let him look at them, he told me that he had two boys and took a couple of small faded photos from his wallet. I told him they were hansom and looked like him which was true and it also made him beam, and being aware that it is not polite to ask about the wife or any female member of the family in Arab society unless you are a very close friend, I carefully avoided that subject.

Our official visits took on a different tone after that. We started by asking about each others family (as much as was allowable) and after tea we got down to business. I can't say our visas got any easier to get after that but it did make things more comfortable. However, this small friendship would prove to be very important at a later date.

That date came about two months later on a Saturday morning, which was the second day of the weekend in UNIKOM. I was the duty officer or DO that week so I had remained in Um Qsar for the weekend. The CAO, Tom had also remained in the compound that weekend and we planned to do a bit of work after lunch, but he wanted to go jogging in the morning.

We left the main gate and instead of going straight as usual to follow the road to the military contingent camp, he turned left and we skirted along the compound perimeter. I assumed he wanted to look at the fence and the burm (deep anti- tank ditch) which ran the entire length of the demilitarized zone.

When we reached the end of the compound fence, instead of turning right which would have kept us in the safety of the demilitarized zone Tom turned left which took us on a narrow path along the back perimeter of the compound, but it also took us very close to the town. We were technically still on UN controlled turf but I was immediately uncomfortable and told Tom that if we were running outside the zone we should take a couple of guards with us. He ignored me and kept jogging. There was a back gate to the compound, but it was a considerable distance away and we were quite exposed until we got within sight of it. Also, since that gate was seldom used, except in evacuation drills, the guards may well be asleep or at least dozing off.

We were drawing attention and soon enough I saw what I was dreading , two armed men in uniforms. They stepped into the path about twenty meters ahead of us and motioned for us to stop, which we did. In broken English they asked who we were and demanded to see our identification.

Wrong Place-Right Time

Tom told them we were with UNIKOM, which I'm sure they already knew, and since we were on UN controlled property we did not need to show any ID. He was polite but firm and I hoped they would let it go. However, they seemed to be in a rather belligerent mood and demanded to see our ID.

I had my identification card in a pocket, and since we did not even go to the bathroom without it, I was sure Tom had his as well. I also felt certain that he would just show it and let them try to read it, rather than risk having this thing needlessly escalate into an incident. Since he was the senior officer I took my cue from Tom and waited for him to make the next move.

When he did not move I began to get worried and said "let's just show it to them", but again Tom ignored me. Then he said "I do not have my identification, I forgot it." OK, we could still go to the gate and have the UN guards identify us or even go get the ID, but neither Tom nor the Iraqi's seemed to be in a mood to settle this. The conversation went on; show me your ID, I don't have an ID. This was getting stupid. I knew what these people were capable of and they would love to get a couple of senior UN staff under arrest.

Ignoring Tom this time, I began to make suggestions to solve this situation, but one thing I could not do was to let them take just one of us, so I did not produce my ID which probably would have at least gotten me through. By this time additional Iraqi soldiers had shown up as well as a small crowd of curious civilians.

Just as things were getting hot and I thought we might indeed get arrested, a vehicle pulled up and my friend, the National Police Officer got out. He immediately sized up the situation and walking over, he gave the traditional Arab greeting Asalaam Alaykum as he extended his hand to me. Wa-alaykum Salaam I responded, eagerly extending my hand, as I noticed the surprised look on Tom's face, as well as the Iraqi officers who were confronting us.

My friend began to talk in earnest to his counterparts and after several minutes they began to relax a bit. When I got the chance I explained that we were out jogging and since we had forgotten our UNIKOM ID we had stayed on the compound path. I also gave them some crap about coming this way because we had never been into the town and just wanted to see some of Un Qsar. I was buying time. I also told them there was a gate into the UN compound less than a hundred meters away and we would proceed directly to that gate if that was agreeable.

Finally they relented and after we thanked everyone, we began to jog cautiously toward the gate. The UN guards had noticed the commotion and had the gate open as we arrived. We waved to them and kept on jogging until we reached Tom's office. As we entered his office he pulled his ID from his pocket and tossed it on his desk. Damn! He had it all the time. Sometimes Tom was hard to figure.

I made a point of thanking my friend for his help at our next meeting, but I did not tell him that Tom had his identification all the time.

Chapter 14: On the Border

The main objective of UNIKOM was to monitor the peace between Kuwait and Iraq, which in addition to overseeing prisoner exchanges and diplomatic relations between the two states, included constant monitoring of the Iraqi border. To this end we had established UN outposts at regular intervals along the entire length of the border, with teams of eight to twelve UN soldiers in each. In true UN fashion, the solders came from the various military contingents so each outpost had a mixture of nationalities. The outposts, located inside the fifteen kilometer wide demilitarized zone, consisted of several of the ubiquitous white trailers including one for kitchen and mess, and another as an ablution unit (bathroom and showers). Each post reflected the character and nationalities of the occupants. Some had dart boards and others a collection of African drums, but all of them had the ever present soccer balls and net. There were also civilian administrative staff members stationed in some of the posts to provide support in such areas as transportation, logistics, communications and facilities maintenance.

Section Chiefs made routine visits to the camps and we made it a habit to take along a box of items and snacks we knew the solders and staff would like. McVities cookies were my favorite contribution, especially the chocolate dipped variety although the chocolate melted in the hot sun so they had to be refrigerated before eating. I once saw a hungry soldier eat nearly a whole tube of them by himself. Another favorite was the processed potato chips that look like pieces of stirofoam and are neatly packed in a tube. (Things packed in tubes are easy to transport and slip nicely into a backpack) The favorite chips were paprika or chili flavor and the Indian variety was much in demand as they had a real bite.

*

I also made a point of riding along with the patrols that went out from each post, in part to establish rapport with the staff but also to see what more we could be doing to support their activities. One of the first such trips I took sticks out in my mind over the others.

It was mid summer and very hot, reaching as high as 55-57 Celsius or 130 -135 Fahrenheit in the afternoon. Large dust eddies (actually more like small twisters) kicked up by the heat, swirled around us occasionally as we drove along narrow dusty roads and trails that wandered back and forth from the Kuwait side, to the Iraq side and back again. My colleagues on this patrol were a Swedish Officer and a Nigerian Officer. This particular patrol took about four hours and passed through an Iraqi village, a Kuwaiti border post and an Iraqi border post as well.

There were a few commercial farms on the Kuwait side of the border, where water was available for irrigation, but mostly it was very sparsely populated by Bedouin herders who did not really claim affiliation with any state and followed the camels and sheep as they grazed on whatever they could find.

As we entered the Iraqi village we passed something that looked like one of the earth Hogan's one would see on a reservation in the American Southwest. It was a mound of earth with a wooden framed doorway for entrance. The doorway itself was covered by a carpet or heavy drape. Not much to look at but quite effective as protection from the weather and the elements. In front of it sat an Iraqi solder in a worn uniform and beside him was an AK 47. I noticed he did not have shoes, but was wearing a pair of plastic flip flops. He was used to UN vehicles and without getting up from the small patch of shade he had found, waived us past.

The village stretched out for several hundred meters along an irrigation ditch, but since there was no river or lake nearby, I guessed it was supplied by a spring. It provided just enough water for the villagers to plant small fields of onions and vegetables which stood in stark contrast to the barren brown desert that took over immediately where the fields ended.

A few people stared at us as we passed the shacks that served as their homes. They seemed to be neither hostile nor friendly, simply there. They were dressed in old worn clothes, the men in pants and shirts, the women in the traditional long robes but I noticed that many of them did not have there faces covered. I also noticed this in Afghanistan, in areas where people are actively working, as opposed to being in the house or walking around, many women do not cover their faces, or only partly so. Perhaps it is just too dammed inconvenient when you are working, and necessity prevails.

Like kids everywhere, some of the children chased after our vehicles as we move slowly through the village. Having just come from Somalia, what struck me was that while skinny and most certainly malnourished, these people were not quite on the verge of starvation. As we passed through the village and slipped into the desert again, it occurred to me that aside from the guard's Hogan at the entrance to the village, I had seen no evidence of any government presence; no school, no clinic. These people were very much on their own.

*

Less than fifteen kilometers further along the winding dirt road I noticed several tall masts jutting above the desert scrub, off in the distance. As we came closer I could make out that they were communications masts for cell phone, TV and the like and the driver told me they belonged to a Kuwaiti Military guard post. As we drew closer I could see that the compound they serviced consisted of several large trailer like structures formed in a square around a central structure which contained the kitchen, mess hall and recreation area. Parked around the central structure, under shaded carports were a collection of large SUV's and top end cars. As we passed the gate I could clearly hear the sound of generators and air conditioners running at full throttle. A sharply dressed guard smiled and waived at us as we continued slowly down the road.

As if to drive home the extremes, which seemed to me to be largely an accident of birth or more to the point of where you were born, a few kilometers further we next came upon an Iraqi border post. Or should I say we nearly ran over it as we came over a small mound and just off to the left of the trail was a single small tent which was actually no more than a tarp stretched over a rope between two poles. It did not have walls and was staked directly into the earth with both ends open. It reminded me of the simple tents we made as kids when we would camp overnight, next to the creek that ran through the cow pasture behind our house. Certainly, this could not provide much protection from the temperature extremes of the desert.

As we drew to a stop in front of it two men scrambled out of the makeshift tent and walked quickly toward our Jeep. I can only describe their appearance as startling. They did not have shoes and were barefooted, not even plastic flip flops. Their pants were thread bare and frayed at the ends and the shirts they wore were once part of a uniform but no insignia or rank could be made out on the sun faded cloth. They did not carry any weapons but I assume they were inside the tent.

They smiled and seemed to know the soldiers but did not pay any attention to me at all. The driver got out and greeted them in Arabic with Asalaam Alaykum and a hand shake. They spoke for a few minutes and then went around to the back of the vehicle where the driver opened the rear hatch door. As I watched he took out several bottles of water and a small box of food and handed it to them. This was a probably a violation as the UN was not supposed to offer support to either side, but common sense told me these guards may have died without this small help which was occasionally given to them.

As far as I could tell, they did not get any food or water from the Iraqi Army or government and in fact were supposed to bring their own supplies or be supported by the local population. But from what I saw of the few villages scattered along the border, this was in no way possible as the villagers themselves were barely able to survive. It was desperate.

It struck me that what I was watching was maybe the purest form of humanitarian assistance. Clearly these two men were as much victims of circumstances as anyone, and as is very common in such areas were quite probably forced to join the military just to survive, or to ensure the survival of their families. They desperately needed help no matter what their nationality or supposed status, and I was proud of my colleagues for letting humanitarianism win out over application of policy. I saw a tube of cookies sticking out of the box, and the two Iraqi soldiers smiled and waved as we left.

Chapter 15: Family Life

It had now been about a year since I arrived in Kuwait and while I was satisfied with what I was doing, it was clear I had made some enemies both in HQ and in the mission. Enemies may be a bit too strong, but clearly I had ruffled feathers. I was learning how the system worked and felt I was doing what was best for the mission, but sometimes that is not enough.

In spite of some ominous feelings about how things were going, my spirits got a big boost one morning when I received a call from my wife. She worked for a large firm that had a big interest in the Gulf in general and in the reconstruction, military and petroleum sectors in particular. Prior to the Iraqi invasion of Kuwait they had a successful office in Kuwait City but were forced to close it down during the Iraqi occupation. They now wanted to open it again which would involve considerable public relations and customer relations, and Tia, my wife had been selected to head up that effort.

She and our daughter would be arriving in about a month while our son was just finishing his first year at university and would visit us from time to time. We would rent an apartment in the city where they would stay and I would join them on the weekends, if I was not the duty officer which required that I stay in Um Qsar over the weekend.

I began looking for an apartment in Kuwait City and checking out the international schools for our daughter, and when they arrived we moved into the second floor of a house we rented from a British couple. They lived on the ground floor. They were good neighbors and their antics were very entertaining.

One afternoon I came home and Neville was literally throwing a suitcase in the car while Victoria, his wife was waiting impatiently behind the wheel with the motor running. Neville looked straight ahead and she gave me a strange smile as they quickly pulled out of the carport and disappeared around the corner. The next morning Vickie explained that Neville had to leave for an unexpected business trip to Pakistan. Things were uncharacteristically quiet for about a month, until Neville just reappeared one evening, as if nothing had happened. He later explained that a "business deal" with a Kuwaiti client had gone bad and he found it convenient to get out of the country until things settled down.

I think what happened was that a shipment of scotch had been accidently opened by the wrong inspector in the seaport, and his was the only name they could go after. His friends in high places told him to get out of the country until they could get it cleared up, which meant they probably had to give much of the shipment away as bribes. Anyway, he resumed his normal business, which was importing antiques from Asia, or something like that.

The house we rented was a bit old and had an unreliable supply of water. In addition it was a considerable distance from the American School of Kuwait where we intended to enroll our daughter. So, before school started that fall my wife found an apartment in the Al Ghanim complex that was also home to a number of other expats. The apartments were western style, it was quite close to the school, and a number of expat families with children lived in the complex. Neville and Vickie were understanding, and we remained friends after we cut short our contract and moved into the apartment. So after an initial rough period our family life settled into a nice routine.

Tia purchased a Jeep (the US brand one, not a Tata) and began the process of reacquainting clients with her company's products and services, and gaining new ones. Being naturally quite successful at this, or anything she puts her mind to, in no time she was a major player in the Kuwait business scene and was being invited to meetings and affairs at all the major companies and embassies in the emirate. She also spent a considerable amount of time traveling in the Gulf and Middle East for business purposes.

The usual antics of kids growing up seems to take on another dimension when you are an expat. Our daughter, Monique fell in with an international group of kids and before we knew it she was speaking passable Arabic which soon became good Arabic. She also developed into a very good football (soccer) player and travelled with the ASK Girls Team to tournaments in several countries. Two of her best friends were the son of the American Ambassador, and the daughter of the Commander of American Forces in Kuwait. Tia was well known in both places (the embassy and the general's house) but when I would occasionally go pick up Monique after a party, studying or whatever, I would have to wait outside while she was ushered out by at least two young Marine Guards, in a fancy golf cart. She tried her best to act oh so bored by it all but I knew better.

Not to be outdone, our son Pablo was doing his best to carry on as well. On one of our trips back home we visited him at his campus and while we were there he received a parking ticket. He and I went to city hall to pay it and I was informed that there was an outstanding warrant for my arrest. Somewhat at a loss for words, I looked at Pablo who did his best to also look surprised but then said "maybe it's for those parking tickets I forgot to pay?" His car was registered in my name. The lady clerk saw what was going down and gleefully informed me that if I wanted to avoid a night in the local jail I had better pay the tickets, and the additional fines, now. Which I did. I am happy to report that Pablo has since become an outstanding musician and model citizen, at least as far as we know.

In retrospect, we were living an ideal life. We had interesting jobs, one or two live in maids, we traveled extensively on my leaves and we made many lasting friendships in Kuwait. We still have close friends and feel very much at home in Kuwait and Dubai. All of this was about to change when I got an unexpected call one Tuesday morning at 01:00 hours, or 1:00 AM.

Chapter 16: Under the Bus

Life in UNIKOM was good even though at times it was quite stressful since I always seemed to be cleaning up a mess left by my predecessors. The latest such project required reviewing all the financial and personnel files for the first two years of the mission's existence, which involved about seventy five staff members. Due to a misinterpretation or misapplication of policy, many of the international staff during that period had been overpaid on their living allowance, also known as mission subsistence allowance or just MSA .

MSA is composed of three parts and is meant to cover the cost of housing, food and incidental expenses. Although MSA is not considered as part of the income package, by living very frugally many of the staff manage to save much of their MSA and it becomes de-facto part of the remuneration package. This is not surprising, considering that many staff members come from less developed countries and were making much less than the MSA rate alone before they were recruited into the UN. The policies governing MSA are complex and as you can imagine MSA is a hotly contested matter.

In this instance there were indeed overpayments. Once the exact amount of overpayment was calculated for each of the files, we compiled a report which was sent to HQ, and they began recouping the overpayments directly from the staff members. This amounted in some cases to several thousands of dollars, and as was the practice then, when the UN was recuperating overpayments it was done in one payment with no advance notice. In some cases this resulted in some staff members going with no income for several months.

Again, I was getting dirty looks and grumbles from staff only this time from staff around the world, or so it seemed. While I was not the one responsible for the initial problem, my name was signed on each sheet of the calculations so I was definitely associated. For several years after that I would run into staff members, mostly in field missions who would still associate my name with that connection.

With long hours at work, and such things as the recalculations happening on a fairly regular basis I enjoyed the few hours of sleep I could catch. One evening in September, I was in a deep sleep when the phone rang at about 1:00 AM. I recall I was groggy but immediately recognized Tom's voice and my mind quickly imagined the worst. In UNIKOM the worst was usually that someone had been involved in a head on collision with a speeding Mercedes, or had been arrested for selling booze, or their visa had been revoked for some obscure reason.

This time it was different. Tom merely informed me that he had been transferred out of the mission and was returning to his post. He was leaving on the early morning flight to London. I was caught off guard and was silent for several seconds. After he repeated it, I asked if everything was OK, thinking perhaps he had a family emergency but it immediately occurred to me that I knew nothing about his personal life, I was not even sure he was married. We had just completed the calculations of overpayments I mentioned above and Tom knew it was causing some problems, so he said to contact him if I needed any further help with that, and he was gone.

*

The next morning there was an e-mail on my computer that Tom had sent to all Section Chiefs as he was leaving. It did not really give any more details, just that Edward, the Chief Finance Officer would be OIC, since he was the most senior Section Chief after the CAO and asked us all to cooperate fully with him. Edward called a meeting later that morning and assumed the reins.

Wrong Place-Right Time

At lunch I joined several senior staff members at an isolated table and we discussed what had happened. We all knew that the Force Commander did not get along well with Tom. The FC was a strict and somewhat rigid Major General from the Italian Army who thought that the civilian staff were not very disciplined, and I had heard him discussing it with Tom in a heated voice on several occasions. He felt Tom should be taking a much stronger hand with the civilian staff, which are always administered by the CAO. In addition, the FC felt that, what he saw as the liberal availability of alcohol was having a bad effect on his soldiers and again Tom was the one responsible. Relations had been getting worse between them over the past few weeks and we felt the FC may have put enough pressure on HQ to get Tom transferred out. There was also a rumor that the continued availability of alcohol on the local black market was rightly or wrongly being attributed to UNIKOM which proved to be a source of embarrassment with the host governments, culminating in the removal of the CAO since again this was ultimately in his area of responsible.

*

At any rate, Edward, the new CAO did not fair much better with the FC who saw him as having the same weaknesses as Tom, and within one month the tension between their offices was clearly visible. This was unfortunate as Edward had all the skills, the intelligence and experience to be a good CAO and while I personally liked him, it soon became obvious that the situation had not improved with the departure of Tom. Things seemed to get worse daily until the Force Commander was avoiding Edward and going straight to the Section Chiefs.

The situation came to a head when HQ announced that Edward had been recalled to his home office (this was getting to be a habit) and he would be replaced by a CAO on loan from one of the sister UN agencies. His name was Chris Gua. Of course we immediately sent out feelers and found that this guy had a reputation for being a real bastard. In addition to openly spying on his staff and currying informants, he was suspected of absconding funds including taking kick backs from a large development project he headed up in Central Africa, but nothing was ever proven.

Gua was due to arrive in March, and several of the old timers lost no time in using their connections to arrange transfers to other assignments, leaving several key posts vacant. When he arrived, Chris brought with him his hand picked replacements for those Section Chiefs who had left, instead of risk working under him. With this guy's reputation for corruption, even if you were able to keep yourself clean the question would always be there; were you one of his cronies? I have seen staff members passed over by CAO's for less.

It quickly became clear that this gang all knew each other well and were operating as a close knit group. To make matters worse, Gua and the Force Commander seemed to get along well, at least as far as how to handle administrative matters, and they worked together hand in hand. I was now one of three Section Chiefs left over from the previous group, along with the Chief Engineer and the Chief of General Services and we began to feel like outsiders. By April the Chief of General Services had retired, which he had intended to do later in the year but under the circumstances decided to move it up.

*

About this time another event took place that would work to my advantage. My wife had been very successful in re-establishing her company's office and business in Kuwait. Her assignment was now mostly completed and the decision was made to reorganize, and bring the Northern Gulf operations under the companies' regional office in Dubai. Tia was advised that she would be transferred, either back to her previous position which was located in the mid-west, or she could apply for other openings. Since I was working for an organization with headquarters in New York, we agreed she should concentrate on positions on the US East Coast. She was quickly selected for an international post located in Washington, DC and was scheduled to move back in late June.

I was now getting desperate as I would clearly be on Chris's hit list if I remained. He had already informed Karl, the Chief Engineer that he would not be extended beyond September when his current contract expired. Unfortunately Karl had made himself a bit of a thorn in the side of both Tom and the new CAO, and did not have much choice but to scramble around looking for other posts.

June came and my wife and daughter moved to the Washington area and began settling into a house we had purchased on the Chesapeake Bay in Maryland. My contract was also due to expire in the fall and just as I was beginning to expect the same notification Karl had received, I got news from the New York office.

*

Whenever I had visited NY, I made a point of talking to the Director of my division telling him how I wanted to spend some time in New York, to gain experience in HQ. Whether he was aware of the situation in Um Qsar or not, I am not sure, but I assume so since not much got past him. I was offered a position in New York with DPKO and while I would work in New York, I would at least be able to spend the weekends with my family. I could not believe my good fortune, not only to be leaving the situation I was in, but also the opportunity to remain in DPKO.

So, at the end of August I followed my family out of Kuwait and after a few weeks vacation I started my new position in the United Nations Secretariat Building in New York. My office was next to Kid's and I felt like I had come full circle.

*

About a year later I received an e-mail with a copy of a clipping from the New York Times, sent to me by one of my former staff members in UNIKOM. It related how one Chris Gua, a high level administrator with the UN had been arrested for tax evasion. He was picked up at the JFK Airport as he stepped off a plane from Dubai. Seems the US Government was aware of income tax irregularities including failure to declare just over half a million dollars income while he was the administrator of a major development project in Africa. This also forced the UN to look into possible corruption and kick backs from the construction company that had been awarded the contract for that project.

I had avoided being thrown under the bus and Gua had been arrested. I was now ready to move on.

Chapter 17: New York New York

While many staff members were trying to get assigned to New York, I was the opposite. I was afraid of getting stuck in HQ. Of course I was grateful for the opportunity to work with senior staff members, and over the period of a couple of years of this experience, I became quite proficient and knowledgeable concerning UN policy and procedures. After only a few months I was given the opportunity to take an assignment as a Section Chief in the Cyprus mission, which is considered a plum assignment but decided I would benefit more by staying where I was, and further sharpening my administrative skills.

At that time, our offices were located on the twenty second floor of the Secretariat building on Second Avenue and 42nd Street. I had wanted to work for the United Nations since my first visit to New York as a young man. I had taken a tour of the Secretariat building and was very impressed by the ideals the UN stood for, as well as the quality of the UN people I met and had read about. I decided at that time that someday I would like to join the UN. While some of the shine and polish had worn off by the time I got to HQ, still I was now a member of the UN, working in UNHQ in New York and proud of what we were doing.

Most of the staff members I worked with during my years in the Secretariat only reinforced that feeling. They were thoughtful, hardworking and loyal to the UN. Of course, a few were a total waste of space and I did not know how they got hired. In between these extremes there existed a sizable group who had entered the UN as bright, dedicated and hopeful new recruits, only to be slowly ground down by the system. A system in which advancement opportunities were few and your personal connections seemed to heavily influence promotions. It was as if everyone knew who was going to get selected for which position before the vacancy was announced. With this middle group, you could watch the sparkle in their eyes grow dimmer by the month and by the end of a few years it had been nearly extinguished. They either moved on or settled into a routine of meritocracy until it was time to retire. Before this happened to me I was determined to get back to a field assignment, where one faced many of the same issues as in HQ, but where I knew I could survive and even thrive.

Shortly after I moved to New York the Director of our division, who by that time was already a legend in the UN, after many successful years in HQ decided that he needed to get more field experience. He was subsequently selected to serve as the Deputy Director of one of the largest and most complex missions, and most of us were sad to see him leave. Unfortunately, but predictably, no replacement had been groomed before his departure and we drifted for several years, with first one temporary OIC then another. Harkening back to phraseology used by Winston Churchill to describe his difficult years out of office just before WW II, I refer to this as our years in the wilderness.

In a footnote to this section, as I finish writing this book I have just learned that our former Director and dear friend L was killed, along with so many other Peacekeepers in the earthquake in Haiti. He was a friend and mentor to so many of us in peacekeeping.

*

During this time in the wilderness, an important event took place. As part of the efforts to reform the UN, a comprehensive study of the Department of Peacekeeping Operations was conducted and came out in the year 2000. Known as the Brahimi Report, it took it's name from the eminent North African Ambassador and diplomat who headed up the study. The report covered a very wide range of topics, ultimately resulting in various improvements in the way peacekeeping operations and missions are conducted. One of the recommendations of the report was to establish and fund new posts for DPKO, and as a result the General Assembly approved over one hundred new posts for DPKO. Our division received nearly twenty of these posts, which it badly needed.

*

At about this same time a replacement for L was finally selected for our division. Orlando was a rising star, selected from a sister UN agency in Europe. Suave, connected, and mildly arrogant, his most noticeable asset seemed to be his skill at self promotion. In short he had all the requirements for rapid advancement. As is frequently the case when a new chief comes on board, especially in the midst of a frenzy of reform, he seemed to assume that the current staff members were of course the problem, and not potentially part of the solution. We were hoping for a new Chief that would inspire and revitalize the division but from the start it seemed obvious that he did not have much use for the existing staff. He had already made up his mind as to who would not be filling the new posts.

The Brahimi report had recommended that the new posts, which were established at a fairly high level, be used to strengthen the planning, training and support functions for the division. These were concepts which we all agreed with, and in fact many of my colleagues had been recommending such actions for years, to anyone who would listen. (An example was the establishment of a formal training unit, which oddly enough we did not have, and also a training facility for new peacekeepers, which they would attend before being deployed to their first assignment; much like a mini "boot camp"). Given that many of my colleagues were highly qualified and experienced in these regards, it seemed reasonable that at the very least they would be considered in filling the new posts. We all applied and waited in anticipation.

However, aside from one or two of the more groveling staff members, who were also adapt at self promotion, it appeared that others were passed over. The new chief cast his net far and wide to bring in a number of friends, and friends of friends, who settled down to accomplish very little over the next few years. To all appearances, the good old boy system prevailed, and the new posts were mostly wasted.

*

Within a relatively short time after filling the posts and solidifying his contacts in HQ, Orlando went to yet another UN agency and negotiated his next promotion. Over the next couple of years, many of his appointees followed his example and left as well. We were back in the wilderness, where we would remain for another long period.

I will say this for Orlando. He quite successfully dismantled the existing structure of our division, but did not seem to know what to replace it with. Either that or he was just too busy concentrating on his next move, or to be more charitable perhaps he ran into the always present resistance to change. I suspect the first but in any case the division suffered.

Following this episode, we had another series of temporary chiefs, including several good internal candidates who acted as temporary officers in charge, but none were selected on a permanent basis. Again, I think this was influenced by the assumption that the existing staff members (certainly not the organization) were the problem.

*

The next selection was an outside appointment with a military background which is fine, in fact potentially quite useful, but he apparently had little experience relevant to the job. To further complicate matters he was aloof, but apparently not too aloof since during his first weeks he surprised everyone by being caught in his office, in a rather compromising position with one of his female staff members. What little credibility he might have had was now lost. However, after a couple of months his case was quite decisively dealt with when he was quietly moved out of our division and into an empty office where he was assigned rather menial tasks for his level, or could be found on coffee breaks or wandering the halls.

Finally, after two basically failed appointments and various temporaries, an internal candidate was agreed upon. Eventually she restored some stability to the division, but this rapid turnover of chiefs and the resulting power vacuum had a destabilizing effect which the division is still struggling with.

Chapter 18: September 11, 2001

Tuesday, September 11 started as a beautiful day. The first cool of autumn had replaced the dreadful hot humid days of a New York summer, the sky was pale blue with a thin wisp of clouds and the sun was gorgeous. Autumn is my favorite season and I chose to walk from my apartment on 63rd Street and Third Avenue, which I frequently did. I arrived at my office on the 22nd floor of the UN Secretariat at about 08:30. There were still only a small number of staff in the office and I decided to take advantage of the lull to answer faxes and e-mails that had come in overnight from the field missions.

At about 09:00 Hammed came running into my office and said "You will never believe what I just saw". Hammed is a Pakistani staff member, about my age and one of the most decent men I have ever met. Reliable and hard working, his family is the most important thing in his life. Thinking maybe he had seen some movie star, without looking up I said, "OK, what was it?" When he did not respond I looked up and a chill went through my body. His face was pale and his eyes were wide open and staring at me. Clearly he had seen something.

He explained that he was driving across the bridge from Brooklyn and had a clear view as a plane flew right into one of the World Trade Center Towers. My first thought was it must have been a small plane with some rookie at the controls who got all messed up. No he insisted, it was an airliner. Turning quickly to leave he said he was going to listen to his radio to see if it was on the news.

Within minutes he returned and said "Oh my God, another plane has hit the other tower. Come look, you can see it". My office faced the East River, so we ran to an office on the other side of the building, facing west and looking as far to the left as possible, we could clearly see smoke billowing out of the tallest buildings in our view. My first thought was this is no accident as we stood dumfounded and craned our necks to watch.

My second thought was that the UN was a high profile building and if more crazies were out there, we may be the next target. Since the East River is very wide and there are no tall buildings or obstructions on the opposite bank at that point, the UN building would be a very easy target to hit.

I told Hammed to check how many staff members were in our office as we started to round people up to get them out of the building. Many people had the same idea and the elevators were nearly full, but since a lot of staff had not yet arrived, it was still quite orderly. As Hammed and I went back to look out the window, Security came on the intercom. They confirmed that there had been an incident at the WTC and as a precaution everyone was supposed to evacuate the UN building.

Normally during an evacuation, the elevators are shut down or there is a Security person using them to evacuate handicapped and elderly. However, we were the last two off our floor and we had no problem getting an elevator which took us straight to the first basement level. As the door opened we were greeted by a crowd of people milling about, all speaking and shouting and no one seemed to be in control. This looked dangerous. I recognized a lady from our office and asked her what the hell was going on. She said Security had instructed that all staff were to remain in the basement until an all clear was sounded.

I could not believe it, the last place I wanted to be if the building was hit was in the basement where all the fuel would run down and worse yet the building could collapse on me. Hammed, Judy and I worked our way to the nearest exit, which led through a hallway past the library and up to Second Avenue, and sure enough, there were two uniformed UN Security Guards standing in front of the glass doors.

I did not know the guards by name but did recognize one whom I used to speak with in Spanish. I asked him why we were staying in the basement when it seemed like the most dangerous place to be. I finally convinced him to call his boss on his two way radio and after a brief conversation he said it was OK to leave but we should get away from the UN building immediately.

The doors opened and I could feel a surge of people behind me as we literally ran down the hall way and up to Second Avenue.

*

It was now well after 10:00 AM and although there were still a few cars and busses, the streets were already filling up with people as the sidewalks could no longer accommodate everyone. Those who lived nearby or had someplace to go left, the others milled around and stood in small groups talking. A few people were clearly nervous but one thing I recall very clearly is that no one seemed hysterical. I stood at the main staff entrance gate on the corner of 42nd and Second Avenue, wondering if I should walk the twenty blocks back to my apartment. Absent mindedly I tried to call my wife on my cell phone but got a message that the call could not be completed. I decided to just wait for a while and see what happened.

As I stood there, Second Avenue slowly began to fill up curb to curb with people walking north, away from the WTC which was to the south. I was mesmerized. Slowly, as the crowd moved past us it began to take on a different look and then it struck me, they were covered in dust. These people had been so close to the towers as they collapsed that they were covered by the tremendous clouds of ground up concrete, plaster board, furniture, computers and as we would later learn, people. Everything was ground up when those towers collapsed.

It was like watching a column of grey dead people walking and for a second I almost panicked myself. I was struck by the fact that other than the sound of feet on the pavement, it was virtually silent. No one talked, and that is no exaggeration. What also struck me was that no one panicked, at least not on the corner of 42nd Street and Second Avenue, a corner that has seen so much history and so many circumstances that would cause panic. This ghostly grey parade went on for a couple of hours as we watched it head up Second Avenue, over the 59th Street Bridge, over Roosevelt Island and out of sight into Brooklyn. People walking home, or just walking. I could not help but think of the descriptions of masses of refugees leaving before an invading army, and World War I came to my mind.

I wanted to help them but no one was asking for help. Staring straight forward, they trudged along slowly and orderly, as if some unseen someone was leading them. I know it may sound fanciful but in those faces I did not detect panic or defeat. I saw resolution, a determination to get through this.

Many times in the past as I have watched America and Americans (both inside the country and from afar) I have felt for sure that they were nothing like the generations that came before, generations that had risen to the challenge and dared to make America a great country. Felt for sure it had all been lost. But in this hour of real trial and testing, of real blood and suffering and not some made for TV script, this calm, resolute reaction I saw actually made me proud. Maybe we still have it, it is just that in our fat and comfortable world we so seldom have the need to reach down and find it.

*

It was late that evening before I was able to speak with Tia. Her office was only about seven blocks from the White House in Washington, DC and she was there when the third plane hit the Pentagon at 09:43 on the morning of September 11. The entire central area of Washington was evacuated, all offices shut down and the staff sent home. She later recalled how quickly armed personnel in uniforms appeared on the rooftops of buildings in her area. She had tried to call me and our children to let us know she was fine, but all lines were busy. After waiting some time in her office for the traffic to clear a bit, she proceeded home.

*

A final note on 9/11. Soon after the World Trade Center attacks I was assigned to the peacekeeping mission in Afghanistan and in the fall of 2002 was home on a short leave. I accompanied Tia as she represented her organization at the Meridian Ball, which is held every fall in Washington DC. It is a lavish black tie affair where selected members of the political and diplomatic corps, business world and military get together for an evening of dining and dancing and to promote better relations and understanding between America and the world. OK, it's a bit posh but a lot of fun.

The program begins with dining in smaller intimate parties at various embassies on Washington's famous embassy row, then meeting en mass for an evening of dancing, drinks and good conversation. My wife's company provided a driver and limo, so were went in style. We have attended this event several times and there is always some memorable moment at each affair. One time we saw a senior PBS news show host who was famous for his "weekly report", dancing with a beautiful young lady less than half his age. Maybe it was his niece. What was memorable, and still good for a laugh between my wife and I was his style of dancing. He simply planted his left foot firmly in one place and with appropriate hand motions in time to the music, slowly moved his right foot, and his aging body in a circle around his left foot. I was so impressed that I have since adopted this method, and it works.

That particular evening we had dinner at the Italian Embassy with about eight other couples. Everyone was well scrubbed and turned out, with ladies in full length evening gowns and men in tux and black tie. The Italian Ambassador and his wife were very gracious hosts, and after dinner and coffee we mulled about talking to other guests while enjoying the art and the beautiful furnishings of the embassy.

I found myself talking to a man about my age, an inch or two taller than me, and with a bit of grey around the temples. He was quite hansom and I was sure I had seen him or his photograph before. His name tag read simply Chuck. He asked me what I did and when I explained I was on leave from my DPKO assignment in Afghanistan he immediately started asking questions; insightful intelligent questions. This was very unusual since frequently the first question I got was "now exactly where is Afghanistan?"

When he saw me staring at his name tag he introduced himself as a US Senator from the mid-west. No wonder the questions were good, he was the Chairman of the Senate Foreign Relations Committee, and at the time among the most knowledgeable people in Washington on matters of foreign affairs and US foreign policy. His comments and questions showed that even at that early stage he already fully grasped the importance of

Pakistan in the overall battle against terrorism; that it was a regional and not just an Afghan issue. We talked about 9/11 and I related my experience and my impressions standing outside the UN building on September 11, how I actually felt pride in these people and the way they were handling the situation, how for the first time in a long time I felt we still had some greatness left in us. Maybe I got a bit carried away as he just looked at me and listened in silence.

Then he called his wife over and introduced her to me with the comment "this is one of the UN Peacekeepers we were talking about". I stammered something and shook her hand. At that time I saw my wife, and calling her over introduced her to the Senator and his wife. After a few minutes of conversation, the Italian Ambassador announced that we should now proceed to the main ball, which was at another location. This brief meeting was one of the most pleasant and exhilarating conversations I have ever had in Washington.

A few days later on the plane ride back to Kabul, two things occurred to me. First, that it had taken a national tragedy like 9/11 to restore in me a bit of faith in the American people. Second, that there actually were people in Washington who seemed to have an understanding of foreign affairs. This second assumption was to be put to the ultimate test by the subsequent actions of the Bush Administration over the next few years. To be truthful, in my mind the jury is still out on both questions, but I still have hope.

Chapter 19: I pull off Afghanistan

As the American military geared up for a quick reaction after 9/11 it also became clear that DPKO would be in Afghanistan right behind them. I saw this as a chance to get back to the field in a high profile mission that had real consequences for the US. It was also an opportunity to get unstuck from the tar ball that is UNHQ. I took a lesson from the more brash members of my office and began to immediately, and shamelessly push my name and express an interest whenever the opportunity came up.

In December 2001 I was selected to be a member of the advance party which was to spend about a month in Afghanistan and make preliminary plans for the mission to follow. The new mission would be called the United Nations Assistance Mission to Afghanistan, or UNAMA for short. However at the last minute the size of the advance party, which had grown to be quite large was cut in half, and being the less senior member of my division, I was bumped.

I was disappointed but I understood, and for that matter agreed with this decision. Keeping the advance party small reflected the concept of a "light footprint" as espoused by the Brahimi Report. The idea of the light footprint implies keeping missions smaller in size, taking in only the bare number of international staff that are needed when starting a mission, and to recruit and train national staff to the full extent possible. It reflects the reality that peacekeeping missions can be so large that they tend to overrun and dominate the local society and economy.

This also has other implications such as keeping a low profile in terms of large numbers of white UN vehicles brought into the country, flooding the local housing market with high rent paying international staff, and other highly visible indicators that that the UN is present. Finally, it also implies having a higher degree of sensitivity to the cultural and national standards of the host country than perhaps has been exhibited in some other missions. No more of the wild parties and excessive behavior, if you know what I mean.

A final note on the "light footprint" concept. It is in theory a good idea but it depends on how it is implemented. Frequently the result in the field is to keep the number of qualified international staff at such a bare bones level that there are not enough experienced staff members to train and mentor the local staff that are hired. Particularly in the early stages of a mission it is not unusual to see sections with one or two lower level international staff member and the rest being new raw recruits from the local area.

When UNAMA was officially launched, my colleague who was on the advance team from our division was also selected to head up our section in the mission, so I bided my time. I requested to work on UNAMA issues when ever possible, and did what I could to keep my name in the fore front.

By May my plan worked. My colleague announced that she wanted to return to her post in HQ. I stepped up my activities to be selected as her replacement, but as it turned out there was very little interest from other candidates. My supervisor endorsed me and in early June of 2002, I departed for Kabul.

Mogadishu 1993, Day of the Blackhawks. Taken on the roof top of UN house twelve.

Street traffic in Kabul, Afghanistan. Spring of 2002.

Jimmy, our house guard and companion in Kabul. This was before his third bath.

My friend and trusted driver in the UN compound in Kabul.

War damaged house in the west end of Kabul. A family with several children were still living in it.

A foreboding looking mountain compound near Tora Bora, Afghanistan.

Gardez, Afghanistan. Child playing in the family compound.

UN staff with onlookers, buying honey and apples in the market place in Gardez.

A view across Bamiyan Valley, Afghanistan. Taken from the base of the destroyed Buddhist statues.

Tomato vendor on the road to Bamiyan.

Small boy asking for money and posing for a photo on the road to Bamiyan.

View of the UN staff housing compound in Bamiyan, the sight of many memories both good and not so good.

Ali's Arms Emporium near the Khyber Pass, Pakistan. Thats OK, we are only looking.

Old man passing on the bridge of time, Band-e-Amir Lakes in northern Afghanistan.

The last of the Ramadan Riot in Kabul. They all got paid their Ramadan bonus.

View of the UN compound during rainy season, Abyei, Sudan. The mud pulled the boots off your feet.

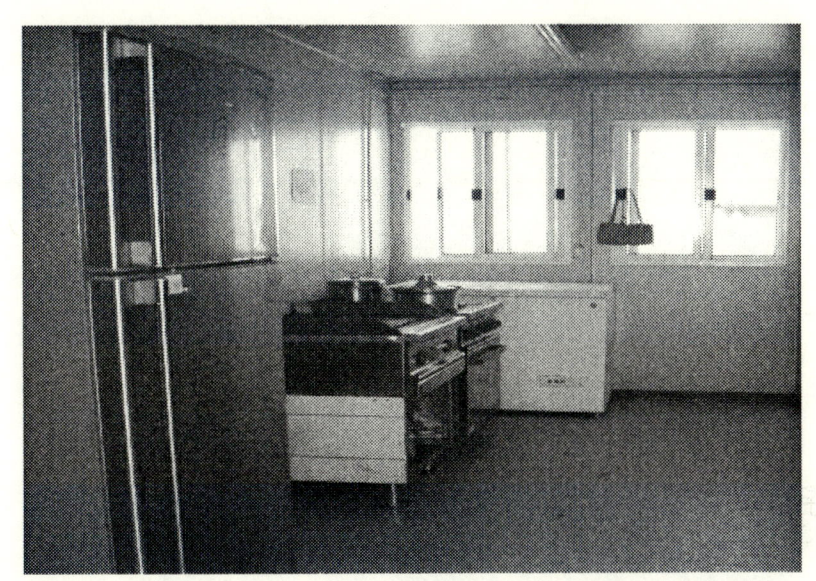

The field kitchens we put together out of odds and ends to replace the vile kitchen tents in Abyei.

Addressing Dinka and Misseriya Chiefs during a development conference in Abyei.

The fantastic and ever present Dinka dancers at a celebration in Abyei, Sudan.

Haboob or sand storm coming across the Nile River in Khartoum, Sudan.

*Taking a break to chain down the "jeep" tires in a
snowy mountain pass in Afghanistan.*

Part Three

Mission Impossible – Afghanistan

Chapter 20: Three Decades to Kabul

I entered Afghanistan through Dubai. The UN plane, a medium sized Antonov left the ultra modern Dubai airport and flying northeast crossed the narrow part of the gulf at the Straits of Hormuz, passing directly into Iranian airspace. All UN flights were required to fly low and slow in Iranian airspace so it was a bumpy and noisy trip for nearly one and one half hours until we got into Afghan airspace where we immediately climbed above 10,000 feet and picked up speed. From there to Kabul, another two hours, the ride was considerably better. The Antonov's leased by the UN are usually combination freight passenger planes and have only one or two small windows on each side. The joke is that the VIP seats are the window seats.

There were two air routes into Afghanistan, one through Islamabad, Pakistan and the other through Dubai, UAE. The Pakistan route had been initially favored as it was the traditional and historical way of reaching Kabul. All the various UN agencies and international NGO's that had operations in support of Afghanistan during the war with the Russians and later under the Taliban, had set up their offices and conducted operations from Pakistan. However, by the time I arrived in Kabul in June of 2002 it had already become apparent that movement of both personnel and certainly goods and supplies was much faster and easier through Dubai. Pakistan is a lovely and interesting country but it is not efficient, rather corrupt, and it is extremely complex politically. It is still difficult to move anything through it to Kabul.

However, from all directions the descent into the Kabul valley and the airport is rather step and abrupt, made all the more so by the fact that the city is nearly ringed by mountains and high plateaus from which it is easy to launch missiles. Pilots tend to waste little time getting through the vulnerable zone between decent and landing. At the airport we lined up to have our Afghan visas processed. Even in the heat of an early Afghan summer the dank stone and concrete airport was cool and a bit musty, and in the high altitude winters it is downright cold and musty. The officials were actually rather friendly but the process was all done by hand and took considerable time.

Once through the visa process we were assigned to hotels and loaded onto a bus to be taken to our respective hotel to drop off our luggage. Then we went to the UN compound to complete our processing with the Personnel and Security offices.

*

I'm not sure what I expected when we left the airport but I knew it would be fascinating. Years ago as a Peace Corps Volunteer (in fact as one of the first volunteers), I was asked to name my top three preferences as far as assignments. I named only two; South America (the Andean region) or Afghanistan. In retrospect I think this reflected my background as an anthropologist. Both areas are similar in that they are mountainous environments, and the way in which the societies have adopted are similar. An assignment in the high Andes of Colombia came up first, but now several decades later I was about to get my other choice and my eyes, my mind, all my senses strained to take it in. But first we had to get past the heavily armed Afghan Army guards at the airport gate.

By this time I was getting used to having scruffy unshaven guys in worn tattered uniforms circling my vehicle with their finger on the trigger of an assault rifle. Actually these guys looked better than many and they actually wanted us in their country, at least for now. But, if you know anything about Afghan history you know that when they no longer want you in their country you had best get out. Ask the British (1842), the Russians (1988), and in their turn maybe the Americans? After a cursory inspection they waved us on.

The airport sets on the far edge of the city and at least at that time it was ringed by farms with small fields green with wheat and vegetables. Trees lined the banks of irrigation ditches and ran up to the small adobe and cement block farm houses which sat back from the main road. Men and boys lead donkeys loaded with burlap sacks and bundles of fire wood, and we shared the highway with horse carts loaded with all manner of boxes and bundles. A few women walked along covered by dark blue burkes, usually with children in tow.

As we got nearer to the city the fields disappeared and the street was now lined with all manner of shops, markets, bakeries, and repair places for automobiles and bicycles. The place was alive with people and I was struck with the level of commerce and activity. Granted it was dirty and primitive compared with Dubai or even Islamabad but it was far more than I had expected. I also noticed a number of children flying kites from ditch banks and roof tops, which seemed a bit unusual at the time as I was unaware of the national obsession with kite flying and kite fighting. As we got closer to the center of Kabul, actually only the west side of the city, there were an increasing number of buildings being patched and painted. I was immediately impressed by the vibrancy, the activity and the spirit of the people and while I would eventually also see the darker side and learn how cruel a place Afghanistan can be, based on my experience it looked fairly good when compared with other locations where we had peacekeeping operations.

*

I was assigned to a hotel known by UN staff simply as the "Wild West Hotel", which was across from the Communications Ministry and close to the main UN compound. As I entered I was greeted by a young Afghan man known as Zaid who said "Hey, how you doing man?" I guessed immediately from his accent and demeanor that he was most likely from New Jersey, maybe New York and he confirmed he had in fact lived in Newark. His family owned the hotel but had left it in the care of an uncle after the Soviet Union took over Afghanistan. He had decided to come back with his aging grandfather as soon as the Taliban were ousted. He assigned me a room, locked my bags up in a closet and said we could finish the paperwork later. The Wild West was an OK place to live and would more than live up to its name, but right now I had to get back to the main compound.

After completing the paperwork, I was directed to the office of Franz, the Chief Administrative Officer (CAO) who was also my director, as I was the Chief of my section. Franz was German by birth but since he also grew up in North America he spoke English like a native. He was a competent administrator and a friendly guy on loan from another UN agency, but as I would find out this was his first assignment with DPKO and he was pushed to his limits by this mission. I thought it odd that his office was located in a building separated by some distance from most of his own staff and separate from the office of the head of the mission. After giving me a briefing on key issues he handed me a copy of the staffing table and said I would need to familiarize myself with it quickly as he was going on an extended leave in a few days. Since I was the next most senior officer I would be the Officer-in-Charge (OIC) of Administration. This was a first, being the OIC Administration, and I could not help but feel a bit proud, even if it only happened because I was senior in rank.

I spent the next couple of days introducing myself around in all the sections, and since I already knew people in most of them I felt comfortable taking over. They were competent enough to do their jobs and really all I had to do was liaise with the office of the Head of Mission (HoM) and the substantive offices. However, it was rumored that the Head of Mission had little time or patience for administrative types, a rumor that was to be confirmed soon enough. I had suggested to Franz that he should introduce me to him before he departed, but he always had something else to do. A day before his leave the CAO called a meeting of the Section Chiefs and handed things over to me. The next morning I called the HoM's office and requested a meeting to introduce myself. I was told to come over at 11:00 AM.

When I arrived I was met in the outer office by Konrad, the Chief of Staff. In the background I heard the theme music to Inspector Morse quietly playing on his radio. A good start I thought as this pensive and slightly melancholy piece is one of my wife and my favorite works. It also evoked many memories since we became fans of this television series from watching it on the BBC while we were stationed in Kuwait. It was rumored that Konrad was born in East Germany but he had jumped the wall when he was a young man, and had risen to a fairly high level in the government of West Germany before joining the UN. He was intelligent and a gracious old world style gentleman. He explained how the HoM did not meet with the CAO but he would see if he could manage to get a few minutes since I was new.

I could not imagine the head of the mission not meeting, and meeting often with the officer in charge of all the administrative aspects of the mission which included such important things as budget, finance, security, communications, personnel, logistics, air operations and on and on. Without good administration a peacekeeping operation is doomed.

He then said a curious thing, that the Head of Mission did not drink or smoke and was a very busy man. From his rather intense look, I immediately grasped this as a word to the wise but before I could further consider its meaning he returned with a smile and said the HoM would see me. I'm sure he felt he had scored a bit of a coup just getting me in.

Konrad opened the door and motioned to me, so I lead the way into the office. I recognized the HoM from the photos I had seen of him. A rather thin man of average stature, he sat behind his desk and without extending his hand he gave me a quick glance and motioned for me to sit down. I judged him to be in his mid to late sixties, with white hair, a bit frail but healthy looking. I introduced myself and extended greetings from several people in HQ, who had specifically asked to be remembered to him. I then explained that I had just arrived and would be the Officer in Charge of Administration for a few weeks while Franz was on leave. With a distant and slightly bored look, he commented that he had little to do with administration and did not meet with them. Konrad would call me if he had need of us. After a few brief words of welcome to Afghanistan, he quite literally gave a slight Pope-like wave of his hand to signal that the audience was finished and looked back at the paper he had been reading before I arrived. Konrad sprung to his feet and ushered me out of the office.

Overall I was left with the impression of a bored, somewhat aloof man. As I would find out, he kept most people at a distance, communicating with staff only as needed. This was further complicated by the small circle immediately around him, who actively shielded him from others. He was difficult to see unless you were on his "A" list.

I would also be told by others that he considered administration to be much like the hired help; necessary but there mostly to fix things and stay out of the way. However, Franz had apparently contributed to this situation as well. He had a reputation for being a bit of a drinker and a cigar smoker, both of which were not too uncommon in the world of peacekeeping, but which apparently infuriated HoM no end and he seemed to look down on Franz, and administration in general, as a result.

Having said this it cannot be denied that the HoM was a respected diplomat, intelligent and a positive force overall. Although he made life difficult for administration, because of his reputation and experience he was perhaps the best person to be the HoM in the early days when the Afghan government was struggling to get on its feet. In that regard he was the right man at the right time. It was Franz who was out of place in this environment and he did not last long. In fact he left for another assignment shortly after returning from his leave and was replaced by an American, who was both a former military officer of high rank and who had considerable experience with DPKO. Although he found it necessary to take a firm stand with the HoM from time to time, the situation did improve.

*

I quickly forgot this strange first meeting, since as OIC I had many other concerns, the first being to close negotiations on a warehouse. We had a huge shipment of everything from computers to drinking water coming in by air in three days and the owner of the warehouse we preferred was nowhere to be found. Just as I was about to direct the Procurement Office to look at other facilities, the owner came back from a trip to Herat, in the west of Afghanistan near the border with Iran. We arranged to meet him at the warehouse the next day. One of the selling points of this facility was its location near the airport, in fact it sat on the edge of the main runway. We arrived at 10:00 AM and began a final inspection before we signed lease papers. We immediately noticed a large wet spot on the floor, and looking up we saw a leak in the roof large enough that pigeons were flying through it. No one could explain how this was missed in earlier inspections, but other than that glaring defect the facility was fine. Located near a paved main road, it was surrounded by a walled compound and had a guard house at the main gate so it was easy to reach and easy to secure.

As we were completing the inspection we heard the roar of a jet making its final approach, in fact as it landed it flew directly past the open door of the building. It had UN lettering on the tail and it was obviously the freight plane we were expecting from the huge UN warehouse and logistics center in Brindisi, Italy. The only thing we could do now was to sign the lease and do a quick repair on the roof. I immediately called the Engineering Officer and explained the situation. He promised to have the roof fixed before nightfall, so we signed the lease and took possession of the warehouse. Within an hour the first pallets of goods arrived. Everyday was filled with hectic activity like this, especially in the start up phase of the mission when I acted as the OIC on various occasions. At least I had a nice quiet hotel to return to, or did I?

Chapter 21: Life in the Wild West

If one did not mind a bit of uncertainty and unpredictability in their life, the Wild West was a good hotel. Located on a busy corner near the Ministry of Communications building, there was a constant stream of busses and taxies outside from early morning to late evening, and vendors gathered near the main door selling everything from vegetables to black market CD's. At least two military police officers with rifles were stationed at the door at all times. Less than a block away was the start of the famous "Chicken Street" which joined up with "Flower Street". They got their names from the fact that in the distant past mostly chickens and eggs were sold on Chicken Street, and you guessed it, flowers and plants were sold on Flower Street. Since several embassies are located close by, along with the relatively well healed people that go along with embassies, the shops in this area had evolved over time into western oriented food stores that had fresh vegetables and canned goods, bakeries, and shops that sold carpets and souvenirs. However, other than one store that still sold flowers you would be had pressed to find either chickens or flowers on either end of the street.

Being centrally located in the midst of all this the Wild West was always busy and this applied equally to life in the hotel. The hotel itself was nothing special. Each room had a bed, one or two chairs, a wardrobe and a fan. Linen was changed once a week and some of the young male staff had the habit of showing up late at night to change the linen in the rooms occupied by women. They were chased off. Without air conditioning the rooms could get hot and it was difficult to leave a window open due to the traffic and noise on the street. It took some getting used to before one could get a good night's sleep.

Breakfast consisted of toasted flat bread with jam, instant coffee and powered Tang like drink which I never drank since I did not want to risk getting some bad water. Evening meals were usually some kind of grilled meat, beans, and rice or flat bread. Weather permitting, evening meals were served on the roof which was very pleasant as it was cooer and at that altitude the views of the evening sky were spectacular.

The mixture of residents in the hotel came straight out of a spy novel with the UN staff probably being the most common, even though we came from every continent and many countries. We were not usually long term residents and moved into houses with other UN staff as soon as possible for the convenience and to save money. Other regulars in the hotel were several Americans who were obviously ex-military and simply identified themselves as "consultants" with some construction or training firm or another. Some of them behaved as if they were acting a role in a movie, the strong silent type that kept to themselves. Others were more outgoing and friendly and even shared a bottle of whisky with us when we could find one. They were all careful not to talk much beyond generalities, as I guess we all were. Just better not to get to close, you never knew who you were really talking to. Then there was a group of about ten Chinese who were working on a project to reconstruct the local hospital, which was only a few blocks from the hotel. They did not speak much English and although we nodded and even shared drinks with them they remained a separate group. Evenings in the roof top café were usually boisterous affairs with no less than six or seven languages being shouted at any one time.

After about two months I went on a short official trip to one of the regions and when I returned the hotel was buzzing about the shoot out that had happened the night before. Seems Zaid had gone to dinner with a guy who was staying in the hotel, and with whom he had gotten to be friends. Sometime after midnight they came back to the hotel and apparently finished half a bottle of vodka in Zaid's office. A disagreement started over something, nobody knew for sure what it was, the score to a football match maybe, and fueled by the vodka it soon got out of hand. The guy went back to his room, which was just down the hall from the office and got a handgun. Not to be outdone Zaid pulled a gun out of his desk and they started shooting at each other down the hallway. Luckily everyone else was either in their rooms or still up on the roof, but the noise and the ricocheting bullets woke up the entire hotel.

Some of the staff started shouting that the Army or Police would come and kill them both, that the UN would pull all their staff out of the hotel and after a few rounds they apparently stopped and just went back to their rooms. The next morning it was as if nothing had happened and life seemed to be back to normal. However, it made you wonder just how many weapons were actually in the hotel.

*

One other memorable feature of the Wild West was the laundry service ladies and the "extras" they apparently provided on special request. The ladies were mostly young women and many of them were alone in the world as they had lost husbands or families to the war. They had to find whatever work they could to survive and I always felt a bit sorry for them as they did not have much standing in society.

Now I always thought the laundry area, which was located in the back of the hotel, was busy, especially later at night but I must admit that in some respects I am very naïve and apparently they never offered these services to me, or I just didn't catch on. Not that I was interested, but to tell the truth I was not aware that for a few dollars or Afghan pounds some of the ladies would invite you in to help look for your clothes. I found this out from a Polish friend a couple of months later, after he and I had moved out of the hotel. We had gone in with several other staff members and rented a house near the central park next door to a hotel that for good reason, we nicknamed the Honeymoon Hotel.

Chapter 22: Jimmy's House

In the early days of UNAMA there were no living arrangements provided in the UN compound so all staff members either lived in a hotel or went in with several other staff members and leased a house. The latter arrangement was the most popular and economical even after you paid for furniture, as well as several guards and house keepers. Having your own house also provided more privacy than a hotel. So in late September, after nearly three months in the Wild West I went in with three other senior officers and we rented a suitable house in what should have been a good location.

It was located near a large old park with a nice stand of fine looking mature pine trees, and which was a favorite spot for weekend family gatherings and picnics. Along one side of the park I discovered a large dilapidated shop that sold very nice handmade carpets, pashmina shawls and furniture. The owner was an elderly Afghan gentleman who served tea to customers and never rushed you to make a decision. The only real problem was finding him open as his hours were irregular to say the least. On the opposite side of the park was a barber shop which one of my national staff introduced me to. They spoke little English so we resorted to pantomime to get the finer points down, but for the equivalent of a couple of dollars I got a decent hair cut and more importantly I never got any rashes or unwanted bugs.

Our house was a two story stucco building with cool tile floors and a small rather poorly kept rose garden in front. It was a decent if somewhat small house located next to a quaint looking hotel that was quiet and reserved, when we moved in. However as we soon found out it used to be a favorite site for weddings and loosely translated was known among the locals as the

Honeymoon Hotel. During the Taliban era there were a number of things that Afghanis tended not to do and one was get married since wedding parties were frowned on by the Taliban. Afghans do like a long and loud wedding party after which they pile ten to a car and drive around town blaring music and horns for another few hours. As a result of the slow down there was a rather large backlog of weddings to be completed after the Taliban were run off.

One of the other things that the Taliban forbad or frowned on was kite flying, I guess because it was fun and frankly they did not like anyone but themselves having a good time (I'll leave the punch line about Taliban good times to you). So the hotel was soon filled with loud wedding parties several nights a week that carried on into the small hours of the morning and the park was filled with people engaging in the national pastime of flying kites and challenging each other to a form of aerial dog fights with the kites. The kites were fine, the wedding parties were not so good. However, we got adapt at sleeping through the noise and music and at least the hotel owners kept the area clean.

*

But for me the best thing about that first house was Jimmy. Jimmy was a somewhat bedraggled looking German Sheppard mixed dog that belonged to the owner of the house. As we came in the front gate he looked up from a well worn bed he had made between the rose bushes, and when he saw we were with the owner he put his head back down and continued to bask in the afternoon sun. Since the house was vacant at the time, Jimmy and a live in guard were left by the owner to keep an eye on things. The owner was wealthy and owned several houses in Kabul as well as others in Germany, where many Afghans had sought shelter during the Taliban era. He spoke good English and spent more than an hour showing us the fine points of the house including how to keep the finicky water heater working. However, since we were frequently without power we took a lot of cold showers anyway. When I asked about the dog he explained that he had brought Jimmy from Germany, but he was getting a bit old now and mostly slept. On a whim I asked if Jimmy came with the house and he said sure, Jimmy could stay for a while.

We took the house, and the dog, and also hired a couple of young guys the owner recommended as guards and general house staff. One was a distant relative of the owner, but he turned out to be a petty thief who stole fuel, food and about anything that was not nailed down. We eventually let him go. The other was a war orphan who did not have any family or any papers and only went by one name, a name he had been given growing up in the streets. He turned out to be the better of the two, maybe not as intelligent but a lot more honest and I eventually steered him toward a job as a guard cum watchman in the compound. I am pleased to say he was happily married and expecting his first child when I eventually left Afghanistan.

The house came furnished with some rather ugly furniture so all we had to furnish were the bedrooms. We spent the next week or so finding beds, fans and miscellaneous items and getting settled in. The food situation was quite bad, in part because there was not much available, and in part because we worked such long hours that by the time we arrived home, usually around 20:00 hours (10:00 PM) we just opened a can of tuna or corned beef and went to bed, usually to the sounds of the wedding party at the Honeymoon Hotel.

At any rate, Jimmy was always happy to see us and I know he was eating better than we were. Every time one of us went on leave we would bring back a large bag of dog chow and chew bones. One of our group, Chris had apparently raised dogs and he made sure Jimmy got wormed and even arranged for Jimmy to get a warm bath. I swear the first two rinses looked like water straight from the Kabul River, but after half a bottle of shampoo and the third wash Jimmy looked and smelled so much better. He was also responding well to all the love and attention and began to put on some weight.

One peculiar thing about Jimmy was that he would come up to the door but never enter the house, even when I enticed him by setting his food just inside the door. Similarly, we had a dog house made for him but he would not go in it. I suppose he had never been allowed inside and probably was beat every time he tried, and since we knew Jimmy would likely spend the rest of his life in Afghanistan we did not try to westernize him too much. I came out one morning and found him sleeping on several bags near the front door. One of the bags had some sawdust in it, which we used in the heating stove, and he had hollowed out a nice bed on it. I think LL Bean sells the same thing for your pampered Fido but for a bit more money.

From then on that was where he slept. I also noticed he was getting stiff and slow as the mornings got colder and I assumed he had developed arthritis from sleeping on the ground. Chris recommended giving him half an aspirin with his food everyday and after a couple of weeks the difference was really noticeable. Jimmy would be waiting for us at the gate and actually started to prance a bit when we came in. He seemed to be enjoying life a lot more and I even considered letting him out to look for a lady friend, but thought that would be too dangerous. While Afghans are much better about dogs than the people in the Gulf were, still he would have gotten stoned or chased for sure. Muslims traditionally hate dogs and associate them with the devil, and will only tolerate a dog if it is used to work a flock or as a guard dog. I have seen some mean things and did not wish to see Jimmy subjected to that so we kept him in the compound.

Meanwhile life in the house slowly passed as the first Afghan winter settled in. The bedrooms were unheated and reminded me of the old farm house I lived in as a child. When I would wake up on a winter morning the frost would be so thick on the window by my bed that I could scratch my name in it. Still, I always enjoy sleeping in a cool room. As for the rest of the house, the main source of heat was a uniquely simple stove that used sawdust as fuel. An inner chamber was packed with dry sawdust, taking care to leave a hollowed out area in the center for the air to pull through. It was lit from the bottom and slowly burned upward, providing heat for up to five or six hours.

This device was cheap and quite efficient so it caught on quickly with the UN staff, and as a result the price of sawdust throughout town doubled and then tripled that winter. I assume that was a special price for foreigners, at least I hope the locals were able to get it cheaper since we could always resort to kerosene heaters if necessary, but that was out of the question for many locals. What I have found is that there are usually separate price categories for foreigners and for locals, although the overall effect of having so many UN and other internationals move into an area such as this is to simply inflate the price of everything from rent to food.

In addition to heat, the sawdust stove proved to be a source of entertainment, at least in our house. Occasionally the sawdust flame would die down and we would toss a piece of paper in it to get the air moving upwards again. I don't remember who, but one of us took a piece of cardboard and rolling it up stuffed it down the opening in the sawdust core, put the lid back on and forgot about it. After a minute, the cardboard gradually heated up and without warning burst into flame, sending a violent puff of air upward. It sounded like a small firecracker and the stove lid flew several inches into the air.

Since this was about the most exciting thing that had happened since Jimmy got pissed off and chased one of the guards around the yard, we immediately did it again. The result was less dramatic but it worked. We spent the rest of the winter perfecting the "roll" technique as well as the necessary timing to see who could get the highest lift on the lid. For dramatic effect, my favorite was to wait until the others were dosing in front of the stove and load it up.

However the record is held by Chris, who is also an Engineer and knows about these things. He doused one end of the cardboard roll in a bit of kerosene and carefully placed that end upwards, so it was the last to ignite. The lid achieved lift off and flew two feet straight upwards followed by a stream of flaming sawdust. After that we begin to think about the consequences if four of the most senior officers were to get burned or worse yet cause a fire, so we toned it down a bit. Besides it was getting towards spring and time to put the sawdust stoves away until next winter.

Early that summer we moved out of the house by the hotel into an altogether more sedate but nicer house, which also had the advantage of being close to an excellent Iranian restaurant, at least excellent by Kabul standards. But before we did, one sad event occurred. One day I came back to the house and the first thing I noticed was that the front gate was open. I immediately thought of Jimmy and when I could not find him I called to the guards. They were standing sheepishly by the empty dog house and after a few minutes they finally said Jimmy had gotten out and ran down the street. I immediately sent one of them to search the park, another to search around the local restaurants and vendors and I searched the streets around our house. When it got dark we called off the search, but I instructed one of them to be at the front gate all night in case Jimmy came back. He never did.

The house was never the same without that ragged old mutt greeting us at the door or spiting out his aspirin when we tried to feed it to him, and I was frankly glad to move away. Some months later I remembered something that may explain his disappearance.

Shortly after we had begun to look for another place I ran into the owner of the house down on Chicken Street on one Saturday afternoon. He was aware we were moving and was not upset, in fact he sold the house for a good price to the hotel, as an addition. But I asked him if we could take Jimmy when we moved and even offered to pay him, and maybe in some strange way that upset him. It was about a week after that that Jimmy disappeared, and perhaps he just decided to take him back to his house.

Jimmy was getting old and in that tough environment he would not live too much longer. I can only hope his last days were good ones.

Chapter 23: On to Gardez

Gardez is a town of about 50,000 if you include the surrounding areas. It is located sixty miles south of Kabul on the road to Kandahar at an altitude of 7,600 feet or about 1,700 feet higher than Kabul. What makes Gardez notable in recent history is that it is the capital of Patika province, a conservative Taliban area, and relatively close to Tora Bora, the last hold out of al-Qaeda before they slipped across the border into Pakistan in 2001. That may seem like quite a distance but when air strikes were called in to that area shortly after I arrived, the deep rumbles could heard and almost be felt in Kabul. But in late 2002 the situation was relatively quiet so I took the opportunity to go along with one of the regular caravans to Gardez to check up on both the staff and the general administration in that area.

There had been an incident at the UN compound about a week before when a grenade was tossed into the compound one night. It had broken windows, blew a door off its hinges and one security guard was slightly injured on the hand by flying glass, and I wanted to talk to the staff and see how repairs were going, as well as take stock of the neighborhood. We seemed to have quite good relations with the local people and this was the first such problem.

The convoy of three vehicles left the UN compound after breakfast and drove through the center of Kabul to pick up the gravel and dirt road which continued on to Gardez. The Chief Security Officer, a good friend and a large Fijian guy named Swami was in the first vehicle. I shared the second vehicle with a national staff member from Finance who was going to check up on salary payments, and the third vehicle carried two staff members from Communications section along with their equipment, going to do some routine maintenance on the comms tower.

Our route skirted the edge of an area of Kabul which had been one of the main battlefields for the Taliban and the Northern Coalition forces and as a result had been very heavily damaged. The buildings were so shot up with both large and small arms that they were barely recognizable as structures. Even the street lamps and signs were riddled with holes. Abandoned military vehicles and trucks were scattered around and had been stripped of everything that could be removed or used. It was a scene from Dante. Yet even in this total destruction you could see that people were living in the ruins. When we stopped once for traffic, several children poked their heads out of a hole in the side of a building from which the door had been blown away or stolen, and seeing us scurried out for a closer look. They just seemed to be curious and I could not help but wonder what effect growing up in such an environment would have on them as adults.

As we left Kabul we passed small farms and orchards located in broad pleasant valleys, that stretched away to the low lying mountains in the distance. It was peaceful and pastoral compared to the man made hell we had just left. We dosed off and on as the SUV's slowly bounced over ruts and around puddles until we came to a fork in the road, where the lead vehicle pulled to a stop. We got out to stretch our legs and pointing to the road that turned left, that is to the east, Swami explained that Tora Bora was about forty minutes in that direction. Gazing in that direction, we watched a shepherd driving a small flock of sheep and goats down from a rocky hill. As he approached , the shepherd stopped momentarily to look at us and then continued on.

We climbed back into the vehicles and almost immediately began to climb into the Hindu Kush mountains that seemed to come from out of nowhere, and there was no way around them. The road got narrow and steep as it climbed upward, and the mountains closed in until they seemed to be just outside the window. Then within a few meters, the environment seemed to change completely. Not only was the ground covered with snow, it was falling at a fairly heavy rate. I could feel the all wheel drive vehicle skidding a bit as we pulled over and parked behind several trucks that had also stopped. The driver explained that we would be a while as they had to chain down so we could get through the pass.

Stepping out of the vehicles we could see the road winding and twisting into switch-backs as it seemed to climb straight up into the mist. This was the pass and it looked formidable. The clouds had settled in and although it was mid morning, we had our lights on and there was an eerie iridescent glow to the sky. Just then a large truck loaded with firewood loomed out of the mist into our line of sight, coming straight towards us. It was trying desperately to maneuver the last hairpin curve so it could get to the relative safety of the small plateau we were sitting on.

It must have been a Pakistani truck as it was painted in the way they typical do. It had a pale blue background with hand painted murals in bright colors on all sides and on the tale gate as well. It had lush tropical scenes with red and green birds on one panel, a village scene with a lovely veiled lady on another and on the tailgate a mountain scene. I suspect the paint cost more than the truck did. By the time the truck skidded ever so slowly to a halt, it was nearly off the edge of the road. Looking at the driver and passenger, they had the largest eyes I have ever seen on a human. Slowly, the driver maneuvered it back onto the road and they crept off as the clouds began to swallow the truck up before it had gone more than thirty meters. They had made it through the pass.

With four wheel drive and tire chains, and by driving slowly we managed to get through the pass with little more than the occasional skid which none the less had our driver muttering oaths in Pashto. On the other side of the pass we removed the chains and continued on to Gardez. When we got to the small compound they had lunch and pots of hot green tea waiting.

*

The compound house was a beautiful old fashioned rustic hunting lodge. It was made of pine logs and stone walls, with wooden floors and windows that looked out at the mountains in the distance. It was heated by several stoves and the smell of the wood smoke was better to me than the most expensive perfume. It was reminiscent of a lodge our extended family owned in northern Michigan when I was a child. Some of my most pleasant memories are of fishing in nearby streams or being snowed in for several days at a time while we kids played in the attic or made snow forts outside.

The only drawback was that the Gardez house sat inside a large walled in compound surrounded on three sides by a muddy area that had been chewed up by vehicles churning in the soft earth. After lunch The Chief Security Officer and I got a briefing from the Regional Security Officer, and then I spent the rest of the day visiting with the other staff members assigned there.

I was most impressed with Dana, a young Dutch woman who was working with local women's groups. Under the Taliban, women were severely restricted but now they were eager to emerge and Dana had managed to organize several women's cooperatives and support groups. Many of the women had lost husbands and sons and were left as the main breadwinner for their families. In addition, the women often had more of a stabilizing effect in the post war community than did the men.

Shortly before we left to return to Kabul in the late afternoon, the Regional Security Officer asked to speak with Swami and me. He said that one of his local staff guards had confided in him and explained how the attack on the UN compound actually came about. It seems that some local boys were walking down the street one evening, and found a small cash of handguns and grenades that had been left in a ditch running past the compound. It is common in Afghanistan, as in many countries to have a rather deep open ditch along the side of the road or street that serves as a catch all for everything from rain water to ... well you name it. In towns the ditch has little foot bridges crossing it and is usually lined with stone or concrete so it can be cleaned from time to time, so it is not too bad. It is a good low tech way of handling a common problem.

The boys had noticed a package or bundle in the ditch and upon opening it found the handguns and several grenades. Boys being boys, and having probably been brought up with weapons since they were small, they tucked the handguns under their belts and began to play catch with the grenades. One thing lead to another and soon someone playfully pulled the pin on a grenade and tossed it to his friend.

I guess it dawned on them that they had a live grenade on their hands and whoever had it last tossed it over the nearest wall, which happened to be the wall to the UN compound, and they ran like hell. Fortunately it was late at night and everyone was either inside or sleeping. Relatively little damage was done and one Security Guard who was about thirty meters away got a shard of glass in his hand, which proved to be minor. It was not an attack on the compound, just some youthful high jinks, Afghan style.

Before we returned to Kabul we stopped at the local market to buy the two products that Gardez is rightfully famous for; locally grown apples and honey. Anyone who goes to Gardez always brings them back. Munching small red apples, I couldn't help but smile on the trip back to Kabul. The kids got off with no injuries and our relations with the local community were still good, thanks in large part to the efforts of UN staff like the Dutch Civil Affairs Officer.

Chapter 24: Mission Impossible

After serving nearly twenty years in various UN Peacekeeping Missions on three continents I have observed that in some regards all missions are pretty much the same, yet in other respects they are unique and different. From the standpoint of just trying to do your job, UNAMA was to be the most difficult mission I worked in, but not the most dangerous (that would be Somalia) or the most demanding (that would be Sudan), or the most personally rewarding (again that would be Sudan). But to explain this I will need to give you a bit of background, so please bear with me.

Peacekeeping Missions are composed of two basic components. The substantive side is the most visible part of any mission and to be honest it delivers the "product" if you well. We all admit that it is the real reason the mission exists. Composed of Political Affairs, Humanitarian Affairs, Civil Affairs, Diplomatic staff and similar sections it is responsible for delivering and implementing the overall program. It is what we read about in the news. The Administrative side exists to support the substantive sections in these efforts and is composed of a wide range of admin sections such as Finance, Procurement, Engineering, Communications, Human Resources, Transportation, Air Operations and a massive logistics requirement..

Due to the nature of the places that Peacekeeping Operations are conducted, typically there are few if any local organizations or services available, at least in the early stages of the mission. Accordingly the administrative side of the mission is extensive and must cover every thing including even medical services and security. In effect, a peacekeeping operation must be self sufficient.

The United Nations is a large organization and the Department of Peacekeeping Operations, with over 20,000 civilian staff members (both international and local) in approximately 17 operations on four continents, has become the most high profile part of the UN. It is not a small mom and pop NGO (Non-Governmental Organization) with its membership reflecting most of the 192 plus member nations, and with each member state having a vote in the General Assembly as well as on numerous committees and review bodies. With an annual budget of about US$ 5.5 billions dollars (which is reportedly still less than the annual NYC School Board budget, or the budget for the Tokyo Fire Department), and with staff members flung around the world and in the most dangerous places, DPKO naturally has very complicated administrative policies and procedures. Very much like a modern military operation.

*

Given this, each DPKO mission is still unique and has it's own feel or personality. One of the key elements determining that uniqueness is how well the substantive and the administrative sides of a particular mission function together and get along. To put it bluntly, do they cooperate and support each other or do they not. This in large part depends on the tone set at the top by the senior most office as well as by the senior officers within the two areas, substantive and administrative. I suppose this is a natural division found in most organizations (production vs. administration), but most missions I have known are able to manage this natural tension and still establish a relationship of support and mutual respect. Afghanistan proved to be most difficult in this regard.

In addition to the generally poor relations I immediately detected from my first day, and which were to continue at least during the initial period of the mission's existence, many of the recruits for the substantive sections were new to the UN and DPKO. They seemed to come in with a "different" attitude than most of the older more seasoned staff, who had served in a few missions. Many of the new recruits apparently felt they were superior to the administrative staff, whom they seemed to view as inferior or at best not so "well informed" as they were. They gave the impression that since they were on a mission to save the world, or at least Afghanistan, this put them above the rules. This attitude of superiority on their part was seldom challenged or even questioned by their superiors and in many cases seemed to be given a tacit "wink" of approval, so naturally they took their cue from this.

*

In an effort to be balanced on the subject, the situation was made worse by the slow pace of administrative procedures in the UN which is frustrating to everyone, but especially to the substantive staff even in the best of times. In DPKO, administrative authority is only reluctantly delegated down to the field. Rather than delegate to the officers in the field and hold them responsible, many administrative matters require review and prior authorization by HQ in New York, which adds immensely to the time and work required. Meanwhile, as the actions of even a senior officer in the field move through the bowels of HQ, they are scrutinized and questioned by junior officers and clerks. Only recently have some missions been entrusted with a bit more autonomy in making decisions, but even this comes with such restrictions as to frequently render it progress in name only. As a result, any administrative process can easily become bogged down.

*

With this reputation for slow administrative action on the part of the UN, and as mentioned above the elitist attitudes of many of the substantive staff in Afghanistan, the schism between the two branches of the mission seemed to spread to all levels of the organization. I would have to say that the disregard for administrative procedure, and for those whose job it was to implement and oversee them, overall, was worse in Afghanistan than any other mission I have worked in.

There were of course notable, and much appreciated exceptions. The Political Affairs Section was headed up by an experienced French diplomat and scholar, who had previously served as the SRSG for a mission in Central America. While, like everyone he chaffed under the administrative requirements, he understood the need for substantive and administrative staff to work together and he sat the example for his own staff members. As a result I always found the Political Affairs section much more pleasant to work with. They could be demanding, but their expectations were much more in line with the possible, and they exhibited an underlying respect that was all too often missing in many staff members.

*

On more than one occasion senior substantive officers went so far as to make on the spot offers of employment to individuals, and would send them to administration to be processed so they could start work as soon as possible. While I understand that the recruitment and hiring process in the UN can be extremely time consuming and frustrating, as is the case in all organizations, all offers of employment must be made in an official manner and by the Human Resources Department. I even had one individual who had resigned his position with another NGO on the assumption that he would be given an immediate contract, that day. I was put in the difficult position of explaining that he could not be given an appointment as he had not yet even applied for a position with the UN, let alone been recruited.

In these instances, when I explained that there was a recruitment procedure that all UN staff had to follow I was usually accused of throwing needless administrative rules and procedure in the way. On one occasion, when I explained this to an individual who said he had been offered a position at a party the night before, he stormed out of my office and about thirty minutes later I received a call from the office that had made him the impromptu offer.

After much discussion, I suggested a solution to the officer on the other end of the phone line. We could try to get him on a special appointment as a contractor, but such an appointment was limited to six months. A better solution would be to have the candidate go ahead and apply for a position, which would get him entered into the UN recruitment system, then I would do my best to see that his application was cleared immediately for the post in question. I even offered to have our staff assist him with the application, as this could be done immediately by e-mail. He grumbled about needless administrative procedures and hung up. I later learned that he was complaining to his colleagues about how uncooperative we were.

*

One problem that seemed to occur in both the substantive and administrative sections was what I refer to as "constructive promotion". The term "constructive" as used here, is as a legal or labor relations term, which simply means that you set up the situation such that the desired outcome is inevitable. For example, making the environment and employment situation so bad that out of frustration the person quits, is known as constructive termination. It is a prohibited employment practice in most countries, but for many years this was the preferred way to rid your organization of minorities, females and union organizers. And let's face it, it is still used.

Constructive promotion happened as follows. A unit or section recruits someone at one level, let us say against a P-3 post. After a short period of time they are quietly moved to a higher level post, let us say a P-4. Now that is not against the rules, in fact it is quite common to fill a higher level post with a lower level appointment, but no promotion goes along with this reassignment. What is not allowed is to then claim, dare I say insist that the person be promoted to the higher level, simply because they are against a post of that level. An analogis situation would be if a Lieutenant was placed in a Captains post, and then was promoted to the rank of Captain without having to go through the promotional procedure. You can easily see how friends would arrange for the rapid promotion of friends, and countrymen for each other. One of the main problems in Afghanistan was that so much of this clandestine movement from post to post had taken place that in many cases there simply was no reliable history of such movements. But again this is a common tactic if you are trying to set up a promotion without going through the normal and required procedures.

When an administrative officer would explain that in order to be promoted, the individual would have to apply for the higher level post and be recruited, like everybody else, well they of course were just being obstructionist and not helping to support the overall objectives of the mission. One of the most persistent, vocal and abusive of those demanding a constructive promotion involved a staff member who was very close to a senior administrative officer, and who repeatedly used that connection to pressure and even threaten others. While I defended the administrative staff members and stood up to the situation, it ended up putting a great deal of pressure on my relationship with that senior official, and it affected our ability to work together. Still, I am sure I did the right thing.

*

However, perhaps the most persistent problem also involved the smallest section, which had a total of only seven international staff and four local or national staff. This section was a high profile one, so I grant that selection of the correct candidates was important. However, a review of the records showed that his section also had the highest turn over rate of any in the mission, and in addition there were currently no female staff members in that section.

When you first met the Chief of this section, I will call him Alejandro, you were immediately struck by his condescending and sarcastic attitude. He could be pleasant but usually only to those he felt he had to impress. Over the next three years the Personnel section was recruiting on a nearly continuous basis for this small unit, and they spent more time per capita on that small unit than on any other single group.

After much effort we finally did recruit a female candidate for this section. When she arrived I was hopeful, and quite impressed as she had worked in a professional capacity with a large international news agency, and had also been in a similar post with another UN agency. Although she was qualified and had a proven track record, in less than one month she was in my office begging to be transferred to another section or she would resign. The reason she gave was the constant interference and attitude of mistrust from her Chief. She also said other staff members in the section would not speak with her and she felt shut out of the unit.

When I discussed this with Alejandro he had a number of excuses about how she did not make an effort to fit in and her writing was not all that good anyway. When I asked about the other females who had left his unit after very short periods, he got quite defensive and the conversation quickly broke down.

A few days later I got a call from the Head of Office in one of the regions, asking if the lady could be transferred to his staff. I facilitated her transfer, but soon after that she was offered a post in Sudan and departed. About a year later I got an e-mail from her, thanking me for my assistance and telling me that she had recently been promoted to Deputy Director of her new section. Not bad for an under qualified person who cannot fit in.

*

Some issues concerned only the administrative sections and while they were also complicated, were usually more easily handled. In this regard, perhaps one of the most interesting and ultimately sad events involved the disappearance of one of the national Afghan staff, who worked as an Administrative Clerk.

One afternoon a rather attractive young Afghan lady came to my office. She was dressed modestly in loose pants and a long skirt like blouse and had her head covered with a scarf. She looked sad as she explained that she would have to resign at the end of the week as she was going to Germany to get married. I considered telling her she had to give the usual one month notice but sensing she was already quite stressed I instead told her to just give an official letter of resignation to Personnel as soon as possible. I could see she was upset and when I congratulated her on her marriage she quietly thanked me and without looking up left my office.

The next morning Swami, the Chief Security Officer was waiting in my office when I arrived, to brief me on an incident that had taken place the previous evening. The mother of the young lady had shown up at the main gate late in the evening. She was very distraught as her daughter had not come home from work and she feared she had run off. Slowly the story came out that the daughter had been promised in marriage to a friend of the family who was some years older than she and who now lived in Germany. Arranged marriages are the custom in Afgan society, and in fact seem to work out with a much better rate of success than do western marriages.

In this case, the mother thought her daughter had a local boyfriend and the girl did not want to go to Germany to marry an older man, even if he was a friend of the family. After checking with his staff, Swami assured the lady that her daughter had gotten on the bus after work, as usual and left for home. He also assured her that if she returned to work the next day he would tell her to immediately send word to her family. After more than an hour of further discussions and reassurances the poor lady left.

I immediately sent a copy of the security report to HQ, asked for their advice and advised them we would continue to monitor the situation. But before Swami could leave a young man who worked in the same section as the missing lady came to my office and offered an explanation. He was a friend of the family, as well as her, and knew she had a boyfriend. He feared that they had run off but there was really no place they could go to get beyond the reach of either family. He was concerned for her safety.

His prediction proved right as they were found hiding out at the apartment of a friend later that week, and both were arrested. After being held for a couple of days they were released to their respective families. The last I knew the young man was sent to live with relatives in Pakistan and the young lady was restricted to her family's house where pressure was being applied on her to accept the marriage in Germany. Since this was a personal matter and did not involve the UN, there was nothing we could have done.

*

Sometime later I was discussing this incident with a member of my staff, a well educated young Afghan man who held a professional level appointment with UNAMA. His was a very interesting case. His family had left Afghanistan when he was young and moved to New York where he attended several years at PS whatever in the Bronx. They returned to Kabul for a visit and were unable to get out again so they had to make the best of it under the Taliban. Eventually they did manage to get to Pakistan where he attended university. His family now lived in Peshawar, Pakistan as did many Afghans who had left to escape the war years. I would visit Peshawar with Haamid eventually and meet his wife, a delightful lady who doted over their two young boys, and I never met a more loving and devoted couple.

Haamid explained that his was also an arranged marriage, with a slight variation. He explained that when he reached the age to get married, he had a discussion with his parents. He respected tradition and asked them to arrange a marriage, but if they picked someone whom he had strong feelings about he would refuse and remain single. Having lived for a while in America they apparently had a broader view of the world and agreed. Haamid explained that they had settled on a young lady whom he had known for some time but to be honest had not really considered for marriage. His mother explained that this girl had many virtues and they had many things in common on which to build a relationship. He liked her so he agreed, and while facing the problems common to any relationship, it had indeed prospered.

In many respects Haamid was wise beyond his years and observed that the success of arranged marriages depend on a wise choice being made by the parents. Family is all important. The implication was that the family of the young lady had made a poor choice, and I think the mother realized that. I do not know what became of the girl but I felt as sorry for the mother as I did for the daughter.

*

I am happy to say that Haamid subsequently got an international appointment as a Human Resource Officer in the Congo, where he is laying the groundwork to become a Chief Civilian Personnel Officer someday. I am also proud to say that I have tried to assist worthy national staff from every mission I have served in, to get international appointments. None of them have been disappointments.

*

A final and actually rather comical example of disregard for administrative procedure occurred when I called one of the northern regions to speak with a staff member, whom we will call Martin. I was speaking with a very competent local staff Administrative Officer, who was being uncharacteristically evasive about letting me speak with Martin. Finally he admitted that they did not actually know where Martin was but they thought he was home in Ireland. After more questioning my colleague explained that Martin had gone for a weekend trip to Tashkent, Uzbekistan (just across the border from his location) but had not returned. When was this, I asked. Nearly two months ago he replied. He was quick to add that he had wanted to report this immediately but the Head of Office for that region had said no, that Martin would return.

The HoO got on the phone and in a huff explained that Martin, who by the way was very knowledgeable about everything Afghan, having read nearly every book on the subject, wanted to take extended leave to spend with his spouse but did not have that much leave built up. I tried to explain the problems with this arrangement. In addition to his being absent without leave, which compromised his insurance, how would we explain to HQ that he was being paid when he was in fact not working? When I got no assistance from the HoO, I attempted to explain the situation to the office of the Chief of Staff, hoping for some support. Instead, I was told it was my job to support the Head of Office and Martin, and I should figure a way out of it.

I did. After explaining the situation to HQ, and calling in a few favors, they agreed that Martin would be placed on annual leave retroactively, which as it turns out covered more than half of his time off. The remainder was retroactively approved as unpaid leave, which would be recovered from his salary once he actually returned to work.

None of it was against policy, but it did require the obstructionist and uncooperative admin types to think outside the regulations. It appeared that Martin had wanted to take an extended leave without using his vacation time. The comical part is that about six months later Martin "disappeared" again after a weekend trip, this time to Islamabad. The Section Chief and HoO were furious this time and insisted that Martin's appointment not be extended. Again they left it up to administration to take care of it.

Chapter 25: Peshawar and a Visit to Ali's Arms Emporium

One of the best perks to a life in peacekeeping is the opportunity to visit exotic and interesting places, and I took advantage of this whenever possible. So, one fall when Haamid asked for time off to visit his wife who was visiting her family in Peshawar, Pakistan I said of course, as long as I can go along. We were friends by now and he had extended the offer before so I did not feel like I was too far out of line. Actually he seemed pleased to have the company so we booked ourselves on the next UN flight and packed our bags.

I had been to Islamabad and the old sister city of Rawalpindi several times, mostly on business since UNAMA had a regional office there. I had usually spend any free time just looking around the market areas, or in shops that sold everything from furniture to knock offs of every luxury item you can imagine, but I had not felt comfortable taking the bus alone for several hours to places like Peshawar or the Swat Valley. I feel comfortable just about anywhere, with normal people, but if there is a real chance of being killed, kidnapped or abducted, it is better to take extra precautions.

We landed in the Islamabad airport and headed directly to the bus station, where we purchased two tickets on the next express. It was a sunny warm day so we sat in the shade and drank a Coke. As we waited for the bus to arrive I got a few looks from customers and the general public, but they seemed to be more out of curiosity and none that made me feel uncomfortable. Nearby the local busses were loading and it seemed like every passenger had a large bag of vegetables, furniture, some chickens or even the occasional TV or microwave oven to load into, or onto the bus. It reminded me of the years I spent in South America, where I think the wildest bus trip I took was an overnight run with some booze smugglers in an ancient bus loaded with home brewed hooch in Ecuador. I should have suspected the extremely low fare. Or maybe it was in the "Turkey Express" (so called because it had more turkeys on board than people), up the side of a mountain to a market town in Bolivia.

Finally the ticket agent came out of his office and said the bus was ready to board. As we lined up to file on, two armed members of the Pakistan Military carefully eyed everyone and checked ID's. The bus was Pullman style with seat backs that reclined, and it was air conditioned and clean so this promised to be a good trip. After we found our seats, the two military guards got on the bus and this time one was carrying a video camera. Starting at the back they asked each person to hold their ID up next to their face and they filmed both the individual and the ID. Haamid explained this was just in case the bus ran off the side of the mountain, crashed and burned, the bodies could still be identified. Then laughing at his own humor, he said no, it was actually so that if the bus was bombed or robbed, they could try to trace the people involved. This time he did not laugh. I wasn't sure which explanation I preferred, both seemed equally lacking in humor.

The bus pulled out of the terminal and heading west it followed a paved road which had been build over the old road used by the British as they tramped back and forth between Kabul and the major cities of the old Indian Empire, which in turn was built over the ancient trade routes that had joined up with the Silk Road to the north in Central Asia. It occurred to me that this was symbolic of just about everything in this part of the world. Everything has its roots running so deeply throughout history and is so connected to everything else that it is not possible to understand anything, or any event on its own. It is so intertwined in history and everyone else's business that it seems to take on a life of its own. In the end it does no good to just observe events, you have to live them. This was not a western way of thinking. Either I was beginning to get the hang of things here or I was getting completely lost. Then again, maybe they are in reality much the same.

Wrong Place-Right Time

As the bus glided along the old Grand Trunk Road through the afternoon heat, the amazing panorama of Pakistan unfolded. The highway was lined in places with trees so huge that they must have been hundreds of years old. Everywhere there were fields of wheat, grain and vegetables being harvested by men in baggie white pants, the oversized legs pulled up and neatly tied like a dipper to keep them off the ground. The houses and villages were white and drab in comparison with the gaudy and colorful trucks, vehicles and even farm carts and tractors, that had the most fantastic and intricate trim and even complete murals painted on any surface large enough to be used. I tried to guess where the driver was from by looking at the works of art his vehicle sported. A high mountain village meant he was from Swat or the Kashmir, a lush tropical house and a flowing river signaled he was from the south. Some even had paintings of notable figures and popular musicians.

At about the half way mark the bus pulled into a shaded rest area, and as the door opened my other senses came into play. First was the smell of fresh naan (flat bread) followed by the snap of curry and biryani, mixed with the lazy smoke raising from the kebob grill. Then as I stepped off the bus, the sounds of people hawking their goods, the bray of donkeys in the distance, a flock of birds gleaning grain from the fields, and the clip-clopping of horse hoofs as a cart passed by on the road.

Standing in the cool shade of a massive tree taking it all in I felt connected, transported not just in time but to another reality. Watching children chasing each other and running between makeshift tables as their parents tended to business, I understood how one could be happy growing up in this place, how it could seem like the best place in the world. I have had that feeling, if only briefly in other places. In a small peasant village in the Colombian Andes, standing by the trout stream that runs through Bamyian Afghanistan, watching from a small mountain side farm as the sun sat below on Florence Italy, and listening to the breakers roll in off Lake Superior at Pictured Rocks, to name a few. How can you choose just one place, or for that matter any place to live?

*

Back on the bus we continued west, and as the sun began to dip slightly in the afternoon sky we entered Peshawar. At the old Fort Bele Hissar we turned left off the GT and continued south west until we were across from the main train station, where we got off the bus. From there we took a taxi and Haamid gave the driver directions to the hotel/residence where I would stay. His wife and boys were on an extended vacation from Kabul and were stayed with his wife's family so the in-laws house was rather full, and besides I preferred to have the privacy of a hotel room.

The hotel was actually a private home that also rented rooms and provided meals. Sitting back from the road behind a tall brick fence with an ornate iron gate, it was a relatively new brick building surrounded with trees, flowering bushes and a large green lawn. It was clean, cool and very inviting. Haamid spoke to the owners in Urdu, which is similar to his native Pashtu, and since he had lived in Peshawar and attended university there as well, he spoke like a native. Seeing I was a foreigner they responded in English. After I settled into a room and we made arrangements for Haamid to pick me up the next morning, he departed.

My room was on the second floor and looked out over a cricket pitch and a football field that were part of a boy's school. As I was watching a group of young boys in blue school uniforms picking teams for a cricket match, a young man knocked on my door and said afternoon tea was being served in the garden. Following him down the stairs I was struck by the mixture of local culture and classic English influences in everything from the furniture, the art, even the layout and construction of the building. It was a comfortable feeling, reminiscent of similar places in Kenya, Egypt and other corners of the old British Empire.

*

The next morning Haamid picked me up and we toured Peshawar, especially the old town which with its classic colonial houses and traditional sukes (markets) selling everything from gold to pungent spices, is like steeping back into a history book. After lunch at a KFC (Haamid's favorite) we went to his in-law's house. A modest but well kept house it was located on a side street in a quiet tree shaded residential area not too far from the main university. I had briefly met his wife once before in Kabul and after we greeted each other Haamid introduced me to her parents and brother.

We passed the afternoon discussing the UN mission in Afghanistan, the

Karzai government and the next round of elections, and the antics of the two grand children who played in the garden. Of course they insisted that we eat again, after all Kentucky Fried is not really proper Afghan food, and that was followed later by tea.

By nightfall we had mapped out our plan to go to the Khyber Pass and if we could get around the guards we would go part way through and come back, since it is really not all that long, but very historic and dramatic. After everyone approved of the plan, we ate yet again and Haamid dropped me off at my hotel. It was all I could do to waddle up stairs and collapse in a chair on the veranda to enjoy a cigar in the cool evening air.

*

The next morning we departed immediately after breakfast to take full advantage of the light. Haamid did not want to chance driving in unfamiliar territory so we hired a car and driver from a friend of the family and headed west to the Pakistan-Afghanistan border, and the start of the Khyber Pass. The trip was uneventful until we got about half way to the border, where the Federally Administered Tribal Area or FATA begins. Laying on the Pakistani side of the border with Afghanistan, this rugged mountainous terrain is technically part of Pakistan, but since it is basically ungovernable it has been granted self rule. The federal government and military have limited rights. More to the point, they know better than to interfere with the fiercely independent and quarrelsome tribes (some would say prickly) that live in this remote area, and which have remained essentially independent and unconquered since the beginning of recorded history. One of the few government outposts found in this area are the road blocks that check identifications and frequently turn back travelers if the situation is too risky.

And so it was on the day we chose to visit the Khyber Pass. We had stopped by the provisional government office in Peshawar the day before and asked what was needed to go into the Khyber Pass. They assured us nothing was necessary but of course it all depended on the situation in and around the pass; if it is clear you can go, but if the boarder guards stop you at the road block, you cannot.

From a distance we could see the road block which consisted of a long sturdy steel pipe painted bright red, with barbed wire loosely wrapped around it. In the middle of the pipe was a hand lettered sign with the command to stop in several languages. It was on a swing stand and could be lifted to allow vehicles to pass. Standing in front of it were three soldiers in the ill fitting brown uniforms of the Pakistani Military. Two of them held their rifles in their hands at a semi ready position, the third had his slung over his shoulder and was checking id's and vehicles. Off to one side was a guard house with at least two other soldiers visible, and a short distance behind that lay a barracks and a mess building. It looked peaceful enough but everyone was fully alert.

In front of us were a truck, a van and several cars waiting to be inspected and hopefully waived on. As we slowed to a stop at a respectful distance the truck made a slow u-turn and started back down the road. Not a good sign, but maybe he did not have the correct papers. Then after several minutes, the next car in line did the same. As they passed us I could see a driver and a teenaged boy in the front, and a women in a black burka with her face covered and several children in the back. On the roof of the vehicle were a rolled up mattress and two large bags. If a family was being turned back it looked less promising. Each vehicle was turned around until we were next in line.

As the soldier looked through the open window and asked for our papers, I noticed his two comrades take a couple of steps forward. I guess three men with no women or children in the vehicle put them a bit on edge. I had given him my UN Laise Passé for two reasons. It does not list a nationality, only that the individual is a member of the UN, and if they for some reason decided to keep them it was much easier to replace the LP than a national passport.

One of the other guards, who had an officer's insignia that I could not make out, stepped forward and also looked at our ID's. He looked long at the photo on the LP then looking at me again he asked if I was in the United Nations. When I responded that I was he asked why the UN wanted to go into the FATA. With Haamid translating I explained that I did not want to go into the FATA, I just wanted to see the Khyber Pass and would turn around and come back. He was unimpressed and said it was closed, no one was allowed to go any further today. Handing our credentials back he motioned for us to turn around. We tried to ask if we could go in later or maybe tomorrow but he just continued to motion us back. Not wanting to give them any reason to arrest or detain us, we did as told and slowly headed back toward Peshawar.

I was disappointed, to have come all that way and not get to at least see the historical pass. Ever since I was a child I had read about this famous place, how in 1842 the retreating British Army had lost thousands of soldiers and camp followers in the pass trying to get from Kabul back to Peshawar . I had heard its name mentioned in conversations and it never failed to excite my imagination. Maybe we could find a way around this road block, but this suggestion met with silence from my colleagues. I let it drop.

After a few kilometers I noticed a small collection of buildings in the distance, a few hundred meters off to the side of the road and asked Haamid if that was a village. He asked the driver who explained that that was a place where several arms dealers had their stores and you could buy anything from a pistol to a rocket. Hell I thought, if we can't go to Khyber maybe we can still have some adventure. Can we go there I asked, fully expecting more silence, but instead the driver said sure. To my surprise he slowed down and pulled onto the dirt road, that lead to the collection of buildings. I quickly glanced at Haamid and although he looked a bit apprehensive he did not seem to object. Too late, we were pulling up in front of the first shop.

*

OK, I figured as I got out of the car, you are always more of a mark if you appear to be lost or timid. Act confident, not cocky and look like you know where you are going. I had adopted this approach in Detroit and perfected it in Bogota, and with a couple of notable exceptions (such as when I was in the wrong part of Bogota and the police thought I was buying marijuana), it had worked. Just then I heard the sound of gun fire, an AK-47 most likely, but it was measured and regular, not panic-like, so I figured it was someone target shooting or trying out a weapon before they bought it. We walked on.

Haamid lead the way as we walked into Ali's, at least that is what the sign over the door said, just Ali's. In fact it also had some Urdu writing and drawings of a hand gun and a rifle, but in English it said simply Ali's. That's what I like, a simple direct man. Ali was behind the counter and barely looked up from what appeared to be a Glock handgun he was putting into a holster. As he hung it back on the wall he spoke with the driver and said we were welcome, everyone is welcome at Ali's.

He was dark skinned, with jet black hair, in his thirties, about five feet seven, muscular and stocky. I judged that Ali could more than take care of himself, but he smiled and asked if we were buying or looking. Looking, we assured him. He seemed entertained by us and taking the Glock back down from the wall said he could give us a discount, if we bought a lot of them. He showed us several guns including a well polished AK-47 that he said had been "left behind" by a Russian soldier, and since it had been made in Russia or Czechoslovakia, it was much better than the same model made in other countries. I asked who else made it and he took down a model made in Pakistan. It is called the "Birthday Special" he explained since it is a common gift to a boy, usually on his thirteenth birthday. He said the quality and workmanship aren't as good but it works OK and is much cheaper. I immediately thought of the .22 bolt action rifle my Grandmother bought me on my fourteenth birthday. Maybe there were not so many degrees of difference between Ali and I after all.

After a few minutes, he told us he kept the bigger stuff in the back where he also had a target area, if we wanted to try anything. At this point Haamid gave me an apprehensive look and I thought it best if we got out of there before we drew a crowd. I asked if we could take some pictures and Ali said sure, just don't take my picture. But after I had taken a couple of general shots of the place, he grabbed a "Birthday Special" and stepping in front of the camera said OK, you take Ali's picture. After that we shook Ali's hand and thanking him for the tour we confidently and casually strolled back to the car, and got the hell out of there.

I was still a little disappointed that we did not get to go through the Khyber Pass, but we did get to visit Ali's Emporium, and get our picture taken with Ali, and not many people can say that. After relaxing a couple more days in Peshawar, we took the bus back to Islamabad and caught the UN flight to Kabul.

Chapter 26: The Ramadan Riot

The Holy Month of Ramadan is one of the most important events on the Islamic calendar. It calls on devotees to fast during daylight hours, observe the five pillars of Islam including attending prayers five times a day and giving to the needy for an entire month. And by fasting I do not mean in a Christian style of limiting yourself to one Big Mac and no fries, this means no food or water, in fact nothing can pass your lips including cigarette smoke. The end of this highly religious month is marked by a three day celebration known as el-Eid during which you visit family and friends, give gifts and especially give to the poor and indignant. Like Christmas to a Christian it is a very special time but also one that requires extra spending for food and gifts, which everyone is willing to do. Ramadan puts a strain on the pocket. Therefore, in Islamic countries it is common to pay a Ramadan bonus, usually equal to one month's salary paid just before the Eid. People are usually in a very good and charitable mood as Eid approaches, but one way to really upset them is to not pay the Ramadan Bonus.

The second year I was in Afghanistan, Ramadan fell during the winter months, so at least the daylight hours were short, it was cool and fasting was a bit easier. The last working day before Eid we had issued the bonus to all the local staff, or so we thought and were winding down for the long Eid holiday. I had been out of the office looking at a possible site for the new compound we were building and at about 10:00 hours, as we rounded the corner to the main gate my driver muttered something and slowed down. Looking up I saw a mob of nearly fifty people milling outside the main gate to the administrative compound. As we pulled up the only UN staff I recognized was the new Chief of Technical Services, a large and imposing retired Canadian Air Force Colonel named Berry, and two Security Guards. As I opened the window Berry smiled and asked if I had any experience negotiating with mobs, which of course I did from Somalia and elsewhere, and he knew it. The people looked upset, but not violent so I stepped out of the car and through a translator asked what was going on.

One of the group, a young man who spoke pretty good English came forward and explained that all of these men were local staff, construction workers, who worked for the Engineering Section. They had come to the main gate to be paid their Ramadan bonus like everyone else, but had been told there was no money for them. By this time the shouts from the back of the crowd were getting louder and the mob was pressing forward. They had also spilled into the street, closing it off and I could hear car horns blaring as traffic began to back up. This was beginning to look bad.

I immediately told the young man to tell everyone that we would get to the bottom of this but I needed him to act as a spokesman for the mob. I asked him to explain that to the crowd and to get them lined up and out of the street. I turned to Berry and asked him to get more security guards but keep them out of sight inside the gate, just in case we needed to be rescued. Seeing that Abdul, the newly appointed spokesman was having trouble getting the attention of the group, I jumped up on one of the concrete barriers that are placed to slowdown or stop any vehicles from ramming the gate. I motioned for Abdul to join me on the impromptu podium. Now in a position where we could see the crowd, I had Abdul explain that I would find out when the bonus would be issued but since I had just gotten there they needed to give me some time. I hoped like hell the bonuses could be issued or I would never dare show my face again.

Just then a small door opened in the main gate and I saw the face of the Chief Finance Officer peering nervously out. Raul had just recently been assigned to Afghanistan from a plush post in Asia, but he had a wealth of UN background and experience. At first glance he appeared to be rather thin, a bit jumpy and nervous, and we had taken advantage of this and played some rather mean tricks on him after he first arrived. The worst was once when we convinced him that the Taliban had vowed to kidnap a UN staff member that evening. He piled all of the furniture against his bedroom door before he went to sleep. I must confess I was a bit sorry for the tricks after I found out some of the extreme situations he had survived in other missions, such as in Rwanda. But it was all in a good natured way, at least I hoped he saw it that way. Raul would prove to be a real trooper as well as a dammed good golfer (or so he says), and after serving together in Afghanistan and again in Sudan, we have become good friends. His assistance was certainly welcome on that day.

He informed me that indeed these guys were eligible for the Ramadan bonus, but that the Engineering Section had failed to process the paperwork and we were in trouble. Engineering had at least provided a list of the construction staff and all the Finance Section was busy processing it now. It would be as much as a couple of hours before they could start handing out money, and he hoped we had enough cash on hand. We agreed to start issuing the payments in groups of five as soon as the paperwork was ready, rather than wait until all of it was finished.

I got back up on my makeshift podium and had Abdul explain how we would proceed. By now the crowd was calming down a bit and the tension seemed to be easing. At least there was a bit of order and I just hoped we could keep it that way until the bonuses were processed.

*

About this time I noticed a very old man standing near the gate in a tattered coat and well worn felt hat. Clearly he was too old to be working, so I asked Abdul who he was. He smiled and said the old man was just walking by and thought he would try to get a bonus as well. I found this quite comical so through Abdul I asked him where he had been working. The old man replied I have been digging ditches, which got a laugh out of everyone around us. I appreciated his spunk so I responded, yes, you do look stronger than I do, which got a real howl. By now people were pushing forward to watch and I asked if he had any UN identification. He looked up at me and through a gap toothed grin he said no sir, I lost it. I shouted get this man a chair, I can't see our father standing in line, which had everyone in stitches. One of the guards came forward with a chair, which the old man took and placing it at the head of the line he sat down.

This could not have been staged any better and by now everyone was nearly doubled over in laughter, including me. On the spur of the moment I reached in my pocket and pulled out the equivalent of five US dollars in Afghani Pounds, a pretty good sum. Handing it to the old man I said let me give you your bonus now, and wish you Eid Mubaric (Happy Eid), but you be sure to come back to work next week. The old man smiled and took the money. He looked at it for a few seconds, stuffed it into his pocket and hobbled off to buy Eid sweets, or fruit, or cigarettes or something.

*

Just as I was wondering what we could do as a follow up to this, the gate opened and motioning me over, Raul handed over the first list of five names to be paid their Eid bonus. It had been less than half an hour but his staff had worked a minor miracle and had the first group of bonuses ready to go. We read out the names and they stepped forward. After checking their identifications, a security guard walked with them to the pay window inside the compound.

It would take another hour and a half before we were finished, but everyone got their Eid bonuses that day, including the old man in the tattered coat. I still have to smile whenever I think of him, and how in the true spirit of Eid, he helped quell a potential riot.

Chapter 27: The Ancient Silk Road to Bamyian

Many people have their own location to nominate for Shangri-La, that mythical nearly perfect valley usually hidden somewhere high in the mountains. It is always pleasant, cool and green, even though it may be surrounded by hot deserts and heathen populations. It has become a symbol of the haven we all seek, or at least that we like to think still exists. It holds out hope in a world of reality. Of course it is a figment of the imagination, especially in view of the intolerant "in-your-face" culture that seems to be spreading around the world faster than a jet out of Newark International. Still, it is a nice bit of figment to cling to, and I have a nomination from Afghanistan.

Bamyian is essentially a large village that is also the capital of a province with the same name. Setting north and west of Kabul at 2500 meters or about 7,700 feet, it was a stop over on the Silk Road that connected India with Central Asia, and eventually with Turkey and Europe. By small fixed wing aircraft or by helicopter (that is the only airborne way in), it is less than one hour from Kabul, but you have to land on a gravel strip that can jar your teeth. By land the most direct route is along the old Silk Road following river valleys and snaking through several villages that people warned me about but which I found to be friendly enough. The dirt road finally reaches a series of passes that lift you to the rare air and other worldliness of Bamyian valley. If the weather is agreeable and there are no muddy sink holes or snow drifts, that route takes about seven hours.

Bamyian is populated mainly by Hazara. With Mongolian features they are related to the people of north central Asia, and walking through Bamyian one could easily imagine they were in a village in Western China, which in reality is only a scant few hundred miles to the east. However, about every forth or fifth house is Pasthu and the inhabitants exhibit the longer angular face and round eyed features. They live together in relative peace. Being separated from Kabul, both physically and culturally, the people of Bamyian have been protected by their remoteness and the nearly impenetrable Hindu Kush Mountains. This was the only region in Afghanistan that remained under Buddhism and refused to accept Islam until recently. It was also here that the giant statues of Buddha were carved into the side of the gigantic stone cliffs on the east side of the Bamyian Valley, nearly fifteen hundred years ago. They were famous through the civilized world and many Buddhists made religious pilgrimages to the valley to pay their respect.

This was among the last areas to fall to the Taliban in 1998 and they suffered greatly as a result. Many innocent people were killed simply because they were Hazara. After establishing a harsh provincial government the Taliban eventually decided that the statues were graven images and in the year 2001 they blew them up. Today, the rubble still lays in chunks at the base of the cliffs as a tribute to the sheer stupidity and narrow mindedness humans are capable of, but an international effort is being made to restore or reassemble them.

*

I had been to Bamiyan several times by plane and always enjoyed the spectacular view coming into the valley. As the craft settles slowly onto the airstrip, a sheer cliff hundreds of feet tall rises abruptly from the east side of the valley floor. Carved into the solid rock face of that cliff are the opening for the statues; two tall sitting Buddah figures nearly 80 meters high, and one reclining Buddah. In addition, the cliff face is littered with caves that have been dug as houses over the centuries, with many of them still occupied as residences today.

From the other side of the valley if you stand with the rock cliffs to your back, and gaze across to the high ground where the airstrip is located, the village and the town lay between. It is essentially a peasant farm town so there are still small fields and pastures with cows and sheep sprinkled everywhere between the small stores, the houses and the makeshift markets. No roads are paved and the most imposing building is an adobe prison once used by the Taliban and now by the provisional government, but aside from the barbed wire and armed guards sitting around outside, you would not know it was a prison unless someone told you.

Running through the center of the valley is a small river with white birch, poplar and pine trees scattered along the banks. Coming down from the high mountains, the water is clear and cold and reminds me of trout streams I have fished in Canada. It is a rustic peaceful little town, especially beautiful in the autumn when the birch and poplar turn gold and with the occasional flaming red of a maple tree (at least I think it is a maple), and the babbling of the river as it glides over rapids and rocks, it is one of the best places I can imagine to pass a few hours or days.

I had vowed to take the land route to Bamyian before I left Afghanistan, so late one summer when two of the UN vehicles from Bamyian had been in Kabul for major repairs and were ready to return, I took the opportunity to travel back with the convoy. Also traveling with me was the Regional Administrative Officer from Bamyian, a colorful character named Goran. Our first meeting had been a rather rough one as he had several local staff members who had not been paid for several months. Goran, who was one of the most thoughtful and concerned people I have met, had paid them out of his own pocket but was understandably angry that DPKO could not seem to get this seemingly simple matter straightened out. He had called me and threatened to send these local staff members to Kabul so I could pay them for a while.

Digging into the case I found that they were in fact staff from another UN agency that had left Afghanistan either right after or during the war, and somehow they had not been transferred over to us. This was not too unusual, in fact I was still finding such cases up to the time I left Afghanistan after nearly four years. I cut through some red tape and got them transferred to UNAMA, as well as all back pay issued. From then on we were good friends. We would meet up again in Sudan and continue our friendship but only briefly, for unfortunately Goran had developed an incurable cancer and died less than a year after I arrived in Sudan.

Some of my fondest memories of Afghanistan involve setting with Goran on his roof top in Bamyian, watching snow clouds roll in over the mountains, swapping stories of our families, or just telling lies in general. However, I do not want to leave the impression that Bamyian, or anywhere else for that matter is perfect. I believe in Sharngri-La as a concept but not as reality, which is mixed with incidents closer to one that happened in Goran's house.

He got a puppy from an Afghan neighbor, who kept dogs to herd a flock of sheep he kept in the mountains. It was a really cute energetic ball of fur and the international staff in the house quickly adopted it. As it grew up it acted like pups do and would playfully tug at your pants legs, run under your feet, and chew on it's toys. The cleaning staff seemed indifferent to it but I'm sure they felt it was being spoiled. Goran usually washed the food and water bowels himself, knowing the local staff would probably be offended if he asked them to do it.

Once when he was going on leave he told the cleaners to wash the bowels while he was gone. Usually one of the other house members did this and I don't know why he did not ask them to do it that time. When he returned the dog was laying, apparently unconscious, under the table. It would not respond and was nearly dead, and all that the staff would say was that it had gotten sick a few days ago and would not eat. Later that day when the dog died, Goran felt sure it had been poisoned but could not prove anything. Sadly, he dug a small grave on a hillside near the compound and prepared to bury the pup. As he lowered it into the grave, he noticed that it's lower jaw had been broken. He was furious and demanded to know how it happened, but no one seemed to know a thing about it. In true Goran style he blamed himself for this, having asked the staff to clean the bowels and all. Shortly after that the cleaning lady just left at the end of the day and never returned. He never did find out what had happened as far as the poisoning, but he speculated that maybe she lost her temper and hit the dog out of frustration, seeing a dog that was more spoiled and pampered than her own children. Or maybe it was just done out of spite, we will never know.

*

However, back to our road trip to Bamyian. Early in the morning on a

Wrong Place-Right Time

late summer's day, our small convoy of Toyota Forerunners rolled out of the main UNOCA compound on Jalalabad Road. We cut through the northwest side of Kabul and almost immediately hit dirt roads. On the entire trip to Bamyian, outside of Kabul I think we had less than two kilometers of pavement. I expected to travel through arid open territory, like one does on the road to Baghram or Herat, but instead we followed a series of narrow valleys , only occasionally cutting through a pass in the mountains or over a short stretch of cactus strewn land to reach another valley. Each valley followed a small stream or seemed to have some source of water such as a spring or a small lake, which in turn supported fields and orchards.

The road was never more than two lanes wide and especially in mountain passes or when crossing ancient looking stone bridges, it was barely one lane. Although the traffic was light, we did end up waiting for the road to clear in several areas. Once we stopped to buy apples and wander off behind some buildings to relieve ourselves. The people were friendly and got a real laugh out of Goran and I as we bargained for apples. Later, in another village we stopped again to rest and I saw an old man selling a few tomatoes. I could not help but think that when necessary he was probably a Taliban and when necessary he sold tomatoes on the roadside. Life is like that for much of the world, adaptation and survival are two of life's main virtues.

As we left the village and travelled on, we came across a road crew cleaning up an area blocked by a recent landslide. It is quite common in Afghanistan, as well as in many parts of the world for local men to work on the road, either to pay off taxes or to earn a little cash. Sometimes they will hold out a hand and ask for contributions as you pass. As we slowed down to navigate through the area, a small hand suddenly thrust itself into view in my window. I glanced out, and down, and saw a small boy not much more than two feet tall, with a shovel taller than he was. He was wearing a bright blue hat and tattered jacket, as he leaned on the shovel like he had been working all morning and was taking a break. He was asking for a donation.

I opened the window and as I handed him some change he broke into a smile. I pulled out my camera and held it up as if to ask if it was OK to take his picture, at which point he glanced at some men standing nearby. When one of the men, apparently his father or an uncle laughed and said a few words, the small boy adjusted his hat and putting his hands in his jacket pockets, looked at the camera as if to signal he was ready. By this time I was snickering, the men were laughing and my colleagues were laughing. I took two pictures and handed him another few Afghan Pounds and an apple. Looking very pleased with himself he dropped the shovel and ran off.

At about 15:30 or 3:30 PM we pulled into the UN Regional Compound. It is located within walking distance of the airstrip and close to the ISAF (International Security Assistance Forces) compound, which serves as headquarters for the New Zeeland Army contingent for that area. Goran immediately called the local staff together and we held a general meeting to discuss administrative issues such as salaries and promotions, and to answer questions. This lasted until nearly 17:00 (5:00 PM) after which some of the staff members hung around a bit longer for individual questions. I would meet with the international staff members the next day, and spend any spare time with the administrative staff going over finance and personnel issues. We were trying to get the official matters out of the way so we could spend a few days touring around the valley and visiting the Band-e-Amir lakes, located a few hours further on in the highlands.

*

After we finished the meetings with local staff we walked to the housing compound where most of the international UN staff lived. The compound consisted of four wings, three of them single story and one with a second floor. Together they formed an enclosed square with a large open patio in the middle. The building was made of mud and adobe block with a white stucco finish, and with the dry mountains in the background it reminded me of farm and ranch houses I had seen in the highlands of South America. One wing of the complex held the kitchen, dining room and three bedrooms. The other wings had bedrooms, a common sitting/living room and storage rooms.

The compound in Bamyian was unique in that it also had an authentic Swedish sauna (which I think was the only one in all of Afghanistan). It had been built by two Swedish Police Officers who had been assigned to Bamyian with UNAMA. They had built it from scrap lumber and a few fixtures they brought with them when they returned from home leaves.

At an altitude of over 7,000 feet the evenings can get quite cold and this sauna was certainly a welcome addition. Since it was used by a mixed staff of men and women, we had to wear shorts when we used it. Instead of rolling in a snow bank to cool off, we just splashed ourselves with a bucket of well water, which was like melted snow.

The staff had gone in together to rent and refurbish the compound, which was a common arrangement both in Kabul and in the regions. They had hired some cleaning and house hold staff but usually did most of their own cooking. I always took along a box of food items to add to the storeroom and while the meals were simple, with the mix of nationalities in the house including English, Indian, African and Scandinavian (Goran himself was Croatian) the meals were never boring, much less predicable. Going to Bamyian always involved official duties for me, but because of the surroundings and especially the friends I developed among the staff there, it was a welcome break from Kabul.

*

One of the natural wonders of the Bamyian Highlands are the series of five lakes known as Band-e-Amir, or Dam of the Amir, which lay about 3 hours west of the town of Bamyian at 2,900 meters (nearly 9,000 feet). This is a high enough altitude that it affects the performance of normal vehicle engines, as well as one's own body. Like La Paz, Bolivia it is best to take it a bit easy when you get there. The last third of the trip to the lakes is quite spectacular, especially when you first view the main lake, stretching out like a huge blue crystal gem set in a gorge, hundreds of feet below the road. Even those who have seen it many times before are taken by its beauty.

About thirty minutes after you leave the town of Bamyian you are already above the tree line and the only plant forms are shrubs, grasses and a form of tumble weed whose dried out remains are deposited by the wind into piles and blown into long rows that stretch out like fence lines. The first part of the trip takes you over an endless expanse of highlands, with a few scattered farms where families live in mud and stone huts. Planting potatoes, barley and gathering what they can, they scratch out a living and from the looks of it, barely hold onto life. We passed a man and little girl leading a scrawny looking donkey loaded with a pile of tumble weeds strapped to its back, the main source of fuel for the fires they use to cook and heat their primitive houses. At least the load was not heavy. The little girl had a smile on her face as she clutched very two large carrots which they would likely have for dinner. As we drove on, the driver explained how this area had been mined to prevent the Northern Coalition Forces from bringing tanks and trucks down from Marzar-i Sharif in the north to attack Kabul.

As if to prove the point we soon came upon the twisted remains of a passenger van that only several days before, had pulled off the road a bit to allow an oncoming vehicle to pass, and had hit an unmarked landmine. It had been blown further off the road and was laying on its side. The windows were broken out and through a hole torn in the bottom you could see the distorted seats and dash board, with traces of blood and flesh still evident. The driver said several people had died but the biggest problem was that it took officials nearly a day to reach it since it was in such an isolated area.

Mine clearance in such remote locations is difficult and presented more than a few problems to us, particularly during the run up to the elections of 2004 when we had to establish so many remote helicopter landing sites for the elections teams. Many polling sites were in areas barely accessible by four wheel drive vehicles, so the only practical solution was helicopter. However, for a copter to land the site has to be inspected and certified as clear of mines before it can land. A real catch 22; you cannot land if the site is not declared clear of mines, but you cannot clear it of mines if you cannot get to it. We had nearly thirty remote sites and the job of visiting and certifying them fell to one of the Aviation Officers. He cleared the sites in record time, much to the amazement of the Director of Administration.

Several years later when we happened to cross paths in Africa, he explained how this was done. During one of the early remote site visits, one of the local farmers said the site was clear of mines, and to prove it he confidently walked across and around the area in question. When the AO asked him how he knew it was cleared he explained that he had cleared it, and pointing to his herd of goats he explained what is a common practice in Afghanistan and for that matter in many parts of the world. He drove a large herd of goats back and forth through the area. When no goats are thus sacrificed, and after a further visual inspection, the locals feel free to use the land again. I was also told by another friend that in Palestine, the preferred method is to use cows as they are heaver.

After that, when my friend would arrive at an un-cleared landing site, he would hire local herders to drive their goats back and forth over the area. This may raise the hackles of some, but absent anything else, it is better than letting children wander into the area. I might also point out that happily, no goats were blown up during these rather unorthodox mine clearing operations, and no incidents were reported during the elections as well.

To anyone who glorifies war I would have them spend a few days in Afghanistan, Iraq, Somalia or any number of such places. Being careful to stay well on the road, we proceeded on.

*

As we neared the lake and followed the twisting road down the mountainside for the final approach, the views were amazing. Finally we reached the floor of the valley and the driver pulled to a stop on a bridge, facing a rather sorry looking restaurant and small hotel at the head of the lake. As we got out to have a better view he pointed out that here in the valley, we were actually below the level of the lake.

In front of us was a sheer wall that stretched across the valley. It almost appeared to be man made, it was so vertical. Here and there were small streamlets of water that seemed to ooze from it, and Goran explained that the lake was directly behind that wall. These walls, that at first glance appear to be rather fragile and ready to give way at any moment, are all that is holding back acres and acres of cold clear mountain water.

The water is very rich in calcium carbonate, and over the eons it has evaporated at the edge of the lake and formed travertine walls. These walls, with a glassy appearance are about 15 to 20 feet wide and raise straight up to a height of about 25 feet. They act as a gigantic natural dam and have trapped the water behind them to form these incredible lakes. The same phenomena occurs naturally in other parts of the world but no where as dramatically and with such effect as here at Band-e-Amir. During the winter the streamlets and water seeping out of the walls freeze and take on the appearance of solid sheets of cascading ice, creating a dramatic picture indeed.

As we were stopped on the bridge an old man in robes and a turban, riding a donkey, passed our vehicle and at the risk of seeming rude I snapped his picture. Although I have other photographs of the lake itself, my favorite from this trip is this one, which in my mind I have entitled the bridge of time.

Chapter 28: Scorpion House, the beginning of the end

In late summer of my third year in Afghanistan, we finally completed the new staff living quarters in the main compound on Jalalabad Road. The offices and warehouse facilities in the compound had been completed and occupied for over a year already. The location was good in that it was on the outskirts of the city and was sat back a considerable distance from the main road, so security was easier to maintain. With a series of barriers and gates which we installed, it would have been difficult to get a car or truck bomb close to the main buildings. In addition, it was also relatively close to the airport in the even we needed to do an evacuation.

The disadvantage of living in the compound was that being so close to the office, you would never really be able to get away from it. All in all, I was not sure I wanted to move into that situation as I would be constantly surrounded by the same people with whom I worked. The questions and complaints would never stop, and we had some very persistent staff members, who because of their close connections to senior staff, or just because of their cantankerous and prickly personalities were constantly demanding that the rules be bent or overlooked for them.

Still, living in the compound had its advantages as well. Located on a forty acre site that was completely surrounded by ten foot high block and concrete walls, it had originally been an industrial or commercial site in the Soviet era, and construction of the walls and several buildings was nearly completed before they left. When we first went to view the site much of it was covered with destroyed trucks and abandoned equipment of every description and had only recently been certified as being free of landmines. However, The Chief Administrative Officer at that time immediately saw its potential value, and negotiated to get it. He saw it as the perfect spot for a well protected compound, large enough to provide offices and warehouses not just for DPKO but for other UN agencies that wanted to share the compound. It could also accommodate housing for UN staff, which would be far better than having them spread all over the city of Kabul.

In short, it was a site on which he could leave his legacy. If he had not become a Chief Administrator for DPKO, Ripp probably would have been the head of a large construction company, or maybe a demolition firm. He was always building, tearing down and re-building something and his ideas seemed to get a bit more grandiose each time. He was also the only Chief that could get along with the head of the mission, and could usually bring him around to his view.

Even though we also thought it was a good idea, Raul and I jokingly referred to the new compound as Ripp-Landia, and suggested that he also build a big water slide and indoor ice rink. Depending on the particular day and his mood, sometimes he smiled at our suggestions, sometimes he just growled. We knew when not to offer our helpful suggestions as we had learned to read his moods, and when disturbed, he was the most gentle man to ever put blade to throat. However, Ripp had good insight. Putting most of the UN agencies and staff in one location seems to be the direction things are going. It saves money by eliminating the cost of multiple facilities and duplicate maintenance and security staff. It also makes it easier to provide adequate and secure living quarters in one location, as opposed to having staff and facilities spread out in what is frequently hostile or at least unfriendly territory. In the end, the administrative compound in UNAMA would set the standard for what is now being used in many other places.

*

In spite of the advantages of living in the compound, I was still not anxious to move. At that time I was living in a comfortable house, which was my third or forth relocation since arriving in Afghanistan. I refer to this house as the Scorpion house. I named it after an incident that occurred one morning when I got out of bed barefooted, and nearly stepped on a two and a quarter inch red Scorpion with massive pinchers and an impressive stinger. Actually, a scorpion sting is painful and swells up, and puts you out of commission for a few days, but rarely more than that. Still, it is painful and you don't want to encounter one. We had noticed a few of the critters outside in the yard, but never that large and this was the first one in the house.

I considered just throwing it outside but after a half hearted attempt to carefully maneuver it into an empty jar, and nearly getting hit by its tail, I reconsidered. Instead I dropped a copy of "The Great Game" by Peter Hopkirk on it. In addition to being essential reading on the history of Central Asia it is also quite a heavy book. Then I had the cleaner move every box and piece of furniture, looking for more of them which we thankfully did not find, and spray the entire house with the local Pakistani equivalent of Raids Scorpion-be-gone. In the next few weeks however, a combination of scorpions, the noise from next door and other events would convenience me it was time to move to the new compound.

*

I shared the Scorpion House with a new cast of characters, since by this time the old group from Jimmy's House had either moved on to other missions or had drifted off to other houses. I have always tried to be careful about choosing house mates and this time I was sharing quarters with an interesting group. We clicked and had immediately become friends. My house mates were the Staff Counselor, a hyper- energetic French women with short red hair who seemed a bit crazy but kind; a female German Civil Affairs Officer who looked like a model and spoke with a killer accent; and a Security Officer who was actually a Police Officer from Québec Canada. He was without a doubt the most fit and one of the most handsome men in the mission. I of course was the dud of the group but they humored me. We all travelled frequently on official business to other regions and offices, so much of the time it was as if only one or two people actually lived in the house.

My room was in the back of the Scorpion House and shared a wall with the house next door, which also doubled as a bakery and bread store. It was relatively quiet except from 5:00 to 6:00 AM nearly every morning when they would slam the bread dough on a table, which would bang into the wall with a thud, stretch it out and slam it again. At first I though they were fighting and expected to see a dead body being carried out of the house. But, as I did with the noise from the Honeymoon Hotel, I got used to it. Actually I always carry ear plugs just for such instances, and especially when traveling on planes.

Besides, I enjoyed observing the activity at the bread store, which was actually just a window and a counter in the front of the house. To advertise, they used a method that is common in Afghanistan; they hung loves of flat bread on nails on the wall outside the store. Likewise, if it is a shop that fixes bicycle tires, they will hang a bike tire on the wall or tie it to the limb of a nearby tree. Shops that repair radios and electrical appliances will hang an old radio on the wall or set it in plain sight on the roof. Whatever the product or service, it is advertised by hanging either the item itself or if it is too large, something representing it, outside the shop.

One of my favorites was a repair shop near our office that had two full sized electric stoves (or cookers as they are commonly known) setting on the roof. A real "red neck" approach to advertising. In the case of some bakeries, it was common to see many loves of bread hung outside on nails and customers just take what they want and pay for it, sort of a variation on the self serve concept. One last observation, many people ride bicycles and they come up with some clever ways to carry the bread such as tucking it under an arm or in one case I saw a young man sitting carefully on the bread as he peddled home. At least the bread was wrapped in newspaper.

*

So, in spite of the scorpions and the noisy neighbors the house was still pretty good. We all got along well which was not always the case for some of the other houses. Some were a constant source of arguments and hurt feelings, not to mention good gossip, which kept the Staff Counselor busy, but I won't go into those. Well, maybe just one of the more dramatic but also rather humorous examples.

There was a house that had been successfully shared by two women and two men for about a year. They were friends, colleagues, but nothing more. One of the female housemates completed her assignment in UNAMA, and went back to her previous UN post in Geneva. At about the same time, the girlfriend of one of the fellows in the house (her name was Cabrita) was transferred into the mission. Naturally Cabrita moved into the house with her boyfriend, and the two of them resumed their relationship. Cabrita immediately began a not so subtle competition with everyone to dominate the house, insisting on changing the household routine and insisting that they move to a new house and purchase new furniture. She especially tried to marginalize Dolce, the other woman in the house. Considering Cabrita's personality it was not too surprising as she was that way with everyone. She was at her best when she thought she had a juicy rumor or dirty little secret about someone. Needless to say, Cabrita and Dolce had at best a strained relationship and it all culminated in a nasty and rather childish scene.

When Dolce went on home leave to Belgium, Cabrita made her move. Seems she had been pushing her boy friend, whom she had under tight control, to look around for another house but to kept it a secret from Dolce. Unexpectedly Dolce came back from her leave two days early and found her roommates in the process of loading the last of their things into a van. When she grasped what was happening she asked if they had intended to at least leave a note that they were leaving, or to just sneak out. Looking rather embarrassed the two guys made some excuse about finding a place that was just too good to pass up, but unfortunately, you see it was only big enough for three. But the rent was paid up through the end of the month and of course, she could stay until then. They even graciously agreed to leave much of the jointly owned furniture, which they would only sell after she had made other arrangements and moved out. With this lame excuse, they high tailed it leaving their former roommate to herself and an empty house.

Some friends made room for Dolce where they were living at the time, and she soon found a good place to live. Being an altogether bigger person than her former roommates, she did not seem to be adversely affected by this and in fact found it rather amusing, in a childish way. So, the moral of the story is pick good housemates, or at least ones who do not have unresolved personality problems. I had good mates at Scorpion House, but that was about to change.

*

The breakup of Scorpion House started when the Staff Counselor, Rouge as we called her, announced she had been offered a position in a French speaking mission which she wanted to accept. I was actually her supervisor and encouraged her to take the opportunity for the added experience, and to build up her resume. Alicia, with the models looks and Marlene Dietrich accent, was being transferred to one of the other regions. Cisco, the Francophone flat foot was to be sent to Haiti by DPKO to help do a security survey, and would likely be transferred there full time. In short order our happy house was dissolving.

One Saturday afternoon, after working the morning at my office in the compound, I was setting in the patio considering my options. It was a lovely autumn day in Kabul, with a few feathery clouds in an otherwise blue sky and although the sun was still quite strong, a cool breeze coming in off the Kush made it ideal. The patio was actually a lawn which the owner of the house kept watered and in good shape, as well as the rose bushes which ran along the back wall. There were also several fruit trees in the patio; a couple of apple trees, an apricot and a small mulberry. At one time Afghanistan was a major exporter of fruits and raisins to Russia and Europe.

I had just opened a tin of Dunhill Standard Mixture and loaded my favorite old briar. There is something about the smell and taste of a good Latakia English mix that just seems to clear the mind and I was looking forward to a quiet afternoon.

Rouge was in Herat investigating a potential sexual harassment case, Alicia was visiting friends at another UN house across town, and Cisco had already departed for his temporary assignment in Haiti. Other than the neighbors cat who seemed to like our backyard best, I had the patio to myself. Old Tom was sitting on a sack of cement, halfhearted cleaning himself and I was setting on a chair under one of the apple trees. Drawing slowly on my pipe I was absentmindedly watching a bee as it crawled on an apple that still hung on the tree and thinking of my leave which was due the next week. My wife had been sent back to Kuwait for six months by her employer and I was going to meet up with her there. She had found an apartment not too far from the house of some close friends we had made during our last assignment in the Gulf, and they were all planning a grand reunion.

At about the same time as I first heard the loud hissing sound overhead, I saw the cat spring straight up on all fours. The hissing grew much louder as a shadow moved quickly over the house and across the lawn. The hair seemed to stand up on my head and arms as I jerked around and looked upward toward the sound. I knew instinctively what it was having seen missiles and rockets in Kuwait and Iraq, but never this close. I was certain this one was going to hit us and unconsciously I braced for the blinding light and bone shattering blast. That is a very strange feeling, knowing there is nothing you can do but hope for divine intervention or chance, or luck, whatever you believe in.

Everything seemed to move slowly. I quickly reasoned that since it was a hissing sound, almost like a sucking sound, that the propellant had burned out and this thing was on its way down. It had cleared the house by less than twenty feet so it was going to hit very near, if it cleared the patio. Since we were in Afghanistan I knew it was a Katusha Rocket, left over from the war with the Soviet Union. They were old by this time and not being very reliable, the Taliban just pointed them and set them off, hoping for the best. Almost as soon as it appeared, it had passed over the patio, leaving the cat and I dazed and feeling very lucky. At least I felt that way, the cat went back to his cleaning.

Now I was waiting for the thud as it landed and then the deafening explosion, but I did not hear either. I cringed in anticipation as I recalled the incredibly loud explosion that woke up the entire city of Mogadishu at about 3:00 AM one morning. It occurred when some faction or another blew up the one Catholic Church still remaining from the days when the Italians had colonized Somalia. Even though that explosion was a few kilometers away, my ears rang with the sound for a couple of hours.

Hearing nothing I quickly ran to the gate, and looking out onto the street saw people running in all directions. As I later found out, the rocket had managed to go a few houses into the next block before it crashed into a small kitchen, hitting and killing an old lady sitting at a table fixing dinner for her family. The rocket did not go off, as sometimes happened with the left over Katushas, but of course hundreds of pounds of weight falling from the sky is also deadly.

The more I thought about it over the next few days, the more reasonable living in the relative safety of the compound sounded, so in early November I moved into my new quarters at UNOCA. They were actually quite comfortable, and since I was a senior officer it came with a small kitchenette and my own bathroom. In addition, Raul and Ripp shared a suite next door, where I spent most of my evenings, so it was almost as if the old crew from Jimmy's house was back together, minus Jimmy of course. We did not have the sawdust stove for entertainment but we did have satellite connection and the BBC news channel. To celebrate our reunion Raul asked me to fix his favorite meal, a large cumin and tuna omelet, an old standby which I had first concocted out of desperation one evening at Jimmy's House, when all we had were eggs, a can of tuna and ground cumin. The best that can be said is that it is filling.

Chapter 29: The Last Christmas in Kabul

The holiday season was coming on, and as always during the period between Christmas and New Years everyone wanted to take leave at the same time. Over the past two holiday seasons I had managed to take off, so this year it was my turn to serve as OIC so others could leave. I really did not mind, and after all the years we had lived this vagabond lifestyle, my family was used to this eventuality by now. Instead we planned to take a couple of weeks in January after the holiday rush. We had decided to meet up in a small Swiss village near the Reichenbach Falls, a place made famous in the Sherlock Holmes series by Sir Arthur Conan Doyle. It is a little known village with surprisingly good skiing, but being out of the main tourist area it is frequented mostly by locals. I will not share the name of this lucky find since I do not want to see it overrun by noisy Americans and trendy Europeans.

So, a few days before Christmas, I again found myself as the Officer-in-Charge. About half of the staff were on leave but the compound was still full of activity with impromptu parties and more than a few bottles of beer and wine. Limited alcohol was available at the commissary stores that had opened in several of the International Security Assistance Force (ISAF) compounds. My favorite was a Spanish PX next door to our compound and although it only accepted Euros and was a bit expensive it carried excellent cheese and sausage perfect for tapas, and some decent Spanish wines. Life in the compound was turning out to be good, except for the Boxing Day bomb scare.

*

For those who are not familiar with Boxing Day, it is the day after Christmas which was traditionally when household staff (if you had any), were given a small box of gifts and the day off. In our house it was set aside for boxing up the Christmas decorations and putting them away for another year. My wife insists that the boxing refers to all the shopping that needs to be done at the after Christmas sales, hence boxes. At any rate, Boxing Day happened to fall on a weekend that year so there was no work and it was a slow day of recuperation following Christmas Day. By afternoon the level of activity began to pick up in the staff housing wing of the compound. The PX stores were open so we were able to get more supplies and a few parties were planned for the evening.

I checked in with the various sections to be sure all was quiet and walked over to the Security Section, which was located in a separate building. I spent a while talking to Little Swaimi the Deputy Chief Security Officer, who was OIC while Big Swaimi was on leave. Both the Chief and Deputy Chief Security Officers were from Fiji and both were named Swami. The Chief was only marginally larger, but we called him Big Swami anyway. He reported that as least as far as the UN was concerned it was a quiet day in Afghanistan. Returning to my office I made a few notes to myself to be entered later into the daily log and walked back to my residence, taking the long way around the compound and past the communal kitchen. You never knew what smells you would find in that area and I was greeted by the usual Indian curry, the smell of pancit and adobo (two popular Filipino dishes), an African okra stew and the universal fried chicken. I spoke with everyone and made sure I left the kitchen with invitations to several parties that evening.

As planned, I visited a couple of parties that evening and as usual ended up eating a combination of foods. That is one thing about peacekeeping missions, everyone likes to fix food from their own country and culture and most of it is good. It is a good way to get your countrymen or women together and it is also good for the homesick souls. I have been in this business so long now that in fact I seldom get homesick anymore, at least for the food. I remember the first few years I would occasionally miss a good hamburger or my Grandma's raspberry pie, but then when I was home I would equally miss a good Lamb Briyani or plate of hummus and green olives, so it all balances out.

About the only bad thing that happened that evening was when one of the guys, not Middle Eastern but I won't mention nationalities beyond that, started laughing about American soldiers getting killed in Iraq. Even though he was the host of that party I told him it was wrong to laugh about any soldier being killed, friend or enemy. He kept talking and laughing so I told him he was drunk and talking like an asshole, at which point some of his friends quickly took him into the hallway and shut him up. After another quick glass of wine to smooth over any hurt feelings I moved on to the next party. A couple of days later when I saw this guy again he acted as if nothing had happened. He said he was drunk and did not remember what he had said. I let it go at that.

I quit the party scene at about 23:00 hours and went back to my room where I went to sleep before midnight. Sometime after 1:00 AM I was woken up by an urgent knocking on my door and a voice I recognized as one of the Security Officers yelling sir, we have found a bomb. I opened my door and he told me they had found a box with batteries and a wire hooked to it, and it was in a trashcan near the kitchen. For some reason the alarm system was not working so he and two others were knocking on all the doors and alerting everyone to get outside, where it was winter in Afghanistan and a few degrees below freezing. He suggested that the staff be evacuated to the Transportation warehouse, a few hundred meters from our building, and I agreed.

I quickly got dressed and as I was about to step out of my room there was another knock on the door. This time it was a tall thin blond man in a military uniform that I recognized as being from the Finnish Contingent of ISAF. He introduced himself as Sergeant Hanski of the bomb disarmament and disposal unit. He asked if I was the OIC and as we walked toward the warehouse he briefed me on what had happened.

*

One of our Security Officers was doing a routine check of the building when he saw a suspicious looking package in a trash can. Following the protocol for such instances, he immediately called it in to the Duty Officer and Little Swami, who alerted the ISAF bomb unit. The building was nearly cleared, in fact my wing was the last to be alerted since we were the furthest away from the package. As we approached the door to the warehouse Little Swami met us and reported that everyone had been evacuated from the building and were now in the warehouse. Sergeant Hanski said he would report back on any progress and as he left to go back to his duties, Little Swami and I entered the warehouse.

There were about two hundred people crammed into the facility, some had time to dress and were in regular clothes, some in pajamas with a coat thrown on, some who had evacuated on the run were still wearing flip flops. They were milling about in groups, some sitting on the flatbeds of trucks, a few were fortunate enough to find chairs. I immediately asked Swami how many security officers he had and where they were. I did not expect any problems but was just planning in case of a panic. Including the security officers from other UN agencies we had seven or eight and he introduced them to me. I told them that Swami would be in charge of security, since I was familiar with him and they all nodded.

One of them told me he was keeping an eye on a group of three guys who were rather drunk and loud and while they were not causing any problems he was just watching. They were speaking some language that sounded vaguely like English but with a lot of hoots and hans and sounds like that. I immediately recognized them as some Scottish friends from the Engineering Section and figured they would not be a problem, but still best to watch them. Another told me there were several people who did not have coats and were not really dressed for the cold. As it turned out most of them were from the tropics and this was probably their first winter in snow country. There was a good sized office area that was heated and we intended to put them there for the duration. It was locked and while we did not have keys, a South African Security Officer who looked like Grizzly Adams, worked some "credit card" magic and got the door opened. There were no Medical Officers in the crowd but as it turns out we did not need one. People began to laugh and joke a bit as everyone settled down for the wait.

About that time Sergeant Hanski came back and said his Commander wanted to see me. I took one of the Security Officers with me and with Sergeant Hanski we walked to a mobil command vehicle sitting between the two buildings. The Commander explained that a dog named Junior, trained to sniff explosives had been sent into the building and had not found anything else. They were now sending a robot in to see if the package could be moved. The robot had a camera so we were able to watch a live video on a computer screen as it was slowly maneuvered down several hallways toward the kitchen area. It finally came to a stop directly in front of the guilty trash can and as the camera focused we could clearly see the object that caused so much trouble. It was tube shaped, but not metallic like a pipe bomb. Rather it was cardboard, like the middle part from a roll of paper towel. A flashlight battery was clearly visible sticking out of the end that we could see, and a wire was fastened to the battery. Another wire was sticking out of the other end as well. Although it did not look like anything we had seen, it could be a bomb.

The Commander had a discussion with a couple of his staff and after several minutes he announced their plan. Since it could not conveniently be blown in place, the robot would gently pick it up and bring it back outside where it could be more carefully examined. As we watched, Robbie the Robot extended two steel arms and with crab like pincers carefully grasped the tube. To our relief there was no explosion, no smoke, no liquid nor power dripped out of the package. Holding the roll out in front of it, the robot slowly turned and maneuvered back the same way it had gone in. Tension was high as it could go off at any moment and we stepped back even further as Robbie cleared the last door. Stopping at the top of a small flight of steps, Robbie extended his arms several feet and gently deposit the package on the ground, in front of the steps. The arms retracted and the robot moved back into the building, out of harms way. In these tense minutes, the robot almost took on life, as we came to think of it as alive.

Dressed in protective gear and a heavy face protecting shield, one of the soldiers cautiously set up the device used to blow the suspicious package. It was essentially the chamber and short barrel of a 12 gage shotgun, mounted on a stand. It is placed less than two feet in front of the package, and aimed directly at it. When everyone is well out of the way, it is detonated remotely, and a 12 gage slug is sent into the package. If there are explosives it will set them off. Instead, pieces of the package flew in all directions and into the air.

After waiting for things to settle down a bit the bomb expert, dressed like the Michelin man waddled over and looked at the pieces. There were the remains of four or five flashlight batteries and two pieces of wire, that was all.

As we were trying to figure out what the heck it was, one of the Comms staff, a Filipino, pulled me aside and said he thought it "might be" what he called a homemade power pack. He explained that if larger batteries known as powerpacks are not available, it is common to hook several flashlight batteries together, maybe in an empty toilet paper roll. On one end a wire is attached to act as the positive source, on the other end another wire is attached for the negative source. He thought that someone had just discarded one when it had worn out and had not taken it apart. Since he was also of a friend of mine from a previous mission, I asked him who might have done it, and he sort of smiled as he shrugged his shoulders. I asked him if there might be anymore of them lurking around and he replied oh no, that was the only one.

*

After the bomb squad did one last sweep of the building we finally got back to our rooms after 03:00 hours. The next day we all woke up late, to be greeted by one of the weather fronts that frequently settles in over Kabul in the winter, bringing days of snow and overcast low ceilings.

At that time there were no landing lights or radar at the airport, and these fronts usually meant there could be no flights in or out for several days at a time. But even during these gloomy periods, with no warning huge shafts of golden sunlight would occasionally burst forth, more like rip through the clouds, affording an absolutely brilliant view as they danced off the high mountains surrounding the city. Covered in snow pack as much as twenty feet thick, these mountains seemed to just twinkle and shine so brightly you could hardly look directly at them. With the sun shining on them it seemed that you could see in such detail, that I imagined if even a small fox ran across the distant sloops, I could have seen it. Then almost as quickly as this fantastic view appeared, the sun would slip behind a bank of clouds plunging us back into the gloom. Afghanistan, at least the higher altitudes, is one of the most memorable and remarkable places I have lived. To be sure it was difficult and dangerous, but so often it takes your breath away with it's harsh beauty.

Christmas was over, Boxing Day was over, the bomb scare ended successfully and life returned to normal. As I prepared to join up with my family, I had a deep feeling that this would be my last Christmas in Afghanistan.

Chapter 30: Out of Afghanistan

During my leave that January it became obvious to me that I needed to spend time with my wife and family. We had continued to grow and develop as individuals, and being apart for extended periods we had also become more independent, more self reliant. That is good and I would not want to have a relationship that stifled either one of us, but you reach a point where the things that hold you together are placed under stress. I had witnessed so many among my friends and acquaintances in peacekeeping whose relationships were pushed to the breaking point. Similar to military, police and other high stress occupations, the divorce rate for peacekeepers is high, and I did not intend for that to happen to us.

Having spent so many years in this lifestyle was also having other effects on me. This was made clear when I awoke in one morning in Switzerland and could not remember who I was or where I was for what seemed like several minutes. It was probably no more than a minute or two but I had to make a conscious effort to recall who I was, how I had gotten there and sort of trace my steps before it slowly came to me. This had happened before but only when I was extremely tired and it usually lasted only a few seconds. I recall once, after I had just arrived from Iraq, waking one morning and hearing my wife and Pablo speaking in the next room. I thought it was the TV and only after several minutes did I realize who it was and where I was. It is a very strange feeling when you honestly do not know, even momentarily who and where you are. At first this was sort of amusing, but as the periods grew longer it became annoying, then a bit frightening. What if at some point I was not able to get out of that in between state?

Another sign that my life was sort of spinning out of control occurred when we were casually discussing favorite restaurants. I realized that my favorite restaurant, and more to the point the one I seemed to frequent the most was in Schiphol Airport in Amsterdam. I always felt at home in the Amsterdam Cafe, which is located in the back part of the main concourse near the national flight terminal and train station; between the Mac Donald's restaurant and the old Mercure Hotel. But I always seemed to arrive in Amsterdam after an overnight flight and while it was technically time for breakfast, my body said it was just late night. I usually compromised by having breakfast and a beer. Two eggs over medium, toast and ham; or sometimes rye toast and a slice of Dutch Gouda. As for the beer, anything on tap as long as it was Belgian or Dutch. German beer is a bit heavy for breakfast, don't you think? I was not the only one doing that, and I even began to recognize some of the same people from time to time. Among them were other peacekeepers, a heavy equipment salesman from Germany, IT consultants from Ireland, football hooligans from Manchester, and no doubt others who did not want to divulge their names or where they were from. I used to imagine that we were lost time travelers, condemned to eating breakfast with a beer.

One of my best memories of the cafe was the Cockatoo that set perched in a large cage just inside the door. His name was Arri and he was everybody's favorite. Arri would shift from foot to foot, squawk and mumble in several languages as people walked by. He looked like a little old man. He was dusty green with streaks of orange and piercing eyes. Once when I asked a waiter how old he was, he replied about twelve years. Considering these birds can live to be nearly as old as humans, I always sort of pitied Arri having to spend a lifetime in this cage, even if it was large and he was well fed.

But Arri made his great escape. Several years later when I went through Schiphol again on my way to Sudan, his cage was gone. I asked the lady behind the bar where Arri was and she told me how they used to put him on a perch when they cleaned the cage, with a tether on his leg. He managed to get it untied and flew to the top of one of the umbrellas outside Mac Donald's, much to the delight of some Japanese tourists. Everyone tried to coax him down but he eventually flew up further into the rafters and once he got his wings he disappeared over the train station ticket booths. They would see him occasionally up in the rafters of the building but after about a month he disappeared. There was plenty of food around, and there were numerous places he could just slip out of the airport and be gone. Run Arri run.

*

I also got to thinking about the mission in Afghanistan. In reality it was rather discouraging and depressing. Not the country or the Afghan people, they were the good part. But of all the missions I have served in or visited, UNAMA was the most difficult to take. I think that was largely because of the attitude of indifference and disrespect on the part of so many of the staff towards each other, especially towards the administrative staff who were so often forced into a corner by requirements and procedures.

So, when I returned I made it official that I wanted to return to my HQ post in mid March, and three years and nine months, fourteen days and seventeen hours after I arrived in Afghanistan, I was once again on the flight to Dubai. As the Antonov lumbered across Iran to the UAE, I put my ear plugs in place and lost myself in thought.

I started taking mental stock of my career. In each mission assignment throughout my career, I had taken on more responsibility and had grown both professionally and personally. I was given an SPA (Special Post Allowance) which is the equivalent of a field promotion, to a higher rank. Making that into a permanent promotion in HQ seemed out of the question, but I felt I had done my best and if it was not sufficiently appreciated there did not seem to be anything I could do about it. My father had always said that in the end you have to answer to yourself, and judging myself I felt I had done a good job. In fact I would later meet some of the same people who had gossiped so viciously and caused so many problems in Afghanistan, and they would act as if we had been friends. In time I would view them in the same way, but on the flight to Dubai, the only future I could see was to return to New York, go back to a rather mundane position, and finish my career with DPKO. I knew I would always miss being in the field. As I said, it gets into your blood.

Part Four

It Comes Together – Sudan

Chapter 31: Last Tango in New York

In spite of my expectations to the contrary, my luck began to change for the better as soon as I got back to New York. I was assigned to a recruitment unit that reviewed and confirmed the qualifications and backgrounds of applicants for the various field vacancies in DPKO. Once the candidates had been cleared and put on a roster, a short list of the candidates would be sent to the field mission for vacancies they wanted to fill. It was a chance to put my background to good use, as I understood from first hand experience what the requirements and expectations were for field positions.

The Director of the unit was Claudia, a French lady with considerable field experience. She had a long career in the UN and had just finished a lengthy assignment in Africa as a Chief Civilian Personnel Officer. Being another "field rat" she understood my eccentricities picked up in various assignments and did not get upset when I would occasionally walk around the office without shoes, or jump under the desk when there was a loud noise. Besides being very competent and an excellent manager, she is one of those classic French women who just seem to have natural grace and charm.

I had to share an office, but again my luck held and I could not have asked for a better office mate than Rafael. He had retired several years earlier, but he had the energy of someone thirty years younger than he. With his natural energy and quick mind he could not stay retired long and soon finagled a temporary appointment to keep from going crazy. He was Spanish, and since I am mostly bilingual we spoke our own brand of Spanglish while working. We would switch back and forth between languages at such a dizzying rate that we were accused of creating our own language. Before he retired he had been a special assistant in the Office of the Secretary General, and of course he understood very well how the UN worked.

*

The work load for our unit was heavy and demanding but with my extensive experience in the field and Rafael's knowledge of the UN, I soon found that other staff members were bringing their problem cases around to our office, just to get another opinion. I also found that I knew many of the people in the field, or at least we were familiar with each others names.

Familiarity may breed contempt, but it can also grease the skids and I soon found I was getting e-mails and phone calls from people, some who had only recently been cursing me out, asking for unofficial advice on how to handle a particular situation. I was asked my opinion on such things as how to get an appointment with the UN, if the person should accept a particular offer or wait for a better one, but most especially on how to get DPKO to live up to it's policies on granting Special Post Allowances, which of course involved an increase in salary for the recipient since they were filling a higher level post.

This was a particularly sensitive subject and caused a lot if ill feelings among staff members. It seemed as if some people just automatically got their SPA's easily and quickly, while others would go for months or even years with nothing, even if they met all the requirements. To make it worse, in some cases the SPA was actually granted even before the person left HQ for the field, which is not part of the policy. Finally, it seemed that SPA's for the substantive staff members were more likely to be granted than were those for administrative staff members. All in all, what should have been an incentive, all too frequently became a source of frustration.

I had sat on a number of SPA review panels and had fought the system on numerous occasions, both for others cases as well as for myself. As a result I had professional and personal knowledge in these areas and I found my advice was in demand.

*

While all things considered, it was going rather well inside the office, outside the office I took additional steps to help make this a reasonably good assignment. Whereas in the past I had shared apartments or lived some distance from the office just to save a little money, this time I rented an efficiency apartment less than two blocks from the UN Secretariat. It was in a pleasant older building in Tutor City in which is known as a "pre-war" building, meaning it had been built before World War Two. It was a bit old fashioned with classic architecture, well maintained and with nice community gardens across the street. We also had a doorman who wore a uniform.

I had wanted to live in Tudor Gardens ever since I happened to walk through that area on my first visit to New York City, at the age of eighteen. It is located on a rather quant and quiet side street near Second Avenue and 42nd Street, and the area is frequently used for filming movies. The doorman once told me that Robert De Niro was running through the lobby one weekend with cameras following him, but I was in Washington so I missed it. On several occasions, instead of me going to Washington for the weekend as I usually did, my wife would come to New York and we would take in a play, go to a museum, visit friends or just relax.

This was to be my most pleasant time in New York and at UNHQ, but true to form after about a year I began to feel the pull of the field. This is something that gets into your blood. Even though I was finally close to my family, and I was working with people whom I liked and trusted, still I longed for the excitement and sense of fulfillment one only finds in a field assignment.

My wife could see this as well. Mandatory retirement was looming in the not too distant future and I wanted more than anything to finish my peacekeeping career back in the middle of the action, not setting at a desk even though it was a meaningful job. Several of my colleagues from UNAMA were now in UNMIS (United Nations Mission In Sudan) and I knew it was one of the missions that was difficult to recruit for; nobody wanted to go there. To me that was a draw, since it seems to be my lot to go where others do not want to go. Besides, I find these places are usually not quite as bad as people say, although Sudan did it's best to live up to this reputation.

After promising my wife that this would be the last field assignment, I put my application in for UNMIS. I also called Raul, who had left Afghanistan and was now a Regional Administrative Officer in Darfur, and asked him if there was a golf course in Sudan. He is an avid golfer and while we were in UNAMA he once got a hole in one in while playing a course in Islamabad, or so he claims.

There was a nice course in Afghanistan about half an hour west of Kabul, dating back to when the British were there, but during the war with the Russians the water supply had been blown up and it had turned back into a wasteland. Raul had been the one who spear-headed the efforts to get the golf course demined, refurbished and opened up again, and I had the chance to play it a couple of times with him before I left Afghanistan. It is the only course I have ever played where the problems are not sand bunkers and water hazards, rather bombed out trucks and tanks that could not be moved, and might still have mines and live ordinance hidden inside. If your ball lands in one of them you take a stroke and move on. Leave the ball where it is, do not try to retrieve it.

There was an ulterior motive for contacting Rual, I knew he would want to have an old golfing buddy back if for no other reason than to have someone who would listen to his stories. His wife was also in DPKO and was also assigned to UNMIS, but she doesn't pay any attention to either one of us, as regards golf stories. It worked. A few weeks after I dropped the bait, I got a call asking if I was available for an assignment as a Regional Administrative Officer to a place called Abyei. Sure I said, knowing my friends would not send me to anyplace that was too terrible.

After the paperwork was started, and it was too late to back out I got a call from Randy, Raul's wife who, as I said was also stationed in Khartoum. She was in New York for some meetings and wanted to get together for coffee. As we sat down with a couple of macchiatos her first question to me was, are you sure you want to go to Abyei, which sent a slight shutter through me. What had I volunteered for? Randy explained that Abyei was also referred to as the black hole of Sudan, or worse, but they were sure I could improve things, what with my experience in difficult assignments.

She then proceeded to give me a true briefing on my future assignment.

Wrong Place-Right Time

They had only recently moved people out of tents, after the tents were blown down by a huge thunder storm, leaving the staff standing on their beds holding computers and luggage up to keep them out of the water that was running through the compound, laden with snakes and other critters. There were no facilities for food but there was a good source of clean water. They had not had an administrative officer to this point and the Director of Administration (DOA), who was none other than Ripp, was hoping I would be able to make an immediate improvement. Oh yes, be sure to bring tall rubber boots (known locally as gum boots) as the rainy season was just starting and usually lasts five to six months. Gum boots were the only thing to ware, unless you went barefooted as the locals do.

So there was the truth, my good friends had sold me up the river yet again. But actually it sounded like exactly the kind of assignment I was looking for. It was far enough away from Khartoum that there would not be a constant stream of VIP visitors under your feet requiring care and attention. The situation in Abyei was so bad that almost any improvement would be appreciated and considered a success. Finally, and perhaps most important was the freedom to operate, as long as you don't violate any major administrative rules. In other words, as long as you got results you were given a wide range in which to operate. You would have to pass all the inspections and audits of course, but you can usually clean things up or justify some variation to the rules. As long as you get results first.

*

As I was packing to leave for Sudan I noticed another thing, the more time I spent in the field, the less luggage I seemed to take with me. When I left for Sudan in June of 2006, I had only one suitcase, with a sizable amount of space in that one being taken up by my size 10 gum boots, and one carry on bag. Everything else I would get in Khartoum or do without. Freedom is just another word for no luggage.

Chapter 32: An Eventful Stopover in Khartoum

I still remember the first time I flew into Khartoum. It was during my assignment with DPKO in Somalia, and it was just a stopover on a flight to meet my wife in London. We had left Nairobi, Kenya in the early afternoon and it was just getting dusk as the pilot announced we were approaching Khartoum airport where we would be making a short stop. We should remain in the plane as it was a short stop just to pick up passengers.

As the plane began it's approach I still recall the sight of the city below. The brown of the desert did not change when we reached the city, it was still brown only now it was the brown of houses and buildings, none being over three stories high. The city just seemed to raise up, out of the desert floor. Finally I caught sight of the Nile River in the distance, with the brilliant green border of trees and grass along the banks. The Blue Nile and the White Nile join up just before they reach Khartoum, and it is a massive river as it flows through the city. Historically, this was the life blood of Khartoum and the reason that a settlement of any size grew there.

The city itself, at least at that time was dusty, hot, brown and depressing, at least from the window of a plane. As we taxied to a stop some distance from the terminal and a stairway was wheeled into place, a bus load of passengers rumbled over the dusty tarmac and came to a stop. The door opened and people literally bolted off and ran to the stairway, pushing and fighting to be first in line. Only after they were on board and had found their seats did they begin to slow down. My God I thought, that must be one bad place if they are pushing children and old people aside to get on a plane out of there. And now I was about to land with the intention of staying there.

To my surprise Khartoum had indeed changed, at least somewhat, in the intervening decade since I had spent about thirty minutes on the tarmac. The petro dollars were beginning to flow in from the wells located on the border between north and south providing money and impetus to modernize the city. The underlying cultural differences and problems between the north and south are age old and still remain. However, traditional societies had evolved ways to handle them, that is until the intervention of colonial governments and more recently the addition of potential oil wealth. These influences provided the spark to set off the fires of war. This volatile mix was of course also spurred on by the intervention of outside political and terrorist elements, taking advantage of the resulting chaos to move into the area and use it as a safe haven for their activities.

As we drove from the airport into the city there was a considerable amount of construction going on, with ten and even fifteen story buildings sprouting up in many places and even improvements to the streets and sewers. This construction boom was to continue and even pick up speed during my time in Sudan. It was still hot and dusty with street vendors and beggars lining up at major intersections, hawking everything from watermelon to CD's, or displaying withered and severed limbs to get a few cents. It is always the children that both tug at the heart strings and also frighten me the most. They are going to grow up and at some point realize that they are as deserving of a decent life as anyone else, and if society is not willing to allow that to happen they may decide to just take it. Can you blame them?

*

As I got off the shuttle bus I was met at the airport arrivals door by a young man holding a sign that simply said UNMIS. I recognized him as a hansom young Somali lad that had worked for the UN as a local hire in Kuwait. Samir, as he was called had always been a good worker, and had now gotten an appointment to Sudan. He recognized me as well and we greeted each other with a hand shake and the traditional embrace with a buzz on each cheek, after which he took my papers and whisked me through passport control. Well whisked might be an exaggeration but it was certainly faster than the others, some of whom were still in line when we got my luggage and were headed for the door. By that time it was evening so all the offices were closed and I had been traveling for nearly twenty hours, so Samir took me to the hotel used by new arrivals. After a couple of hours unwinding I went to bed, content that things were off to a good enough start in Sudan. I had my luggage, I was met by a friend and the hotel was old but clean.

*

The next morning the UNMIS shuttle bus arrived at the hotel at 08:30 and I was in the compound at 09:00 hours, waiting at the Personnel Office as instructed to start the week long orientation process. After going through this exercise so many times before I felt like I knew it by heart, but it had to be done. As soon as we broke for lunch I went to the DOA's office to see if Ripp was in. He was, and was in a good mood.

We spent the entire lunch hour going over old times and he brought me up to date on which former Afghan staff members were now in Sudan. He told me how when he left Afghanistan he had been assigned to a mission in East Africa that was closing down. There are two periods in the life of a peacekeeping mission that demand the most work and the best administration; the start up phase and the closing out phase. Ripp had experience in both and had earned a reputation for being able to handle them. After finishing the close out, he opted to come to UNMIS as it was still in the start up phase. He also shared with me his plans to build a new compound (of course), again closer to the airport, and which would be large enough to house many of the military contingent offices as well as all of the other sections in Khartoum. I ended up checking out of the hotel and staying in a spare room in Ripp's apartment for the rest of my orientation period.

*

Near the end of my first week I got a call from the Political Affairs office, asking if I could be there at 15:00 hours (3:00 PM) to meet with the Head of Office for Abyei. As the RAO (Regional Administrative Officer) I would be responsible for all matters administrative in the region, and while the

RAO reports to the DOA, he also has a dotted line reporting responsibility to the Head of Office, who is chief over the entire region. They have to work closely together in order to succeed.

The HoO happened to be in Khartoum but was returning to Abyei the next morning and wanted to meet me before he left. So at the appointed time I went up to his office, which was in the same building as the orientation session was being held. Recalling the strained relations between the substantive and administration sections in Afghanistan, I was uncertain how this would go as I was not in the mood to accept arrogance from some self important person. As it turns out, I was pleasantly surprised as the situation in that regard was much better in UNMIS.

When I walked in I was greeted by Thomas, a stocky man from Gambia with a serious face that easily broke into a wide smile and a warm contagious laugh. I could see he had been reviewing a copy of my resume and background which was still on his desk. We spoke briefly and I sensed that we would be a good team. He was educated in England and the US and showed a good grasp of the political situation of the north-south situation in Sudan. He was forthcoming and seemed genuinely interested in working together as a team. We even had a similar sense of humor. Then, just as I was beginning to relax a bit he dropped the bomb.

He informed me that had handed in his resignation and was due to leave as soon as possible, for family reasons. He was headed back to Abyei the next day and would wait for me there. His replacement had not been chosen, in fact the process was not even close to completion. He had been looking over my background and had recommended to the SRSG (Special Representative of the Secretary General) who is the head of the mission, that I be appointed as his temporary replacement. The final decision of course was up to the SRSG, who was a well known Dutch politician and diplomat, Jon Plont. Plont was well known for freely speaking his mind and for his direct approach (very Dutch in that regard). However, he was also very diplomatic and usually phrased things in a smooth enough manner, but his meaning was clear. I did not have time to get nervous about meeting him as we were already on our way to his office, which was just down the hall.

*

Thomas introduced me to Plont and again I could feel the atmosphere was so different from Afghanistan it was like night and day. Plont extended his hand and motioned for Thomas and I to join him around the small table in his office. Thomas said a few words about my background and experience, how I had been a member of a negotiation team in Somalia, about my experience in Iraq and Afghanistan and then excusing himself, he left the room.

Without loosing a beat Plont explained the situation on the north south border and how Abyei was at the center of it; how the oil fields which were the source of contention as well as wealth were located near the town; and how the north, represented by the Sudanese Army and the south represented by the Sudanese Peoples Liberation Army were both stationed in this area, making it especially volatile. Darfur was just to the west and in fact it bordered on the region, and while Darfur was getting most of the attention it was the border region that had seen the worst of the fighting in the past. The political situation and the implementation of the peace accords were of primary importance of course, but in order to do that the conditions and morale in Abyei must be improved, and quickly. He finished by confirming that he was considering appointing me as the Head of Office (HoO) for this region. I would need to fill both positions as HoO and Regional Administrative Officer until further notice, a tall order. Did I think I could do that?

I immediately flashed back to my first day in Somalia, how Happy was upset with my arrival and had suggested that I be assigned to one of the regions as a Civil Affairs Officer. I had let that opportunity slip away. I was not about to let that happen again, so trying not to sound too eager or over confident I said it was indeed a big job but I was confident I could do it, and would welcome the opportunity. Or some such appropriate statement.

But I think what sealed it was what Plont said next. He again said how important it was to improve the conditions and build the team in that region, and he wasn't sure if I was just telling him what he wanted to hear. Without considering it I replied, well I don't know you and I don't know what you think, so I cannot tell you what you want to hear. I can only tell you what I think. He looked me straight in the eye and for a moment

I thought I had been too blunt, but gradually the slightest smile came to his lips. He said OK, you will get a letter confirming this temporary appointment, but first arrange with Thomas to meet up with him in Abyei.

*

There are rare moments in life when you realize that something important has just happened. I had been given the opportunity to finish my career with DPKO back in the field, as I wanted badly to do. I had been given the opportunity to do so as the RAO for a large and important region and now, quite unexpectedly I had been appointed, albeit on a temporary basis to be the Head of Office, a very important position that had a direct impact on the success of the mission. I was pleased, I felt honored and most importantly I had reached a position I never thought possible when I had started my career so many years ago. There is truth to the statement that a good part of success is outlasting your adversaries. Or, perhaps it is more like one of my father's favorite sayings would have it, even ugly buildings and rich whores get respectable with age.

As soon as I completed my orientation, and after getting my appointment letter and my final marching orders from the offices of the SRSG and the DOA, I left to take up my new duties.

Chapter 33: Arrival in Abyei

The next morning, the Russian made helicopter pounded its way along at 7,000 feet over the dry veldt of central Sudan, from the town of Malikal on its way to the final destination of Abyei. It was late June and somewhere between the end of dry season and the beginning of rainy season. Rivers and swamps had already begun to form anew but the landscape had not yet become a sea of red sticky mud that would suck the boots off your feet as you walked.

The Pakistani chap seated on the bench seat next to me motioned that we were about ten minutes from landing. He had to motion since we all wore big ear mufflers to protect us from the extreme noise but still all I could hear was the whooping of the blades. We had left Khartoum at about 7:00 AM that morning and after a plane flight to Malikal, which is about half way to the southern capital of Juba, we transferred to the helicopter and continued west another hour to Abyei, one of the most isolated UN compound sites in Sudan.

A small town located precisely on the border between the Arab Islamic dominated north, and the tribal Christian south, Abyei is the exact spot where the most recent out break of the ongoing civil war had started over a decade earlier, yet it is not even found on most maps of Sudan. Fighting had quickly spread west to Darfur, which is only a short distance away. With the signing of the Comprehensive Peace Accords (CPA) in 2005, this also became one of the areas in which the two sides having fought to a stand still, now stood literally face to face; the Sudanese Armed Forces (SAF) and the Sudan Peoples Liberation Army (SPLA). The stakes for peace could not be higher, and I had just been appointed as the Head of Office (HoO), the senior UN officer for an area half the size of New Jersey that lay at the geographic and cultural epicenter of this perfect storm. Our job was to oversee and direct efforts to get the SAF and the SPLA to work together implementing the CPA. A real alphabet soup of acronyms, but one with serious consequences.

*

As the Antanov circled for its landing I peered out the window at the clusters of mud and thatch huts below. I guessed there were several hundred huts in small compounds, clustered around three or four block buildings and a central market area. There was one main dirt road from the north that ran past the town, then continued south east through towns with names like Wau and Rumbek, eventually to Juba the capital of the break away south. On the other side of the town the dominate feature was a large swamp where cows and donkeys had gathered to get relief from the late afternoon heat.

We did a fly over of the UN compound and it did not look much better than the village. The entire camp had a shabby military outpost appearance as it was composed of canvas tents and prefabricated, corrugated metal sheds set in rows. A red neck town in the middle of Sudan. The offices were set on the highest ground and the sleeping quarters were raised to keep them out of the water when the rains came in earnest. Compacted dirt walkways, raised for the rainy season connected most of the buildings. At the other end of the compound were similar arrangements for the troops all laid out around the kitchen and mess hall which was in the middle. The entire compound, about twenty five acres in size was surrounded by barbed wire. As we began to settle onto the UN helipad, several large Commodore buzzards (so named because they look like they are wearing black and white uniforms) lifted off from the nearby garbage dump where they had been picking around for a free lunch.

This would be my home for the next year and one half. More than that I was the Officer in charge of approximately two hundred civilian staff as well as a Tanzanian Army Troop Contingent, a smaller Indian Army Communications Contingent and other scattered troops, numbering in excess of five hundred soldiers. They reported to a Tanzanian General who in turn was a member of my senior staff.

We were met at the helipad by the current Head of office with a welcoming committee and after I settled into my quarters, I was given a walking tour by the departing Head of Office, followed by a meeting of all the Chiefs of Section and the commanding officer of the military contingent, General Abasi. By this time it was getting quite late and aside from a small cake and a cup of tea I managed to eat during our layover in Malikal, I had not eaten since early morning. I was very hungry, so at the conclusion of the meeting when General Abasi invited us to eat in the army mess everyone eagerly accepted the invitation and the meeting immediately broke up.

*

The menu was simple sub-Saharan style food which I had eaten numerous times in Somalia and Kenya, and the meal started off with the ever present ungali. Ungali can best be described as very thick white corn meal mush porridge or cake, that is squished with your fingers into small balls which are used to scoop up the stew, meat, beans or whatever else is served. Ungali is usually made from corn but in West Africa it is made of cassava, a root similar to potato but sticky. The meat was beef and chicken stewed with a tomato and pepper sauce which was spread over everything. It was good. Following the meal, I gave a short talk to thank the General and his staff for their hospitality and after some polite conversation we retired to our quarters. As we were leaving, the General told me that as Head of Office I had mess privileges. I thanked him and left.

The next morning at breakfast I noticed that only one or two civilians were present in the mess, so wondering how the others were eating, after breakfast I immediately called the Camp Manager, a Filipino named Bing and asked him to show me the civilian mess arrangement. To my surprise there was none. So how do people eat I asked. Bing took me on a real tour of the compound starting with the two kitchen tents where the civilian staff were supposed to cook their own meals. There were no real mess facilities so people just ate in the kitchen tents, in the open, or in their rooms.

Each kitchen tent had a really filthy electric stove hooked to the generator grid, with only one or two burners that worked. There was a freezer in each tent where staff could store food. I opened one and was met by nearly a foot of half frozen sludge water with green mold growing on it. The food preparation tables were also filthy. All in all the kitchen tents were one of the most disgusting sights I have seen. In fact very few people used the kitchen tents and most people just ate cans of tuna or what ever they could get locally, or bring back from trips to Khartoum.

Bing said there was flat Arabic or pita style bread (nan) that was baked daily in the town which was not too bad, and our local staff brought it fresh every morning. While the bread tasted OK when it was fresh, it had its problems. I did break a tooth on a small stone or twig while eating some of it for breakfast one day. It left a ragged edge that kept cutting my tongue, so I finally took a nail file and smoothed the sharp edges off. This worked fine until I finally got around to getting it replaced nearly a year later. My dentist back home still shutters whenever I make an appointment, never knowing what I will bring her.

Food wise, the military contingents faired much better than the civilian staff. All military troop contingents assigned to the UN are required to first negotiate a contract before they are deployed, which among other things covers provision of food, water and shelter. As a result shipments of food including fresh meat, vegetables, eggs, even butter and ice cream were flown in by helicopter about twice a month for the troops, but not one can of Spam was provided for the civilians. Civilian staff are responsible to take care of themselves and for this purpose are given a mission subsistence allowance (MSA). In theory cafeterias and canteens are supposed to be provided for them, but this depends entirely on the procurement process which is notoriously slow and inefficient. When I departed Sudan one and a half years later, no food of any kind was being provided in this compound. We were very much on our own.

Bing and I went straight to see the Engineer, an Australian named Black, so naturally everyone called him Blackie. Bing and Blackie, along with another Filipino named Bong who could take scrape material and build anything, were to become my "go to" guys in the camp. The three B's; Bing, Bong and Blackie.

I asked Blackie if we had any spare Corimax buildings (the prefab sheds which were made by an Italian company named Corimax). In typical Blackie fashion he quickly "found" a couple, and as he said "knocked them together" in record time to be used as field kitchens. Where as the tents were located quite far from a source of water, we located the new field kitchens close to fresh water and a large utility sink. Only one of the stoves could be salvaged, but we found another one sitting unnoticed in the Generals area. His Cook howled when we took it, but the General stepped in, and being a practical man authorized its reallocation. Next I donated a refrigerator from my office and with some encouragement, persuaded the Chief of Security to donate an extra one which he had "commandeered" for his office. Within a week we had moved from the fly and vermin ridden tents to clean hard walled kitchens with screen doors and windows. They also had hard floors and were raised off the mud. The mood in camp was getting better.

*

Next on the list was to secure a reasonable supply of food, and here our biggest problem was logistics. In theory we were connected by road to a regional warehouse facility and we could order canned and dried foodstuff to be sent on the convoys. However, during all the time I was in central Sudan, we received only two or three convoys. I never understood this since a Chinese petroleum company worked in the same general area and they managed to get supply convoys through except during the very worst of the rainy season. Complain as I might, there was always some reason our convoys could not get through.

The other option, and indeed the only reliable one was for each person to purchase his or her own supplies when they went to Khartoum, and bring them back on the helicopter. The main problem was that we were limited to 15 kilos (33 pounds) luggage on the helicopter, half of which was taken up by your clothes, personal items, and a rather heavy two way radio which we were required to have at all times. Again, in theory, we could ship our excess as unaccompanied baggage which was supposed to be delivered within a couple of days to a week, provided there was space on the bird.

However, it was our experience that unless you actually carried luggage and kept it in your sight at all times, it would most likely get lost. While this was less so in a few of the airports such as Kadugli and Juba which were run by international professional staff, it was especially bad if the flight went through the Malikal airport, which was truly the black hole of Sudan. The local airport staff in Malikal seemed to be untrained and completely unsupervised, and did as they pleased. I once watched a driver run a tractor over a suitcase. It was probably unintentional, but he did not even stop. It was routine for every flight through that hub to have missing bags. It was so bad that the common knowledge among staff members was that when going through Malikal airport, you could only take carry on luggage as everything else would be destroyed, opened or just lost unless it was under your personal supervision.

Proof of this was provided by the experience of two Dutch Police Officers assigned on TDY to Abyei, whose excess luggage just disappeared. When I arrived, they had been living for nearly three weeks on 15 kilos of luggage each, and were reduced to borrowing under ware from their colleagues. I was quite embarrassed for the organization and immediately got on the phone. I called the section in Khartoum responsible for assignment of these Officers and used some rather unpleasant language with them. They in turn put enough pressure on someone in Air Operations and as if by magic the lost luggage was found somewhere in Darfar and arrived in our camp a few days later. Between the new field kitchens and the miracle of the lost luggage, I was getting quite popular.

While we were not able to solve the food supply situation we did manage to greatly improve it by providing clean kitchens. On a positive note, as a result of the canned tuna fish, flat bread and tea diet, I lost 23 pounds in three months, and weighed about as much as I did when I was in university.

Chapter 34: The Lord Helps Those Who Help Themselves

Food was not the only thing we lacked in the way of supplies. During my first week in the office as HoO, I received a visit from Bing who as the General Services Officer /Camp Manager was responsible for dispensing such essentials as toilet paper, soap and cleaning supplies for the compound. Seems we were down to about one carton of TP which considering we had several hundred cheeks to turn, (I'll leave other jokes to you) would not last very long. He explained how TP, or rather the constant lack of it was one of his biggest headaches. He was constantly bridging the gap.

In addition, I had some real concerns about the general state of the toilets, or ablution units as they are correctly called. They were in need of some repair and a good cleaning and I was rather upset until Bing told me we had not had a shipment of basic cleaning supplies for over three months. What about the local market I asked? Even though it was limited I figured there should be something available and we could use the petty cash fund to purchase them.

About that time Blackie (our Aussie Engineering Officer) came into my office and after listening to our conversation for a bit he began to laugh. As he explained in his straight forward Aussie manner (God bless' em) survival is a full time occupation for these blokes. There isn't much demand in town for cleaning powers and the like and anyway, we had pretty much bought out the local market supply. We also needed brooms and brushes since the cleaning staff were reduced to using rags and bundles of grass to scrub out the unmentionables. Blackie had a colorful way of speaking but you usually understood him the first time.

Blackie then explained how when he first arrived, only a few months back, everyone was still living in tents and there was only one portable ablution unit for the entire compound. A typical ablution unit is a prefab trailer unit with three crapper stalls, three shower stalls, a urinal, and a long communal sink. In the ladies units they come up with some cleaver uses for the urinal. Tucked away in one corner is a water heater and a small area for storage of cleaning materials. All you do is put it together, hook it up to a source of water and electricity and it is ready to go. Not fancy but it does keep you out of the sun and rain and provides a minimum of privacy.

However, one unit for nearly 500 people which was the staff count at that time ... well you can imagine the results. The unit was in constant use, most serious business was conducted outside behind the unit, and they were averaging about one or two showers a week. Now with three units for the civilian staff alone and more for the military, everyone thought things had improved considerably. None the less I thought they were pretty bad and intended to improve things. But first we needed cleaning supplies.

To better assess the situation Bing, Blackie and I went on a short road trip to the Abyei market place, such as it was, to see what was available. This was a real eye opener. The market was located in the center of the town. It comprised an area about one block square, but only the main road running through the center was raised a bit, and had at one time been graveled. Once you stepped off this high ground, you had to hop and skip between stones and logs to keep out of the festering mud holes. Vendors sat in front of small tin or thatch huts, or in front of a plastic sheet spread out on the ground with whatever they had to sell. Like good businessmen anywhere they called out to you, held things up and tried to beat out the competition as we passed. I was looking for two things; cleaning supplies and food. It quickly became clear that aside from a few packets of laundry soap, there were few cleaning materials to be had. No scouring power, no bleach, brooms or brushes. As for food I stopped at several shops to examine the cans of tuna fish and sardines only to find they were not only expensive, but the expiration dates were usually expired by as much as one or sometimes two years. There were also cans of pineapple and some peaches, again well past their dates.

There were a few merchants selling a very limited number of fruits and vegetables. They were all dried up, scruffy looking and had obviously been brought in from other areas. I was quite surprised at the lack of locally raised produce, and would later observe that the locals did not even grow much for themselves. While it would be difficult to grow much during the dry season, during the rainy season, almost anything could be grown and in the not too distant past, this region was known as the breadbasket of Sudan. Not far from Abyei are the remains of large fields where peanuts (ground nuts), vegetables and grains were grown when the British were in Sudan, a period which ended only in the early 1950's. I guess the years of war and constant disruption made it impossible to maintain even a household garden.

One encouraging sign was when an old lady several stalls away started shouting "Mr. Blackie, Mr. Blackie, we have beer". Blackie's eyes lit up and he flashed the old dear a huge grin. Skipping around the ankle deep mud and muck we ran to her stall where she showed us several lovely cases of beer from Uganda, which she kept under lock and key. Well actually they were a bit mud spattered and dusty but to us they were lovely. She explained that a friend of hers was now in Uganda and could get her more beer. A marvelous find, I began to see how life here could be bearable. We gave her some Sudanese pounds, took several cases with us, and told her we would be back for more tomorrow. For that evening at least, we would have something besides tea to wash down the flat bread and tuna fish.

*

Back in camp, drinking a warm beer I began to realize that we would have to rely on ourselves to solve the chronic problem of supplies. Besides, the DOA had said to just get things done, and since I had worked with him in Afghanistan I knew he would back me as long as I did not go too far out. Then I recalled seeing a list of new staff arrivals which was sent every week to the HoO's, and recognized one of the poor sots as a Senior Supply Officer I had known in another mission, Jorge by name. I typed his name into the e-mail address list and his details came up on the screen. Not only was Jorge now in Sudan, he was a Senior Supply Officer assigned to the warehouse in our region. Brilliant. Taking another drink of warm lager I tried to recall if I had done anything I needed to apologize to Jorge about before I asked for his assistance.

Just to be on the safe side, I e-mailed him instead of calling direct. To my surprise he responded almost as soon as I sent it off. He had been in mission for two weeks and was glad to hear from a colleague. With that I picked up the phone and after several tries got through to Jorge's office. Now, being in Peacekeeping is very similar to being in the military. There is an instant bond formed between people you serve with and even if you argued and fought with them, if you see them again in another setting or just on the street, it is as if you were long lost pals. Jorge and I asked about families, his girl friends, old colleagues and for good measure we cussed out the incompetent fools in charge of DPKO and the UN in general. Finally he asked me where I was stationed and when I said Abyei, he said "Hombre, you are in the shit, no?" He grasped my situation.

Then I explained how things could be greatly improved if we could just get cleaning supplies, TP and some canned food, in fact about the only thing we seemed to have was beer. I heard him gasp and he said "You have beer?" The negotiator in me kicked in. Well ....yes .... we might have beer, what do you have? Jorge had TP but no way to get it to us since it was balky and there were no truck convoys to our area because of the bad roads and mud. He did not have many cleaning supplies in the warehouse, but the local town was much larger than our hamlet and they had many stores where one could get cleaning supplies as well as good tuna fish, corned beef and even pasta sauce.

The deal we worked out was that every few weeks some of my staff would take the helicopter to the regional warehouse with a couple of large duffle bags filled with cartons of our commodity. They would be provided a jeep and a driver to do shopping in the local town for cleaning supplies and food. The duffel bags would go to Jorge who would exchange it for several cartons of TP. My guys would stay overnight and have a good meal. The next morning they would get back on the helicopter with the TP, the boxes of cleaning supplies and canned food, and arrive at our remote site in the early afternoon.

With a secure source of cleaning supplies we then doubled up on the crews in the ablution units and started cleaning them three times a day. Before long we had the reputation for having the cleanest ablution units outside of Khartoum. In fact, several months later when a Special Envoy of the White House and the US Ambassador visited Sudan and spent several hours in Abyei, they complimented us on our ablution units, but not our food. Still, it was high praise indeed.

*

As a footnote to this chapter, over two and one half years later I made a return visit to Abyei on official business and considerable progress had been made. The compound was now filled with more permanent housing and numerous office buildings, there was a cafeteria and small lunch bar serving decent meals and a small but well stocked post exchange (PX) that even had a selection of canned and frozen foods. We even managed to get cold beer and a friendly conversation from the officers club. On the minus side warfare had broken out between the Sudanese military (SAF) and rebels (SPLA) several months after I had left and much of the town had been devastated. It had been largely rebuilt with a new market just outside the village. As for the UN compound, it just did not feel the same. It was larger and colder. Whereas I knew nearly every person in the old compound, that would be impossible now as it had grown so much. People were not unfriendly, in fact many remembered me and waved or came over and we shook hands but it had a different feel. It was no longer the tight knit group struggling to survive on the edge of the universe and it just had a different, more distant feel. To add to it, a new Head of Office had just been appointed and he seemed to personify that change. Since I was a visiting senior officer, as is the custom I went to his office to introduce myself and explain why I was there. He did not want to see me and after a quick shake of hands strongly suggested that I come back the next day as he was busy. I did not bother to return.

Chapter 35: Duties of the Head of Office

Tending to administrative matters such as the desperate food situation, clean ablution units and supplies was important, but equally critical were my duties as the Head of Office. These duties were many and varied and were frequently diplomatic in nature.

First was to guide and direct the efforts of the substantive units in our region which included Civil Affairs, Political Affairs, Humanitarian Affairs, Human Rights, and the Disarmament and Reintegration of former rebel fighters. All of these involve matters that are sensitive and must be approached carefully, especially in an area that was so recently locked in civil war and in which the former combatants were still armed and housed in camps close to each other. In each of the substantive units there were international and local staff members responsible for carrying out activities throughout the region.

The major programs in this area included working with community, tribal and business leaders to support efforts to reconstruct, rebuild and stabilize the area. Our staff also worked with other UN agencies and NGO's to assist the former refugees as they moved back into the region. Most of the population had left or been forced out to live in other temporary locations such as Khartoum and refugee settlement camps where they had sought refuge from the war. Some had been displaced as far as Uganda and the Congo, to the south.

One of the more sensitive activities involved monitoring human rights which included the harassment of females, children, refugees and other vulnerable groups. I recall one case in particular where a pregnant female was being held in a local jail, based on a complaint from her husband. The husband did not think the child was his and had accused his wife of adultery. During the day, she was fastened to a tree by a length of chain since there was no secure yard for her to use. While a bad situation, she could walk around and at least she was not being held with the general population which did include some bad characters. Our staff immediately got her released to her family while a more permanent solution was worked out, which included the husband eventually dropping the charges and them moving back in together.

But for me, perhaps the most interesting project was monitoring the annual cattle migration that went from pastures in the north, which were green during the rainy season, to pastures in the south which were still good during the dry season. As the rainy season started again, they would repeat the migration and go to the north. This involved complications on several levels. The owners of the cattle were Misseriya and they had to take large herds of cattle through sedentary farming areas settled by Dinka. They spoke different languages, although they could easily communicate with each other. The Misseriya were herdsmen from the north and were Muslim, the Dinka were farmers from the south and were tribal Christian.

In the past the Dinka had resorted to burning the grass around their villages and fields to deprive the herds of food, and when this did not work some of them even fired guns at the cattle causing stampedes and of course killing some of them. This forced the herds to travel much longer distances over frequently dangerous routes. Further complicating this process was the fact that during the recent war, many people had been forced out of the area with the result that with far fewer people living in the path, the migration was easier. The herders had naturally gotten used to this situation. As the Dinka moved back onto their farms, the situation grew more tense every year.

Our Civil Affairs Officers had used a combination of traditional and modern thinking to arrive at a creative and effective solution. We invited leaders from both the Misseriya and Dinka communities to form a committee to plan and monitor the annual cattle migrations. First they identified the routes that would be acceptable to both sides; those that would be the most direct while minimizing the damage the herds could do to the small farms along the way. Committee leaders from each side agreed to work with their respective communities to ensure they were aware of approximately when and along which routes the migration would take place. Finally, as the migrations began in earnest, we made a UN helicopter available to allow members of the committee to leap frog to communities in advance of the herds, to alert and prepare them. In this way they could turn out members of the local community to guide the herds along, with minimal damage to crops and farms.

As a result of this ingenious program the number of problems and near riots were drastically reduced. The members of the committee enjoyed riding in the helicopter and being defacto members of the UN at least for a few days (we gave them temporary identification and UN hats), and their status in their local communities was greatly boosted. In addition, the members of the migration committees gained excellent experience working together, they acquired a level of trust with the other members of the committee and all of this formed a good platform to build on for other joint projects. Finally, we made sure these migrations were well covered by the UN and Sudanese press, which was not difficult as the cattle are the long horn variety and are very photogenic. The only downside was that I never got to go along on the helicopter cattle drives. One time I was at a meeting of HoO's in Khartoum, and another time I was too sick with malaria.

A final word about my two international staff Civil Affairs Officers. One was from East Africa, and while he was senior in rank he was new to the UN. The other was from West Africa and had considerable experience with DPKO. Together they were a brilliant team who came up with creative solutions such as the helicopter cattle drives. Unfortunately they went through periods when they sniped at each other and could not work together. The senior officer felt the junior officer was disrespecting him, and the junior officer felt the senior officer did not listen to him. Both of which were probably true. I would have a frank discussion with them and all would be fine for a few days or even weeks, only to gradually slip back into the old routine. Finally I was forced to make a decision. I recommended that the senior, albeit newer member be reassigned to a larger unit in another region where he could work under a more senior officer and gain the DPKO experience he needed. My replacement as HoO also saw the need for this and pushed it through after I left. It was a difficult decision as they both had strengths. I have since learned that the more experienced but junior in rank has remained with DPKO while the other has taken a position with another NGO and is still in Africa.

*

The second major area of our responsibility fell under the military, therefore under General Abasi. This involved efforts to get the SAF and the SPLA, the former combatants, to work together on projects and programs with the eventual goal of integrating the two groups into Area Joint Military Committees (AJMC's) as they were known. Most of their projects involved disarming local military groups, community outreach, educational programs and quick impact projects which are designed to gave immediate results. Sports, school and similar programs were an especially popular method of reaching the youth, as there was not much for them to do and trouble was always just around the corner. The Zambian military contingent had a special unit that consisted of a drum and dance troop, which also put on skits and dramas to entertain and educate the local population on a variety of subjects such as AIDS prevention, school attendance and the importance of basic hygiene. This group was talented and very popular, being asked to perform at almost all local events. Being young themselves, and from a neighboring African country, they were able to make immediate contact with the local population, especially the youth. One of the strengths of the UN is the extreme diversity of staff that one has to draw on.

Another AJMC project that was very successful were joint patrols of the market place to curtail the number of weapons being brought in. This was one instance when the joint nature of the patrols was especially important. It seems that members of both the SPLA and the SAF were bringing their weapons with them when they went to town and having members of their own military explaining the need for the ban and turning them back, made it much easier than if only the UN or soldiers from the other side were trying to enforce this rule.

In order to build the necessary cohesion and cooperation, senior representatives of the two sides, SAF and SPLA met on a regular basis under the guidance of UNMIS and the General's staff. They addressed issues and concerns regarding their coexistence in the region, such as the unauthorized movement of troops by either side which was viewed as encroachment, or building up unauthorized troop strength near the oil fields or in sensitive border areas.

Officially, both the SAF and the SPLA disavowed any interest in going back to war and maintained that the future of the area would be settled by plebiscite elections in 2011. This vote is to determine if the south will opt for self rule and form their own government (known as GOSS or Government of South Sudan) or if they will choose to participate in the formation of a unity government between the north and the south. However, it seemed to me rather certain that nether side will just back away from this oil rich area, regardless of any elections. Still, there is always hope and we had to strive for that outcome. Officially we were working toward a peaceful integration of the two forces which would be completed after the elections.

A measure of the guarded stance taken by both sides was the fact that when I arrived in Abyei, the movement of anything considered as UNMIS was rather severely restricted, especially to the north. The SAF, representing the government in Khartoum had placed a restriction on movement of UNMIS staff and equipment beyond a few kilometers north of the UN compound. The reason they gave was simply that it was an order from their commanders and whenever we tried to inquire further it just resulted in a run around. This of course was resented by the Sudan Peoples Liberation Movement (the political wing of the movement) and the SPLA (The military wing) since it allowed the north to move troops around and conduct business unhindered and unobserved by the UN. Several months after I arrived there was an incident that led to the SPLA placing the same restriction on movement of UNMIS staff so we were not able to go the south of the town, effectively boxing us in. Thanks to some diplomatic maneuvering and subtle application of pressure, we were able to obtain some easing of these restrictions, which I will cover in a later chapter.

*

A third area of duties for the HoO was to coordinate support for the other UN agencies operating in the region, such as United Nations Development Program (UNDP), World Health Program (WHP), and World Food Program (WFP). Since UNMIS had the largest presence in the area, and since it was a DPKO mission the HoO was also the Senior UN official in the region. In this regard, we were frequently asked to assist with support such as use of equipment (fork trucks, earth graders, trucks, helicopters to transport people and supplies), as well as use of facilities for meetings and so on.

Whenever possible I also extended such assistance to NGO's operating in the area as well, such as Doctors without Borders (Medicins Sans Frontieres) and MercyCorps. The HoO has considerable leeway in granting such assistance and some of my counterparts were rather stingy in that regard. I felt it was best to cooperate as much as possible since we were usually working for the same ends and it is much better to have them as friends. I also made a point of inviting representatives of the major NGO's and all of the other UN agencies to regular security briefings and to our weekly staff meetings, if we were discussing things that concerned them.

A final area that took up a surprising amount of time was the ceremonial side, of which I will give more details in the next chapter. The HoO was expected to say a few words at all UN functions and nearly every major event, at the start and end of the school year, to open new buildings, to kick off the new youth soccer league, to facilitate at regional development conferences and so on. This took on a special importance in our region since no Governor, and for that matter no high level state officials had been appointed by the government in Khartoum. Aside from tribal leaders and government security officials, there was pretty much a void of officialdom and the UN often had to fill in in that regard.

Chapter 36: The Show Must Go On

One of my first ceremonial duties remains clear in my mind as it incorporated so many levels of activity and influences, from the international to the regional to the purely tribal. As if that is not enough, I had not been feeling well for a few days before the event, which was the dedication of a refurbished school in the town of Abyei. This was an important event as it represented the first large and successful project by the combined SAF and SPLA group, in conjunction with UNMIS, so I could not miss it no matter how bad I felt.

The school building consisted of four classrooms, two on either side of an administrative office and a community room. Before the war this had been the main school for the entire region but it had been occupied by the SAF as soon as the fighting started. They had used it to house troops and in the process it had not been very well maintained, I think it would be correct to say it had been properly trashed. The toilets, located in a small building separate from the main building had been broken after they were no longer serviceable. The water taps had likewise been broken and the well itself no longer worked. Doors and even the frames had been removed.

After the signing of the Comprehensive Peace Accords (CPA) in 2005, the military moved out of the building and it sat vacant for some time. Finally UNMIS took steps to make its refurbishment a project for the joint military committee and with the help of UNMIS equipment and technicians, as well as the work and efforts of the local population, it was set to be rededicated about four months after I arrived.

On the day of the big event I woke up feeling worse than ever with bouts of fever and nausea, but I was not coughing or sneezing, nor was I running to the toilet so I had some breakfast and got ready to brave it. Breakfast consisted of tea and some flat bread, but even that seemed too heavy and after a couple of mouthfuls I just sipped the tea. I did not have to say much, just a few words on the importance of this, the first major project for the joint military committee, then hand it over to General Abasi. I mostly had to be there to show the flag.

The General came to my office about 09:15 and we left for the short trip to the town, arriving after 09:30. A tent had been set up in front of the school building with chairs for the guests. In the center of the first row were several ornate overstuffed chairs, which looked like they had been borrowed from my grandmother's house, with a small end table beside each. These were reserved for myself, the General and a representative each of the Dinka and the Misseriya communities. I was thankful there was a tent so we did not have to sit in either the broiling hot sun or in a tropical rain.

*

Before we could take our seats, we were given a tour of the refurbished building and facilities. I had only seen photos of it before they started their efforts, but I was quite impressed. All of the trash had been removed, the walls were patched and painted white, doors and windows had been replaced and it all smelled new. Even more impressive were the toilets, which now were nearly immaculate and each stall had a door that closed. A new water well had been dug and the sinks, which had been shot up, were also replaced. Finally, the crowning glory was the generator. Somehow, the old generator dating back to the 50's or 60's had been fixed up, cleaned up and coxed into running so there were actually lights, at least in the administrative office. All in all it was impressive and given what they had to work with they had every right to be proud.

By this time I was sweating and feeling rather weak as we finally moved into the tent and took our appointed seats for the ceremony to begin. The Head Master of the Abyei schools welcomed us, giving mention to myself and the General, and then gave the history of the building being careful not to be too critical of the military, as they were present.

He then introduced a local dance group who came out from behind the school building in single file, dancing and drumming as they came. They were dressed in traditional clothing and it is always fascinating to watch them dance. The men were very tall and some carried spears and had grass skirts which only made them look taller. The women were shorter and wore matching t-shirts that looked like they had been tie dyed. Their movements were sometimes graceful sometimes jerky and exaggerated but always powerful. Over the years I have seen quite a few traditional African dance groups and the dances vary somewhat depending on the region the dancers are from. They also vary depending on the occasion and sometimes it is quite explicit sexually, not deviant just based on normal behavior so if you are offended I guess it is due to your own cultural limitations. These dances always get howls of laughter from the crowd.

The men are usually the stars and love to show off. One way they get the crowds approval is to bend their leg at the knee and lift it up as high as they can, in time to the drumming. Since their legs are so long they sometimes actually go higher than the dancers head and it reminds me of a huge praying mantas flexing its legs when they do this move. A more universal move is for a man to keep his legs as straight as possible and bending only at the knees to leap straight up, as high as he can. The taller they are the higher they can leap and I have seen dancers whose heads go well over ten feet straight up. This is a challenge to the others and it goes round the group until someone bests all the others.

Dance groups in Africa are much like Samba groups in Brazil. Every community has at least one and they perform at all local events and ceremonies, even the religious holidays. It is a traditional part of each community.

*

After the dance group finished, the Head Master asked me to say a few words. I gave my usual talk about the importance of the community working together with the UN to implement the Comprehensive Peace Accords, how the school was an example of what people can do when they work together peacefully. I thanked the SAF and the SPLA for assisting in this noble project (although it was their fault we had to do it in the first place) and finished by mentioning that I had started my career as a teacher years before and recognized the importance of educating ones self. Then as I was about to faint from fever, which by now was being reinforced by mild chills, I finished and sat down. The General followed me and gave due praise to the two military groups and how they had worked together to accomplish such a fine outcome.

The only thing left to do now was to cut a ceremonial ribbon that had been stretched in front of one of the classrooms, drink a cup of tea and I could collapse in my Nissan Patrol and be driven back to the compound. Or so I thought, for just then a group of men lead a small cow from behind the building into the area directly in front of the tent. Before I could ask the General if this was what I thought it might be, they had tied the legs of the cow together and threw it down on its side. Several men held the beast down and another one raised a spear above it's neck. The blade was long and thin, knife like. With a sudden thrust he jabbed it into the cows neck and after sawing it back and forth a couple of times the blood began to flow, slowly at first, but more rapid as he continued to cut. I expected to hear the cow bellowing but another man was holding its mouth closed so all it could do was grunt as its life flowed into the sand.

I came from a family where hunting was common, in addition to sport it was done for the meat and I have seen my share of death. I also know that for every peace of meat we eat something has to die, but I have never been comfortable with this reality. Still, I have a certain respect for traditional societies who do not have the convenience of a commercial slaughter house, and who do this to survive. In a way there is more of a relationship of respect between man and nature in such societies than there is in ours, in spite of how primitive and cruel it may appear. Or at least that is what I tell myself in such situations. Finally, the animal lay dead. The men muttered an oath as they each stepped over the carcass to complete the ceremony, and together dragged it off to the side where it would be butchered and a piece handed out to everyone to take home and eat.

*

Finally, the General and I were invited to cut the ribbon and be the first to walk into the school. Stepping around the pool of cow's blood we proceeded to the door and after a few more words of congratulations on a job well done, I cut half way through the ribbon, then passed the scissors to him to finish the job. We congratulated the Headmaster and shook hands all around, but after a few minutes I told the General he would have to carry on for both of us as I just had to get back to my room. I must have looked rather bad as he readily agreed and told me he would get a ride back with the Civil Affairs Officers.

Back in the compound I should have gone directly to the clinic and had Dr. Lal, our United Nations doctor look at me, but I was so exhausted I just flopped down on my bed and passed out. With the symptoms I had, alternating fever and chills with bouts of nausea, I should have recognized it as malaria. I had my first experience with malaria as a youth in Colombia many years before, and that time it had taken nearly a week before I could get from the small isolated mountain village where I was living at the time to a hospital in Bogota, where they diagnosed it and were able to treat it.

Recollections of this long ago event, along with other surrealistic dreams drifted through my mind as I lay half asleep, half unconscious. When I woke up it was nearly dusk and I had a terrific headache. After dinking half a bottle of water I managed to get up and find my radio, and called Dr. Lal, who immediately came to my room. After taking a sample of blood for analysis, he checked me into our small clinic overnight, and the next morning confirmed it was indeed malaria. Fortunately we did not have cerebral malaria in that area, so the treatment was relatively quick and I was able to get back to work after a couple of days, although I was weak for nearly a week. Normal malaria is limited pretty much to the main blood stream, but Cerebral malaria, as the name implies gets into the brain and other organs as well. If Cerebral malaria goes untreated for very long and gets far enough advanced it is extremely difficult to treat, and usually results in death. I would have a couple more bouts of malaria during my time in Sudan, but with this refresher course, I once again recognized the symptoms and quickly got the treatment.

Chapter 37: Grass Roots Diplomacy

A few months after I arrived, near the end of the year, the event I had been fearing took place during a meeting of the Area Joint Military Committee or AJMC. As I stated previously the SAF had imposed severe restrictions forbidding movement of our staff north of the UN compound. This restriction had been imposed long before I took over as HoO and try as we might we could not get the SAF or the government in Khartoum to cooperate in lifting it. This was unfair as it allowed the SAF to move troops freely throughout their area without us monitoring them. The SPLA had so far not followed suite by restricting our movement to the south, in large part because they wanted us to continue with the programs and projects to assist returning refugees, which were mostly Dinka, and which we could only do if we were able to move about freely in the south.

During this particular meeting the senior SAF officer began to question our General Abasi, the Sector Commander about troop movements by the SPLA in the southern part of the sector. This concerned information that was only available because our military patrols were still allowed movement in the south and could monitor such troop movements. The senior officer of the SPLA was furious and said that if the UN could not monitor the north than they should not be able to monitor the south, and they walked out of the meeting. The Sector Commander did his best to calm things down but to no avail. The next morning we got an official message from the SPLA that a restriction had been placed on movement of all UNMIS staff more than five kilometers south of the town, thereby putting all of our programs and projects in the south in danger.

We immediately sent a patrol south of town to test this, and they were turned back by armed men at a road block at the five k mark. We were now really boxed in making it effectively impossible to implement our programs in support of the Comprehensive Peace Accords. I immediately reported this to our headquarters in Khartoum and they instructed the SRSG's representative in Juba to take up the matter with the GOSS (Government of South Sudan). I also sent the Sector Commander to meet again with the SPLA, but they would not discuss it. Meanwhile, we were left sitting in the compound. To make matters worse, the one civilian who might be able to help break this stalemate had been out of the area for several months attending meetings in Kenya and Uganda. His name was Amir Kuak and he was the Paramount Chief of the Dinka for central Sudan.

*

I had not met Amir Kuak but had certainly heard about him. He was younger than many of the other chiefs and sub-chiefs, being in his late forties, but he had the reputation of being intelligent and thoughtful, and had the respect of everyone. Some of the younger Dinka were much more militant, in fact some would qualify as hotheads who wanted to teach the Misseriya a lesson, but even they listened to him most of the time. The only good news we had was that Kuak was due to arrive in our sector later in the week and I had our Civil Affairs office arrange to meet with him as soon as possible.

We held separate weekly meetings with the leaders of both the Dinka and the Misseriya, in part to discuss important local matters and also just to build ties of friendship between them and UNMIS. My plan was to use these meetings with the Dinka to impress on them the importance of lifting restrictions, primarily so we could continue the programs we had in progress in the south. They in turn would apply pressure on the SPLA to do so. This seemed possible especially since there were so many refugees returning to their area and they needed assistance with food, logistics, medicine and the like. If the Dinka agreed this may give us some leverage with the Misseriya to ease restrictions since they did not want it to appear the Dinka were taking the moral highroad. It was a long shot, but even if we just got the restrictions lifted to the south, it would be successful.

*

The meeting was scheduled for Sunday afternoon at 17:00 hours (5:00 PM) and I asked General Abasi to attend so he could speak to the issue that such restrictions put on the projects the military were conducting, if necessary. Kuak's compound was set deep in the village so we had to slowly wind our way through narrow dirt roads, and finally through muddy paths barely wide enough for our Nissan Patrols to get through, even though we scrapped fences and nearly hit houses along the way. When we came to a small store we had to stop and wait for people to step inside so we could pass.

Finally we arrived at the Amir's compound and a small party met us at the gate. Kuak stepped out and immediately greeted Maluk, the Civil Affairs Officer who was with me that day. Since they had not seen each other for some time they embraced in the traditional African (and also Arabic) way, then Kuak introduced himself to me. I immediately sensed an air of calmness and self confidence, almost an air of intelligence about him.

Many times my father's old sayings spring to mind and this time it was "don't confuse ignorance with stupidity". Ignorance can be overcome with education, and this deficiency has nothing to do with the ability to think and reason. A stupid person can do neither and usually must depend on family connections. Kuak may not have attended an Ivy League college but his insight was sharp and he could think and reason with the best of them. He was about my height but a bit heaver, and like most of the Dinka he did not ware traditional clothing, rather he had on slightly worn tan slacks and a sport shirt. If you met him on the streets of London or New York, aside from the worn flip flops on his feet and stubble of beard, he would not really stand out.

He gave us a short tour around his compound which was huge in comparison to others. The larger compounds usually have no more than ten of the traditional houses and huts, or tukos as they are called in Dinka. This one must have contained nearly twenty houses and out buildings, all made with the traditional mud and straw construction, or cob as it is called, and with thatch roofs. The houses, although traditional looking can be deceiving as some are quite large and even have small generators, refrigerators and cook stoves. If the dirt floors and mud walls are kept swept and clean, it makes for quite a decent living arrangement. Those of course are the exception and most tukos are rather small and primitive.

We were ushered into a large tuko in the center of the compound which had plastered mud walls about three feet tall, after which it was open allowing the air to circulate. The thatch roof which is cone shaped, started at about six feet, and topped out at nearly twenty feet in the middle. There were enough cane and wicker chairs with cushions for about twenty people and small tables were placed in front of the chairs. It was cool and shaded and even slightly dark at first. After coming in from the raging sun and heat it was very welcome.

As we entered the tuko there was a line of about seven or eight other chiefs and sub-chiefs and they all shook our hands as we entered. I knew several of them from past meetings. After we sat down, trays of sweets, tasty small homemade biscuits (cookies) and tea were brought in. As a young lady poured tea, I noticed several small goats who were following her stick their heads through the door, and after looking around and seeing there was nothing to eat they backed out. We settled down for a long meeting.

Amir Kuak welcomed us all and as is the tradition, being the senior chief, started with his comments. He said a few nice words about UNMIS but quickly launched into a list of problems and concerns in the sector ranging from the lack of government appointments and the poor conditions of the roads to more serious issues such as how the SAF was bullying civilians, harassing vendors in the market place and continuing to occupy public buildings. He ended by observing that these more serious issues were in violation of the CPA, and it was up to the UN to do something about it.

After his comments, each chief and sub-chief followed with their own short speech, which for the most part was a repeat of what had already been said, but I made mental note of a couple of new items that were added. One involved the upcoming migration of Misseriya cattle herds south which was due to take place at the start of dry season, and the other involved completion of some community improvement projects (Quick Impact Projects) that were waiting for funding by UNMIS. It took about forty-five minutes by the time all the chiefs and sub-chiefs had finished, and then it was out turn to speak.

Being the HoO I gave the first response, and I had been listening intently, looking for a way to bring up and reinforce my main message, that being the lifting of restrictions on our movement. I first responded to the main points raised by Kuak. We agreed that the lack of properly appointed government officials was hurting the sector but as they were aware, only the government in Khartoum could fill those posts. I emphasized how we were working with UNDP to repair roads, but due to the restrictions on movements we were not able to work outside of the town. I gave a list of the things we had been able to do, such as refurbishing the school, and other ongoing projects such as donating tents to rural schools to use as class rooms. Then I moved on to the points raised by the other chiefs with special attention to the mental notes made during their talks.

I gave a short history of the successful efforts to assist both communities (Dinka and Misseriya) during the annual cattle migrations, and how we were already planning for the next round. However, with the restrictions on movement it would be very difficult to do it this year. Moving on to respond to the next chief, I emphasized how the funding of our projects would be much more difficult if we could not send UN inspection teams periodically, as was required. I tried to make it clear that we of course would continue with these programs even with the restrictions on our movement but it would be more difficult.

At the risk of sounding condescending I further pressed the point by gently lecturing them on the importance of taking the moral high ground and removing the restrictions on movement even if the other side does not. It would make you look like the wiser and more mature ones, as well as allowing us to work on important projects, and finally to assist the many returning refugees. In fact most of the assistance to refugees was provided by other agencies and NGO's but they relied on the assistance of UNMIS. Several times during my lengthy response I could hear Maluk in a low voice saying "good, good", and I could see the chiefs listening closely and even shaking their heads with approval occasionally. Even Kuak seemed to be interested.

As I was drawing to a close, I glanced at my watch and realized that I had been speaking for nearly forty minutes. And I was the one who always accused them of going on. With that I asked the General to make a few comments and then we finished with Maluk. Finally the Amir said "Well, that is all we have to say", at which point he stood up and walked over to me and shook my hand. He held on to it for an extra few seconds which is a sign of friendship and respect. We had done our best to make our case, and now we would have to wait and see if we had succeeded.

We did not have to wait long. Two days later one of our UN Interpreters who had been present at the meeting, Anglo by name and who is an older and a highly respected man in the area, stopped me as I was walking through the compound. With a big smile he said that the chiefs were all impressed with the meeting and they had decided to approach the SPLA to see if they will lift the restrictions so the UN can work in the south.

Finally, at the next AJMC meeting held two weeks later, both sides agreed to lift the restrictions on UNMIS for one month, both north and south. They would review the situation from month to month but it appeared the situation had improved considerable. I asked the Sector Commander how they had arrived at that decision and what discussion had taken place. He replied that it appeared that most of the discussion had taken place before the meeting, it was proposed by the SPLA and agreed to by the SAF.

*

The next afternoon I decided to take a drive to the north of the compound to verify that the restrictions had indeed been lifted, and also because we had word that the first herd of cattle was moving towards the south. I took an interpreter and one of the security staff with me and we drove about thirty kilometers north, for the first time in many months. There was one road block at about the ten k mark, but they waved us on. We found the herd, which was small and had stopped for several days in an area with good pasture. The herders were obviously Misseriya, being well over six feet tall and slender. They were friendly enough and told us there had been no problems with the local Dinkas. After talking with them for some time we felt the situation was calm so we left. This time when we reached the road block, there were different SAF soldiers and they abruptly stopped us. Through the interpreter they angrily told us we did not have permission to be there and with their hands on their weapons they prepared to take us to their commander. We tried to explain that the restrictions had been lifted yesterday but they insisted it had not.

As we were talking I noticed that the soldier that seemed to be in charge was staring at a package of cigars I had in my shirt pocket. Bong had recently returned from home leave in the Philippines and had brought me several five packs of Alhambra coronas. On a hunch, I took one out of the pack and made a point of lighting it up. I know smoking in UN vehicles is not allowed, but this was a special case. The longer these guys held us the more opportunity there was for something to go wrong so we had to try to get them to cooperate. I then offered one to the soldier, who took it with a grin and opened it. I offered him a light and for a minute we both stood there enjoying the cigar that advertises itself as "one of the world's mildest and most flavorful". I like them, and so did my new friend. I handed him the rest of the package.

That seemed to break the ice. Now that things were calmed down a bit I told him, through the interpreter that the AJMC had agreed to lift restrictions only yesterday, mentioning the SAF Senior Officer by name, and he finally agreed to let us continue. Before we left he said if I was lying he would come to our office and I would have to give him more cigars. We had a good laugh, shook hands again and continued back to the compound, where I went to my office and was busy until dark answering e-mails. However, the interpreter and driver were busy spreading the word on how we negotiated our way out of a road block, and for several days someone was always asking me for a cigar as I walked around the compound.

*

The end to a nearly perfect day. As I was walking the short distance to my quarters I noticed several local guards shouting and obviously upset over something in front of the ablutions units. As I came near they started warning me to be careful and as I got closer I saw why. About ten to fifteen feet away was a good sized snake with it's head lifted up more than a foot off the ground. "Spiting viper" one of them yelled as he threw a rock at it (actually they are cobras but I didn't bother to correct him). And sure enough it spit at us, and although they can rarely spit more than a couple of meters it is nothing to play around with. Finally one of them scored a hit with a brick and the others joined in until it was hard to even tell it had once been a snake. As one of them took the badly battered body off with a stick to pitch it over the compound fence, I continued on to my room.

Chapter 38: The White House Special Envoy

A couple of months after our diplomatic efforts resulted in a relaxation of the restrictions on movement, we received word that the next day the US Special Envoy to Sudan and his party would be visiting our region. Peacekeeping is that way, sometimes if you have an hour's advance notice that seems like a lot. Nor were we given much direction as to what type of presentation he would like; just give him background information and a briefing on the present situation we were told.

Luckily we had a PowerPoint presentation prepared, complete with photographs that showed the history of how the sector had gone from tents and one overused toilet to the relative luxury of hard sided buildings and several toilets. I also tasked each section with putting together a short briefing on their current activities, and we combined them into one presentation, which I assigned to Frank, our South African Humanitarian Affairs Officer to present. Frank's English was good as were his presentational skills, and I could also rely on him to be concise and brief. His facial expressions were comical and reminded me of a young version of the old American comedian Buddy Hackett. I would give the opening statement and the PowerPoint, followed by the HA Officer, and then General Abasi would chair a presentation by the Area Joint Military Committee (AJMC). After a short break for tea, Chief Kabasha would speak representing the Misseriya, and Amir Kuak would do the same for the Dinka. It was a good plan, what could possibly go wrong.

*

To begin, the plane which was scheduled to land at noon in fact landed nearly an hour late. They had been in Malikal in the morning, and the HoO in that sector was an old acquaintance from Afghanistan days. Bradley was a rather traditional Englishman and had arranged a morning tea as well as lunch and a tour of the town, which had thrown off the schedule. Another complicating factor, the landing strip in Abyei is actually a cow pasture with no lights, and the pilot had to lift off while it was still fully daylight to avoid cows, birds and the huts that were encroaching on both ends.

Still, everyone was in good spirits so we pressed forward. The team included the Whitehouse Special Envoy (who would later be appointed as Director of USAID), the American Ambassador to Sudan, the chief US Development Officer for Sudan, a Security Advisor to the Bush Whitehouse, two other aides and two Embassy Security Officers. It was surprisingly high power, more so than we had been expecting. Abyei and Malikal were background trips, after which they were going to spend a few days in Darfur. Everyone was cordial but tired, since they had started in Khartoum at 0 dark-thirty, and some of them nodded off from time to time. To add to the atmosphere, something about lunch was now kicking in and several of them made a quick trip to our ablution units. As I related in an earlier chapter our ablution units were now the envy of the other regions and our high profile delegation was grateful for that.

The meetings went well but we kept falling further behind, so one of the aides consulted with the security officers and added an extra half hour to the departure time. We had just started the briefing with the Area Joint Military Committee when our Regional Chief Security Officer called me out of the meeting. A small fire fight had broken out in one of the SPLA camps, about ten kilometers south of the compound and it appeared at least one person was dead and several wounded. We later learned that the fight was between two soldiers, one of whom wanted to marry the sister of another soldier. Either the young ladies family objected to the marriage, or the lady was not interested. At any rate an argument ensued and after it could not be settled with fists, the would be groom picked up his rifle and killed the other man. Then a small fire fight broke out before the shooter was finally over powered. It did not directly affect us or the compound area but I notified the Embassy Security Officer anyway.

In my experience such incidents, where a small disagreement or perceived insult explodes into violent confrontation seems all too common particularly in Somalia and Sudan. I suppose it may be a side effect of some thirty-five years of unchecked violence and warfare but I did not see it to the same extent in other places that had been through similar experiences.

Then, a few minutes later I got called out again, this time by the Civil Affairs Officer.

To keep the presentation short we had invited just one community leader from the Dinka and one from the Misseryia to attend. Besides, the Special Envoy had spent considerable time in this area before the war and was already very familiar with the issues. The Misseryia Chief, a man named Kabasha had come alone as requested, but the Dinka had sent a full delegation of seven people in addition to Amir Kuak. I figured Kuak was under a lot of pressure from his more militant sub-chiefs to bring more members.

I called him aside and asked if he could pick just one or two to attend with him, and if he could be the one to speak. He said flat out that that would cause many problems. He also asked if they could meet separately with the Envoy which indicated to me he expected the others to speak out against the Misseriya and the SAF. I could see Kuak was under pressure. I said I would try to get all of his delegation into the meeting, but meeting separately would send the wrong impression, that the Dinka and Misseriya could not get along. I also insisted that he be the one to speak. He agreed.

I explained the situation to Kabasha and asked if he would be willing to meet jointly with all of the Dinka representatives present, but only Kuak would speak. He replied, I know all of these people, they are my neighbors, let's meet. I was proud of him. I went back and proposed to Kuak that all of his people could be present in the meeting, but due to the limited time only he would speak. This gave him the excuse he needed to put the pressure back on his members, and they finally agreed.

By now the meeting of the AJMC was concluding and everyone was headed to the ablution units again. General Abasi quickly briefed me on the AJMC meeting, which had gone well. To gain time we decided to drink tea while we conducted the meeting with the tribal leaders, and I could just envision tea cups flying around the room.

*

As it turned out, the meeting itself was almost anti-climatic. Kabasha emphasized how he had lived among Dinka all his life and the Dinka and Misseryia were like fingers on a hand. They only had problems because they were manipulated by outsiders. He was an honest man and I think he was speaking from the heart, but I was also afraid many of his colleagues did not feel the same way. For his part, Amir Kuak, being thoughtful and articulate emphasized that no final solutions could be reached until certain minimum criteria are met; the Comprehensive Peace Accords are implemented, the findings of the Abyei Boundary Commission (an international body which drew up the border between the north and the south) must be implemented, and a full civil government must be appointed by Khartoum.

The Special Envoy stated that the US was not in a position to impose a solution but it was very interested in reaching a solution that is mutually agreeable to all the parties. He agreed to return for a much longer visit and to continue efforts to reach a solution.

Although nothing new was said, I think the meetings were helpful in that they brought the delegation up to speed before they reached Darfur. At least the Special Envoy and the Ambassador seemed pleased and thanked us on the short drive back to the airstrip. With a fast round of hand shakes the party hustled into the plane and in the gathering dusk, it immediately rumbled down the field, kicking up a dust cloud that stretched nearly back to the compound.

It had been a very hectic day, which is typical of peacekeeping, but usually such behind the scenes negotiations and scrambling go unnoticed.

Chapter 39: A Few Days Off

Not every day was so busy. I managed to get a day off now and again, even if it meant having a heart attack scare to get some time off. Although it is rather funny in retrospect, at the time it caused some tense moments.

Near the end of the dry season, and after my second bout of malaria I caught a mild upper repertory infection. The only symptom was a bit of difficulty breathing and a slight wheezing, nothing more. After one long day of meetings, I continued to work late writing the weekly report that was due in the SRSG's office next morning. I was tired when I finally went to bed, but kept waking up all night, I guess because my breathing was not easy. At any rate, the next morning after my usual cup of strong coffee did little to rouse me I decided to go to the clinic to see Dr. Lal.

*

Dr. Lal was an Indian trained doctor and a good friend, as well as one of the senior staff. He had a rather droll since of humor and we often traded our dry observations. He also spearheaded our campaigns to improve health standards, and in general to get some of the staff to improve their habits. For instance, some of the staff had the nasty habit of clearing their throat in a loud and disgusting manner every morning and then spitting wherever they happened to be. Usually in front of someone's quarters. I mentioned this to Dr. Lal and he took it upon himself to launch a healthy habits campaign. Soon he was presenting hygiene classes and even designed some posters which we put up around the compound. It seemed to work.

The expectorating continued, but at least we got them to do it away from the housing units and walkways.

Dr. Lal's most ambitious project however was even more delicate, and eventually resulted in me issuing one of my more famous memos, one which really tested my diplomatic skills. As many of you may know, there are basically two styles of toilets in the world; the commode on which one sits, and the more traditional squatting arrangement. The standard ablution units, since they are made in the west are made for sitters with the seat that gentlemen are supposed to lift when circumstances do not require them to sit. When squatters use the sitter's accommodations they should do the same before they squat on the rim, otherwise they put their dirty shoes directly on the seat. In addition to being disgustingly dirty, the added weight of them squatting eventually breaks even the toughest seat. Since it was nearly impossible to get even basic cleaning supplies you can imagine the difficulty in getting a replacement toilet seat.

At any rate, after various attempts to educate people, based on the theme of being considerate to other staff members, Dr. Lal grew exasperated and was ready to release a barrage of photos he had taken of muddy and broken seats, meant to shame the squalid squatters. Rather than allow that and see this escalate into the tangle of the toilets, the clash of the commodes, I promised to write a memo on the subject instead.

As is my style, the memo was straight forward. I divided the world into sitters and squatters, but made it clear that both approaches work equally well, and that neither side has a cheek up on the other. Most of the time they exist in separate worlds but when they do coexist, both sides must strain to reach a satisfactory outcome. In essence the rules I proposed were simple. Squatters should lift the seat every time, full stop. Sitters must not complain about muddy foot prints on the rim, just put the seat down and get on with it.

To my relief the memo was met with the mixture of approval and good humor I had hoped for. It was soon translated into Arabic and Dinka and posted in all of the ablution units, even those in the military side of the compound. I even got a request for copies of the memo from a couple of the HoO's from other sectors, who were having the same problem in their areas.

*

But I digress, again. This time Dr. Lal's project was me. As soon as I mentioned that I had some difficulty breathing he had me laying down and the nurse was taking my pulse. Now that may sound innocuous, but not if you knew this particular nurse. She was very cute (I have seen guys walk into walls and light poles watching her) as well as being a nice sweet kid. I think I can safely say kid as she was quite young and all of the guys protected her like she was their kid sister. Any way, with her bending over me, poking and prodding with her stethoscope, it should be no surprise that my pulse was a bit irregular.

This was all it took for the sometimes over zealous Doctor to immediately call in a medical evacuation, his version of an air strike, thinking I was having a heart attack. By the time I learned what he had done, it was to late, the helicopter was on its way from Al Obeyed, the nearest major town, which also had a full fledged UN Field Hospital run by the Egyptian Military. Realizing that an evacuation is nearly impossible to call off once it is started, I decided it would be easier to just go to the hospital and let them check me out, even though I knew I was fine. We would all have a good laugh, I would get some good Egyptian food (maybe even grilled lamb, ful mudammas and nan) and be back in Abyei the next afternoon. When the helicopter arrived less than an hour later, the good Doctor and I walked out to meet it. A man in scrubs descended from the helicopter and with a puzzled look asked where the patient was, as he was expecting a stretcher. The Doctor pointed at me.

As we made our way to Al Obeyed it seemed like the medical evacuation team was disappointed that I was not actually having a heart attack, or at least exhibiting some symptoms they could work on. To hide their disappointment they leafed through some magazines or dozed off. To further show their disappointment, when we got to the helipad, they took their time unloading and driving to the field hospital.

Once there it was a repeat of Abyei. The doctors were anxious to get the chance to use all their equipment so they put me through a series of tests, drew blood and gave me an electrocardiogram. Then, satisfied that I was getting better and would probably live, a couple of the doctors struck up a conversation with me. They told me how they had family in the US, one in California and one in North Carolina. I told them of our family trips to Egypt and how we loved to shop in Khan el-Khalili, the famous old market in Cairo where you can find everything from hummus to hashish. We talked baseball, basketball and cricket, but avoided politics. I don't think they were fans of the Bush Administration. Finally, they had a tray of food brought which at least had a small plate of ful and nan, and said they wanted to monitor my vital signs over night so the nurses would hook me up to monitors before I went to sleep. More nurses. With wires hooked to my arms and chest I slept fitfully.

To my surprise the next morning the head doctor, whose brother lives in South Carolina, said they wanted to send me on to Khartoum for further analysis. By now I was beginning to wonder if something actually was wrong, but they insisted it was just to be on the safe side. So before noon I got on the UN plane and by about 15:00 hours I was standing in Ripps office. Looking up from his desk he said dryly, "Good, yur alive. I didn't know what I would tell your wife". It was reassuring to see that my friends were concerned.

I went next door into an empty office and dialed my wife. We did not usually call each other every day, so the fact that we had not spoken in a couple of days should not raise any concern. However, as soon as she answered the phone she said "Well I'm happy you found the time to call". I could tell she was upset. Apparently she had called my office in Abyei and since I was not there she called Bing. He in turn apparently told her the whole story, with some embellishment I'm sure, and since nobody had any real information on me, she was left wondering. It took a couple of days for her to calm down, put my life insurance policy back in the desk, and get over it enough to speak to me. I think she had already ordered a new Mercedes.

After another round of being poked and prodded and checked by the UN Medical Office in Khartoum, I was given a clean bill of health. However, I took advantage of the opportunity and did some shopping for food to take back, visited with the office of the SRSG and Political Affairs, then before I could leave I got a call from the Payroll Office. We did not have banks in central Sudan at that time, so payrolls were sent in the form of cash. It seems the last payroll for our local staff was short several thousands of Sudanese

Pounds so I had to take a bundle with me. Technically speaking, this was not allowed, since large sums of money are supposed to be transferred by someone form Finance and with Security Guards. However, even though this bundle of cash had to be carried in a small bag, it was not worth very much. We did this often until the first bank was opened in our sector, just a few months before I left Sudan.

The next afternoon I arrived back in Abyei. Only one Security Guard met me at the helipad, and he was there to pick up the cash. I could see everything was back to normal.

Chapter 40: Building A Retirement Tuko

As the dry season dragged on, the afternoon cloud banks slowly grew taller, larger and stayed longer each day. When people speak of the African sky, it is not just the night sky with its fantastically bright stars against the blackest background one can imagine, that stretches unhampered from horizon to horizon. The coming of the rainy season is dynamic as well and provides an equally outstanding show. As the clear morning sky is heated up by the sun, clouds began to form and by late afternoon dark rolling banks tower as high as 15-20,000 feet. Sometimes they resemble mountain ranges slowly moving towards you.

It is also a welcome sight as it means an end to the dust storms, the return of green grass and leaves and some relief from the unrelenting sun. As odd as it may sound, the rainy season can actually be cool and in the mornings it seems cold, especially to a body that is used to daily temperatures well above 100 degrees Fahrenheit, or 38 degrees Centigrade for months on end. Of course, after months of daily monsoon downpours and mud several inches deep that pulls the boots right off your feet as you walk, one begins to look forward to dry season. Life is fickle.

I had been in Sudan for over a year now and we had made remarkable progress in Abyei. Improvements had been considerable in the living arrangements and situation in the compound, refugees were moving back into the sector, and the AJMC was making strides with the peaceful integration of SAF and SPLA. To add to the list of successes, the lifting of restrictions on movement of UN staff which we had managed to get on a temporary basis, had now stretched into months. This of course greatly aided the ability to conduct other programs.

Efforts to recruit a permanent HoO for our sector were continuing and I knew my replacement would come eventually. This was inevitable, for even if the SRSG wanted to keep me in that position, the fact was that I was now beyond the mandatory age of retirement in the UN. To be kept beyond retirement in the UN is difficult and every time my appointment came up for extension it involved a minor battle to convince HQ that I was needed. I was grateful to the mission for taking on that fight, although they were getting a lot out of me as well.

*

It was at this time that Blackie began to look around for some projects he could get started now and finish up during the rainy season. His crews had just completed the concrete walkways, which ran in front of the offices and connected the offices to the living quarters. This was done in time to keep us out of the mud that season. The offices were laid out in a U shape, and we had discussed constructing a sheltered area with a roof, in the opening between the offices, to be used for meetings or for parties and social gatherings. On the drive into town I frequently noticed that new tukos were being constructed, and since they seemed to typify our area, I suggested we build a large tuko with open sides. I made the suggestion in one of our weekly senior staff meetings, and it met with immediate approval.

To start things off I donated $200 to help purchase poles and thatch for the roof. The idea caught on and soon staff members were donating $10 or $20, whatever they could. Blackie got started immediately and within a week his crew was pouring a large round concrete pad for the floor. The local staff also liked the idea and began to scour the local market for the best poles to use for the structure. Soon we had poles, grass for the thatched roof, and a large pile of construction materials beside the concrete pad. Watching the construction and shouting advice to the crew became a daily routine and it began to feel (and sound) like we were living in a village.

*

At about this time I got another piece of news that raised mixed feelings; a permanent HoO had been selected for our sector and would be taking over in about six weeks. I did not know her but was familiar with her work with a sister UN agency. She had a strong background and in fact was considered somewhat of an expert on the petroleum sector in Sudan. An excellent choice I thought, and I knew deep inside that it was time for me to move on to other things, again preferably closer to my family. But still, it was also a bit depressing. I had finally reached what I knew would be the height of my career with the UN and one is never ready to vacate that seat.

I now had to prepare the staff, and the region for this change since they would be getting not only a new Head of Office to replace me, they would also be getting a new Regional Administrative Officer, again to replace me. The fact that the HoO was a woman did not cause much concern, even though this seemed to be a male dominated world. While there were no female chiefs or sub-chiefs, there were a number of female community leaders and the men seemed to accept them. In addition, we had several other female HoO's throughout Sudan and they were for the most part well accepted.

An old problem raised it's head yet again, the Special Post Allowance. Even though I had applied for it and certainly qualified for it, I still had not been granted an SPA, which to me seemed quite amazing since I had been successfully filling a post at least two full grades higher than my own. As it turned out, it would only be after I had left the UN, and then only because colleagues in HQ doggedly pressed my case and chased up the paperwork, that it would finally be granted.

So, while I prepared handover notes for my office and the sector in general, I also pushed to get the tuko completed. We had two deadlines now, the start of rainy season and the arrival of my replacement. I wanted to have at least a couple of functions performed in it before I left so the crew worked overtime. Finally the only thing remaining to be completed was the thatch roof. This requires a particular skill and many of the best thatch installers in our area were women, since they tended to be lighter than the men and put less stress on the roofing poles. I also think they work harder. We hired some local ladies to put on the thatch roof, and again everyone was fascinated by the project and spent a lot of time watching the progress.

One of the ladies, who was wrinkled and older but appeared to be the leader of the crew smoked a pipe, and the entire crew had to take a break when she wanted a smoke since it would have been easy to set fire to the dry thatch.

Finally, after the roof was complete, Bong put on the finishing touches. He dissembled two large wooden cable spools, and with the lumber he salvaged constructed a bar and several stools. His finishing touch was to put up a small sign that dedicated it to me. It was one of the best rustic style bars I had seen and would have been a great addition to any Caribbean resort. The staff began to immediately use it for meetings, as a place to have lunch and take a break, and of course we christened it with a party.

*

A typical party in Abyei was truly a communal affair as it required the efforts of everyone to pull one off. The Indian Military communications contingent shared living quarters with the civilians rather than the larger military contingent. They always volunteered to make a huge pot of curried rice and other dishes, and since being military they had food which was regularly sent in. We took up a collection and got a goat which we roasted and grilled over a spit that Blackie had put together out of spare parts. From the collection we also got beer and soft drinks from the local market. Bing and his crew strung some extra lights and set up tables and chairs. Finally, our IT section set up a portable sound system and the young Algerian in charge of the unit served as the DJ. Everybody provided music. The first party in the tuko was a great success. The music ranged from Jennifer Lopez, to Indian Bollywood, to Egyptian. The goat was a bit tough but done to perfection, and we even hauled a refrigerator into the tuko for drinks. We also used the tuko for the weekly staff meetings and other more official purposes, but of course parties were top on the list.

*

Finally the new HoO arrived and I went to Khartoum to help brief her on the sector. She had actually been working for some time in South Sudan, but as I said with another UN agency so she was already familiar with the history and politics of the area. We would have made a good team and she wanted me to stay on in my capacity as RAO, but I had already made up my mind to let my overdue retirement take place. So after a few days I returned to Abyei to wait for her arrival, and following a couple of weeks accompanying her to meet the local Chiefs, community and military leaders, I prepared for my departure.

*

Of course, the farewell party was centered around the tuko. That evening, I stepped out of my tuko to say good-by and facing me were nearly two hundred people. I was touched that many of them were local staff who had make the extra effort to return to the compound for this event even though it was late in the evening. There were the international staff with whom I had shared hardship and hunger, but who had worked so faithfully to create one of the best sector teams in Sudan. There were even a few dignitaries from Khartoum and the new Head of Office who would replace me. I looked at them for several seconds and I can still remember what I said. I told them I had prepared a speech to tell them how honored I was to have known them and count them as friends as well as colleagues, how they still had very important work to do and I was sure they would continue to do it. But, since they all knew me, they also knew everything I would say, and knew it better than I could say it. I finished by telling them I would always remember them and that they were the best team I had ever worked with, and before my voice began to fail me I took one last look around, turned and walked back into the tuko.

*

The plane gained altitude on its leg to Dubai, where I would eventually connect to Cape Town, South Africa to join my wife who was there attending a business conference. This seemed to be a familiar scene, me on a plane out of some God forsaken place where I had just spent several years. This time however was different. After nearly two decades of working in my own small way to make a difference, to bring some degree of sanity, justice and order to places like Somalia, Iraq, Afghanistan and Sudan I was going home. I wasn't even sure where home was anymore, other than where my family was. I had had the very great honor of getting to know and work with outstanding people from all over the world, people who will remain friends the rest of my life. I had slowly and with great effort risen from the status of a raw recruit to be a senior officer in charge of operations in a large and important area. Along the way I had been helped by many, to whom I am forever grateful.

I knew I would miss this life and to be honest was not sure how I would make the adjustment, but it had to be done. My eyes began to cloud up a bit. I cursed myself for being so silly. After years of living a frequently crazy always dangerous life, of witnessing the extremes of human behavior, of always being in the wrong place but thankfully at the right time, you would think I would be tougher than to be effected by this.

Part Five

*The Case For UN Peacekeeping:
Must all good things end?*

Chapter 41: My Own Bias

Let me preface his section by stating that I do not purport to be a UN scholar or an expert on foreign affairs, international development or the like. I am writing this based on my own experience, insight and bias having been inside UN Peacekeeping for a number of years.

By way of background, I first conceived the idea of writing this book when I was in my teens, a few decades ago. I had no definite idea then what I would ultimately do with my life but I knew that I would someday want to document it, and what it had all meant to me. Not to do that would amount to a life wasted. Not that my life has been so unique or meaningful, there have been many similar lives lived by similar people, and perhaps in the end that is what makes it so important to document it. Perhaps I can serve as a witness for the many others who have had similar experience.

While I was trained and educated as a Social Anthropologist and an Administrator, it has occurred to me that I have always been a historian at heart. To greatly oversimplify, in my view there are two major schools of thought about what constitutes history worthy of study; is it the story of a few important defining personalities that tower above events and times (the Churchill's, Lincolns, and Bonaparte's) and who seem to mold the times in which they live? Is it the untold thousands of worker ants fighting the wars, raising the crops and providing the living fodder for these giants? I believe it lies between these two extremes and that the true grist of history is found in each of us.

Most of humanity is destined to live a relatively quietly life making a living and raising families as best they can. Some of these same people also have the same mark of genius as the greats but due to an accident of birth (into which family), personality traits, gender and other essentially social factors never get the opportunity to stand out in front of others. That is why it is important that lives of all ranks and hue be documented, so that someday others with more insight may understand the contribution made by all of us caught up in the rush of humanity.

As an anthropologist, it is not clear at this time (at least not to me) if this grand experiment of the human species will ultimately succeed or fail. It has the capacity to do either, and examples to support both sides of this argument abound. Nowhere is this more abundantly clear than in the life and experience of a peacekeeper, who sees the most depraved and wanton behavior, and yet arising from the same people and from the same places, sees the most sublime and selfless examples of moral behavior and of the desire to do some good.

Both acts spring forth from the same source; the same group, the same village and from within the same families. In this regard such things as religion, skin color, culture and sex become meaningless. When someone is trying to live a decent ethical life or in more desperate circumstances helping to save your life, you do not ask about religion, color, gender and so on. Ultimately it just does not matter.

*

This brings me to the question, why do we do it? Peacekeepers spend much of their time living and working in failed states and broken societies, places where individuals and families are shattered or barely holding on. Places where Taliban fundamentalists are free to deny basic rights and dignity to others. Places where ruthless so called military leaders are free to recruit children as young as ten and eleven years old, put an AK-47 in their hands and teach them to rape, maim and butcher. Places where a few twisted totalitarian minds steal souls and then force individuals into a society that lives only to serve their needs. But this only happens in places like Somalia, Afghanistan and Sudan; obviously so since that is where we send our peacekeepers, right?

I wish it were that simple, but the truth is that just like natural diseases societal diseases do not respect borders. I am always astounded (more like depressed) when I see on the nightly news things as dehumanizing as I have seen in Somalia, Iraq and anywhere occurring much closer to home. The US border with Mexico, drug and gang infested sections of our major cities are both nearby examples of failed states, or at least failed societies. If these same areas happened to be in Africa or the Middle East might we not be sending peacekeepers now? I dare say one could find examples of failed states or societies within twenty or thirty miles of their home, no matter where they live in the world.

Why do we as peacekeepers do this? We do this because we realize that failed and disintegrating societies can and do occur everywhere and that it is seldom the fault of the people living in those areas. In fact a good case can be made that we all play a part in creating and sustaining failed states through shortsighted greed and myopic economic and foreign policy. We think nothing of destroying other cultures and societies for their resources (or perhaps to feed our drug habit), and justify it in our own mind by saying it is simply progress, the way of the world. Peacekeepers do what they do because people living in such areas desperately need help to bring some bit of sanity and basic security to their lives.

We do this for a very selfish reason as well; like any disease this one spreads. If the necessary conditions exist, the failed state syndrome can happen anywhere. So, if your political or philosophical beliefs prevent you from doing something to help others caught up in such areas, then do it for purely selfish reasons. As long as there are failed states and societies in the world, your little part of the world is also in danger.

Chapter 42: Unique Challenges

The United Nations faces challenges which I don't think are faced to the same extent and in the same degree, by any other organization in the world. This became clear to me when I left the UN and began to review a journal I had kept, with the idea of perhaps writing this book. I was struck immediately by the negativity and impatience I expressed in so many ways. To read these entries it might appear that I had given up on the UN. Nothing could be further from the truth. I am not naive enough to believe that just because it intends well, the UN should not be challenged on its shortcomings and should in effect get a free ride. However, and this is an important point, if we were to apply the same tough standards critics use on the UN to other organizations such as our governments, our military, our churches, and our private organizations they would certainly come up short. I maintain that the UN is no worse and no better than many other organizations. In addition, UN Peacekeeping faces many unique challenges that would probably stop many of the world's governments and organizations dead in their tracks if they were to face them to the same extent.

Multi-Culturalism: Most organizations are grounded in one culture, or at least one group of related cultures, as in the case of a NATO. The UN has 192 plus member states from every conceivable culture and continent, and each member state thinks it holds the deciding vote. Sharing one culture, or corporate culture is more of a luxury than many realize; the ability to ultimately relate back to a shared culture and way of doing things is no small matter. For example while members of the US State Department or military may (and certainly do) hold a wide variety of views and express and pursue them openly, in the end they also share the same assumptions about how organizations operate and about what is ethical acceptable behavior. Based largely on these shared values and assumptions, they can ultimately be marshaled by leaders to move in the same direction, to march to the same drummer. In the UN this is much more difficult. What appears as relative order and calm on the surface at best usually represents a compromise whereas much of what goes on under the surface is not obvious to the causal observer.

For example, to survive in Peacekeeping one becomes aware that various offices, sections and functions while not outright controlled, are definitely overly "influenced" by a particular culture; which is not to say it is ineffective or necessarily corrupt or bad, just that if you want to deal effectively in this environment you had better be aware of that. I learned to do a quick reality check when I went into a new situation to see if one culture controlled or was overly represented. In Peacekeeping, many IT and Communications sections are very heavy to Indian staff, Finance is heavily African, Political Affairs is European and so on. When I joined Peacekeeping the term mafia was commonly used to describe this phenomenon. "Oh that section is run by the Caribbean mafia" or whatever. You learn to become a bit of a cultural chameleon as you slide from one environment to another.

While this concept no doubt exists to some extent in many mono-cultural organizations as well, nowhere is it more pronounced and accepted, even expected than in the ultimate multicultural organization, the UN. I will say I have noticed less of this phenomenon over the years but I cannot be sure if it is just that I became more adept at operating in it or if it is actually subsiding.

Rapid Expansion and Slow Adaptation: In a very real since, rapid and steady increase in the number, size and complexity of peacekeeping operations has been forced on the UN and DPKO in particular starting with the first peacekeeping operations to monitor the armistice agreement after the 1948 Arab-Israeli War. This occurred only three years after the formation of the UN in June of 1945. Between that modest beginning and today, the demand and response to a total of 63 peacekeeping missions to date spread around the world (the Middle East, Asia, Africa and the Americas) has resulted in a positive growth curve that would make any fortune 500 company envious.

This also presents a huge problem in that the UN is not an organization that responds quickly and deftly to growth and change. This relates in large part to the fact that the UN is saddled with an organizational structure and membership where change requires gaining a majority vote or at least support, of autonomous member governments instead of merely a board of directors or even a few contentious political parties. As a result, real change seldom happens at all, let alone quickly and smoothly. It has been adjusted many times but in most respects, the UN remains stuck with an administrative and policy framework that originated and still belongs in the 1940's post Second World War period.

The "Step Child" Syndrome (or the need for more "grass roots" autonomy): The original charter of the United Nations made no provisions for a peacekeeping arm, so when the need arose it was logically put under the Secretariat. Other UN agencies, such as UNDP and UNICEF, while still under the UN umbrella operate independently, which works to their great advantage. Nor was it ever imagined how big this function would become when the first Peacekeeping operation was put together in 1948. In retrospect it is as if Peacekeeping was the step-child that suddenly appeared on the door step and while it could not be turned away, nobody was sure they wanted it or what to do with it. Being part of the Secretariat, it naturally comes under the administrative policies and rules that govern that body, and through centralization and a proliferation of committees and review panels the Secretariat jealously guards the application and interpretation of all such rules, frequently to the detriment of DPKO.

As the step-child grew, it was shunted from room to room and given hand-me-downs until one day it could no longer be ignored; it had become a large, powerful and very high profile adult. Not to push the analogy too far, many of the policies and rules of the family simply do not fit the needs of the once small step child. Most of the UN operates in a predictable environment where changes are incremental when compared to the rapid changes that are commonplace in DPKO.

The life cycle of a mission goes from being nothing, to a concept, to within a few months putting hundreds or thousands of people on the ground along with millions and millions of dollars of sophisticated equipment, not to mention creation of very high profile diplomatic and political functions, and when it is nicely put together you begin to disassemble it. The slow ponderous rules that are clumsy and barely adequate for a body that operates essentially like a stable permanent government, do not fit well with the "Special Forces" mentality and quickness required by peacekeeping.

Perhaps one example will make this clear. In the section on Afghanistan I alluded to the problem of getting HQ approval for unpaid leave, to allow staff members to spend badly needed time with their families during a normal lull in their duties. This did not fit in with the plodding interpretation of the rules by the HQ who would only allow short unpaid leave periods. As a result we lost good staff members who simply resigned to spend a few months with their families, and were subsequently picked up by other organizations who were more flexible. We were then forced to go through the long and unsatisfactory recruitment process and were usually not able to replace them before the next round of elections, so we ended up short staffed.

Another example can be taken from the procedures required to deal with cases of poor performance, discipline and dismissal. Even in the most extreme cases the most that can be done is to send the staff member home on full pay while the case is investigated and a recommendation sent to HQ for "further guidance". The outcome of a great majority of cases sent through this procedure is simply no response while the staff member remains at work or on full pay. Most such cases simply pass into oblivion until the mission is finally shut down after several years.

A final note on this point. In addition to more real autonomy for DPKO and the field missions, real reform is required. There have been many attempts to reform the UN and Peacekeeping, all of which seem to concentrate on the highest or global level. What is sorely needed is a grass roots, down in the weeds reform of administrative rules and polices and it must include representatives of people from all levels in the field as well as HQ. Meaningful reform must take into account the ideas of those who actually work with these rules and policies at all levels. Not just a few high flying Directors who perhaps mean well, but those who actually have to apply the policies and procedures on a daily basis. They really are smart enough to know what works and what does not.

Declining Quality of Recruits: The UN, or at least Peacekeeping has also suffered in terms of the quality of recruits it is able to attract. This can be quickly seen by looking at the levels of professional experience required for recruits over the years and how they have been watered down. For example when I joined in 1993, the advertised minimum requirements for a P-3 Officer (with the professional range being P-1 to P-5) was a Masters Degree and 10 to 12 years of directly relevant professional experience. Today the professional experience requirement for the P-3 has dropped to five years. To put it another way, someone who was hired as a P-3 with no UN experience then, would qualify as a P-5 if hired today, one step below the level of Director. I have seen cases where even such watered down requirements are ignored, but it would not be appropriate to discuss particulars of individual cases. They can be found by an audit if necessary.

However, there are other important factors that have contributed to the general decline in the quality of recruits. First, the rapid and sustained growth in UN peacekeeping worldwide would have placed considerable strain on the recruitment pool even under normal conditions. In addition, there has been a similar growth in other government agencies and NGO's (non government organizations) working in international peacekeeping, and they also draw from the same general pool of candidates. Finally, the UN used to be the preferred employer; they usually paid the best and were in many instances the only game in town. That is no longer the case as other organizations have become increasingly more competitive, both in terms of salaries and benefits, but also (and perhaps more importantly) in the administration of more employee oriented rules and policies. There is greater competition for candidates, worldwide.

Needless and Ineffective Layers of Administrative Oversight: It would be easy to just blame the general decline of quality on poor administration and bad recruitment practices on the part of DPKO, and this is partly the case. However, frequently the problem rests not with the peacekeeping arm of the UN, rather with the larger parent organization. For example after a hiatus of over two years from the UN I returned to take up a short term assignment. When I left at the end of 2007 the general trend in recruitment was to delegate more responsibilities to the field missions, in an effort to speed up the extremely slow rate that recruits were brought on board and it was beginning to take effect. When I returned in the Spring of 2010, I was shocked to learn that the General Assembly had set up a series of final review panels in New York (the Field Central Review Boards) to review and pass on each and every case of recruitment carried out in DPKO. As a result, in the mission I returned to the vacancy rate for international staff had more than doubled. The work on many recruitment cases had been completed in the mission, which in theory had been designated the authority to do their own recruitment, but had now languished before the HQ panels in many cases for nearly six months. While these panels were appointed in the name of transparency (no one trusts anybody) all it accomplished was to add yet another hurdle and had completely stalled what recruitment of international staff had been taking place. A review of administrative procedures would certainly reveal that this practice of one step forward and one and one half steps backward has been the practice in the UN and particularly within DPKO rather than the exception.

Clearly the United Nations faces many challenges, some unique to that organization but many are simply self inflected.

Chapter 43: The Benefits, Why it is worth it

So in spite of these unique, and often times self inflected challenges, I maintain that United Nations Peacekeeping as an organization is no worse than many private organizations or governments. But to merit our continued support there must be more than that. What else is there to recommend it?

Coalition Building: First, each country in the world is allowed, and should be allowed to pursue its own foreign policy. However, history has clearly shown there are many instances when one country, no matter how powerful cannot achieve its foreign policy goals alone. For example the US has been most successful when it has worked in a collation with other like minded allies. Perhaps the most successful period of American foreign policy was that exercised during and right after World War Two. I know this is ancient history to many, but America's diplomatic and development achievements during that period were little short of amazing and stand out in any review of American history.

During that period, powerful countries that had been complete and total enemies, and who were utterly destroyed in war, were converted into allies with dynamic peaceful democracies and strong economies. This could not have been accomplished by the US alone, but only as the leader of a strong alliance of nations. Similarly we were successful in facing down the once powerful Soviet Union because we acted in alliance with other nations, even though we frequently did not agree with them on major issues (reference our frequent spats with France for example). But by playing an active, positive and dynamic role in the UN, the US has shown that it is capable of taking an intelligent and long rang view, which has consistently strengthened its leadership position with the other members of these alliances.

The Changing Nature of Warfare : The wars we are fighting today, and probably will fight into the foreseeable future are far different than the well defined wars of the first half of the twentieth century. While we may again fight major wars with well defined enemies who are courteous enough to remain within well defined nation states, and meet us head to head on the battle field, that certainly is not the case now. Today's enemy, since it is not closely defined in terms of a nation state, is only loosely defined and moves freely from country to country, from failed state to failed state or even territory to territory. Look how easily the central focus of Al-Quida has moved from Somalia, to Sudan, to Pakistan/Afghanistan, to Iraq, back to Pakistan/Afghanistan and is now quite likely shifting back to Somalia and Yemen.

This enemy cannot be defeated decisively, once and for all at some famous battle, after which we sign a treaty with them and they elect a democratic government and we all go home. The wars of today are protracted and involve civilian populations as much or more than they do enemy combatants or soldiers. Since we cannot easily find and engage the enemy, in effect the only way to win these dammed messy wars (besides making sure our own diplomatic goals are well defined and on target before we even engage) is to take away the support, or the indifference such groups are able to gain from the civilian base where they are operating. A base that more and more exists in failed states, ungoverned tribal areas and the like.

War as a Cultural Phenomena:

Wars have always had a cultural element but have traditionally been viewed as springing from essentially political or economic root causes. However, most of the situations I have been involved in could only be understood if viewed in a more holistic way. To be more specific, most peacekeeping operations take place in areas where ethnic and tribal conflicts are present. Conflict in such situations is as much culture driven as economic and political, in fact some would say more. To state it in another way the cultural element has always been present in warfare, but in the past it was usually the economic or political agenda that was seen as the most important cause. When an enemy was defeated they were made to pay a tax or perhaps their territory was annexed, usually under loose administrative control. They were seldom forced to adopt the culture of the victor. However, the objective of much warfare today seems to be to either eliminate the other side outright or to force changes in their core culture, more so than simply enacting ones own political or economic agenda.

We know that sustained political or economic change, and certainly cultural change, is very protracted (long and drawn out) and such change is frequently effected over a period of years or even decades not just months. No one country, even a superpower is willing to or can afford to commit it's self to such a protracted effort (although seven years in Iraq and ten years in Afghanistan is longer than one might have expected possible for American political will). Furthermore, even if it does undertake such a commitment it is far less likely to succeed if it insists on going it alone. For example, it is conceivable that Sudan might eventually change as a result of diplomatic and economic pressures applied by the US, China or any one country alone. But it is much more likely to react positively to a broad coalition which includes representatives of other African states as well. The world has such a body already, and the most direct way to use it is to support UN Peacekeeping as part of the overall approach.

How Terrorists Succeed: But why do people support or even allow groups such as the Taliban, Al-Quida, and the like to operate in their territory? There is probably no one reason, but there are certainly some common themes. Besides suffering from governments that are inefficient and at best indifferent, most of the people in these areas have been shut out of the world economy or worse yet have been exploited by it. For most of them, getting rid of government corruption or joining the larger world seems about as remote as going to the moon, let alone just making a decent living, getting education for their children or even basic medical care for themselves and their family.

In the past this may not have caused much problem as such people were basically isolated and powerless. Such areas only posed a problem if you were unfortunate enough to share a common border with them, or if they had resources the rest of the world needed. But relative isolation has become a thing of the past.

Today, no matter where you go you find cell phones and lap tops, and even these are rapidly being replaced by computer-phones such as iPods, blackberries and the like. I recall being absolutely fascinated one time while driving down a rutted dirt track in western Ethiopia, seeing a man clad in a dusty white robe and sandals with a long walking stick, following a small herd of cattle while talking on a mobil phone. When I asked him through an interpreter who he was talking to, he explained how he was going to sell his cattle in the next town and was checking on the price of cattle in other locations. He was doing market research. Similarly, people in remotest parts of the world now have much the same access to BBC, CNN and Al Jazeera that a person in Tokyo or Idaho does, and don't kid yourself they are looking and listening. They are becoming very aware that they are at a relative disadvantage, essentially shut out and one common reaction to being shut out is hatred and despair. In such situations if someone offers some hope, even if it is false hope it is not surprising that it is snatched up. Terrorists and extremist groups everywhere are experts at playing on fear, hatred and despair. Frequently they seem to offer the only alternative to the desperate state of reality faced by many.

Providing Basic Security and Justice: Aside from relative economic hardship, one of the most compelling problems residents in such areas face is that of basic security and justice. In Somalia for example, one of the biggest problems refugees faced when they tried to move back into their homes was securing their home and property. It had usually been occupied by armed groups who were unwilling to move, and there was no legal or court system to appeal to. The only real alternative was to fight to regain ones house and property, which just perpetuated the state of chaos.

As the state fails, or worse yet turns on it's own population such as in Darfur, security and justice are among the first casualties. I know from experience there is nothing more disturbing and destructive than living in chaos and in these circumstances if some group offers an alternative it usually looks better than reality. The Taliban used exactly this road to power in southern and eastern Afghanistan. To oversimplify, society had broken down into warring factions and the rule of the gun after the Soviets had been pushed out, and when the Taliban came into an area they at least offered some predictability and order. Even if it was harsh and inhumane, in the absence of anything else they took it.

Access to Failed States and Troubled Areas: These areas, even though they may seem like desolate wastelands to many outsiders still fall within somebody's sphere of influence, it is in somebody's neighborhood and they are not too anxious to see outsiders come in. This is especially so if the outsiders represent one dominate culture or world power, even if it has good intentions. We need to understand that cultures can be overwhelmed, and it is only natural that not everyone wants to ware blue jeans and eat burgers and fries. Or looking into the future, perhaps to ware a Mao jacket and eat dim sum.

People should not have to give up their identity and their dignity in order to enjoy the benefits of stability and participate in the world economy. This is much less likely to happen if the assistance comes in the form of a multinational force which does not represent just one culture or one nation, rather from a group that is predisposed to see other cultures and other ways of living as normal and even dignified. The presence of outsiders, such as peacekeepers, will always be resented by some but if it is represented by various cultures working together, it is more likely to be accepted by most as less threatening. To state it clearly, peacekeeping is best done by a mixed international body, not by a single national body.

A Question of Time: Many of the issues and situations that require the intervention of peacekeepers are very complex, usually with a long and tangled history that only slowly yields to the light of knowledge. It is not at all unusual for these matters to take years, even generations to reach a conclusion, or in some cases just to reach a degree of stability. In this equation time is one of the most important elements; time to let the feelings subside, to let the sides make the slow but necessary changes that may allow future generations to reach a solution. This may be strange to the western and especially American mind that wants immediate solutions, and perhaps this "need for speed" has bedeviled US diplomacy in the last few decades. But history abounds in examples of very difficult problems taking years or generations to play out. Northern Ireland, East and West Germany, the division of Cyprus into Turkish and Greek sides of the island come to mind.

Another complication is that many of these situations have roots that go back generations or even centuries and a settlement on one level may not have the desired effect on the deeper root causes. One example that comes to mind is the problem between north and south Sudan. Even aside from the Muslim-Christian issue, even aside from the Khartoum-Juba matter, even if the oil money is split 50/50 down the middle, the problem has deeper roots. In Abyei it also involves Dinka and Misseryia tribal relations. Now to be honest, they did coexist relatively peacefully for many hundreds of years and no doubt could again, but feelings of real distrust have been created and spread between them by the recent wars and it may take years for the former relationships to reemerge.

In practical terms this means the presence of some kind of peacekeeping efforts, if not actual UN Peacekeeping operations, for a long time. Again, no one country is capable of sustaining such a long range effort, either economically or politically. It is best done by a shared long term peacekeeping effort in which UN Peacekeeping can and should play a central role.

*

In the mere sixty plus years since the founding of the UN and its Peacekeeping arm, the world has changed dramatically and fundamentally. Organizations all over the world, be they private, religious or governmental are struggling just to keep up with rapid changes in all areas technological and perhaps more importantly in social attitudes. Historically speaking, at the very least we are heading into an era when one culture, one economy and one military can no longer dominate the world as in the recent past. Those days are over, if they ever truly existed, and success more and more depends on the ability to organize and maintain coalitions on a cross-cultural, larger and more complex level than ever before. As flawed as it is, the United Nations presently offers the only real opportunity for all cultures and states, from wealthy and powerful to poor and emerging to participate in meaningful dialog and action. If we overlook the United Nations and in particular Peacekeeping in these efforts, we do so at our own risk.

Chapter 44: The Day the Music Died

Fast forward if you will to the year 2060, fifty years from today. China, as expected is the largest economy in the world but by less than expected. Inherent problems in their labor sector, once hidden by seemingly endless economic growth have surfaced. In addition, competition and resistance has grown to their increased demands on the worlds resources. The wheels turn more slowly and with more resistance. Meanwhile the US has again reinvented and revitalized itself and thanks to its continued draw of immigrant populations and innovative higher educational system has remained the strong second economy of the world. China and the US are the only true superpowers, followed by an array of regional powers. The world is indeed a different place but not the living hell many would have predicted.

It is a winter morning as you sit in your favorite Starbucks sipping a latté. You flip on the hologram screen of your wrist computer and check your personalized news source. Half way through the index of stories a short piece entitled "UN Still Has Some Role in Peacekeeping" catches your attention. It relates how the UN (read DPKO) was relegated to a support role in peacekeeping some years ago, in favor of a conglomeration of regional groups, NGO's and special commissions that stepped up to take its place. The demand for peacekeeping is more active now than ever before but it is carried out by ad hoc groups tailored to the needs of a particular region or set of circumstances. They reflect the groups and organizations that have a vested interest in the given problem or the geographic area in question. This has proven to be both a strength and a weakness. The UN is still involved but mostly through its various agencies and commissions.

The General Assembly still echoes with debate but as for peacekeeping, any action on its part is limited to advice and guidance given to its commissions and agencies. The UN Peacekeeper is for the most part an odd bit of history.

*

What happened? How did the once powerful mammoth succumb. Was it due to the realignment of north south member states in the UN? Was it the result of political blunders and misguided decisions that lead to a lack of confidence and the withdrawal of support worldwide? Perhaps it was the inability to actually solve once and for all the complex diplomatic, civil and social issues faced by peacekeeping operations. No. To be honest most people do not really expect these matters to be solved quickly or easily and are content with some progress even if it is slow. Besides, there really is no definitive way to actually measure progress in the substantive area so any progress is hailed as good. We count the number of weapons recycled, the number of food packets distributed and the areas we have cleared of mines.

Nothing so dramatic or easy to pinpoint would explain this catastrophic failure. It was a lingering death that took place day to day over a period of years, the way that an infection while small at first, untreated grows into a major problem and eventually brings down even the largest beast.

In this case the cause of death was the inability of the organization to regulate it's self administratively; to take the necessary administrative decisions and actions needed to make essential adjustments. DPKO administrators, very aware of the problem attempted on numerous occasions to correct things, but were subjected to an endless seizure of administrative centralization on the part of the larger parent organization and simply unable to do enough. As this archaic outdated approach was left unchecked and in fact became the standard operating procedure, DPKO became more mired and bogged down in layers of irrelevant and ultimately self destructive procedures. This growing mass of endless administrative delays, of mandated committee reviews followed by panel reviews followed by appeal, slowly built up until finally nothing was ever allowed to happen. No decisions implemented, no actions taken. In a state of rigor, the organization could not maintain itself and in a rapidly moving world it became irrelevant. The critical vacuum was filled by smaller more autonomous and effective organizations. Once those organizations learned to work together and gained the begrudging recognition and approval of UN member states, gained the authority to act if you will, they had the clear edge and the end of UN Peacekeeping as a viable organization followed rapidly.

Far fetched, even impossible you say. Let me offer a few examples of just how far this administrative paralyses has already advanced. Examples could be taken from any of the administrative areas but I will limit myself to those of which I have the most knowledge.

*

The life blood of any organization is ultimately its people, that is to say the staff coming into the organization. They are in fact the only real source of ideas, of energy and vitality it has. In this regard DPKO is chocking itself to death. It is quite literally tightening the noose around its own neck. Over the nearly twenty years I have been in DPKO I have seen the UN add layer after layer, procedure after procedure to the process of recruitment. The most recent, as I have mentioned before is the addition of a series of review panels mandated at the headquarters level and forced on DPKO, to review every detail of every case of recruitment for international staff. All of this after each case has already gone through the usual exhaustive procedure conducted by Human Resources. As a result literally months have been added to the already snails pace of recruitment, and the overall level of vacancies among international posts worldwide has risen I would estimate by an additional twenty percent or more.

Recently, a private organization that monitors the UN obtained a copy of a leaked memo from the SRSG (head of the mission) of a very large and high profile mission in Central Asia. He took the highly unusual step of issuing a direct and dire warning to the Security Council that if the backlog of recruitment of international staff was not lowered immediately his entire organization was in absolute danger of failing to meet its mandate. Likewise, in the case of a major African mission, there was recently a six month period in which essentially no new international staff members were recruited, although more than fifty recruitment cases for that mission were pending in HQ. Month after month went by with no feedback and no action taken. During that same time various staff members were transferred in from other missions but with roughly an equal number sent out to other missions. Thus there was some shuffling of staff from mission to mission but no new staff members were brought in. One is reminded of the sardonic saying "shuffling the deck chairs on the Titanic" to describe futile panic like actions taken during an emergency. Actions that completely miss the mark. Given that this same state of affairs exists to some degree in all missions it seems clear that the vital flow of new staff has been chocked off. What would happen to any organization that did this to itself?

Now let us assume that a few recruits do get through. Let us look at them. To be honest they are simply not what they used to be. As mentioned before, DPKO is in a real competition with other organizations for the same recruits and I believe it is losing the competition. During a recent six month period in a major mission I personally saw six senior mid level staff resign, all of whom had excellent work reviews and were very badly needed. These are the staff members who are actually implementing programs in the field, on the front line if you will. Four left for other organizations such as the European Union and USAID while two (who were both in mid career) simply resigned to go home and reassess their options. They saw no future in peacekeeping. During that period not one new international recruit was brought in. A few cases of "staff shuffling" but nothing more. It is clear we are losing them much faster than we can recruit them.

To make up for this recruitment gap over the years DPKO has resorted to other, sometimes desperate measures. First, as I mentioned in an earlier section, the minimum requirements for new recruits have fallen dramatically. To compound this, many of the few recruits who do make it through are being pushed into higher categories to encourage them to accept the appointment. As a result many new staff are coming in with no DPKO experience and far fewer qualifications than existing staff, but at much higher levels. It rankles one to be supervised by someone with worse qualifications, less managerial experience and no knowledge of the organization.

Second, and perhaps more detrimental in the long run is the tendency to recruit national staff (staff members from the local area who are hired locally) from one mission simply to fill international posts in another mission. Traditionally international staff have been of the highest caliber and considered as experts in their field. There is absolutely no problem with this practice of recruiting national staff into the international levels if the national staff member is truly of the caliber of an international staff member, in fact many senior international staff members started their careers as national staff members. The problem is that there is such a dire need for staff that many of the national staff that are being recruited as international today do not meet these more stringent requirements. Many may have specific knowledge of a particular area within their discipline but do not have the experience nor the depth and breathe of knowledge that one expects of international staff. In addition, many simply do not adequately speak one of the official UN languages (English or French) making communication, training and management nearly an impossible process.

I will give one more example in the staffing area. There is no formal or recognized procedure to identify and develop talent within DPKO. As a result promotion is accomplished primarily through ones social networks and through ones work connections. In the absence of an objective and organized system to develop and promote talent it is the socially connected, but who are frequently not the best managers nor the most knowledgeable, who win out and get the promotions. Are you connected is the true test of success. Very frequently the best and most qualified get overlooked or simply pushed aside year after year and the organization suffers as a result.

Any organization that cannot identify and recruit the best and the brightest, or at least the good and the adequate and that takes no serious steps to identify, train and promote it's best employees is destined to go in one direction only.

*

Let me turn briefly to another area which sadly illustrates again our inability to deal with basic administrative requirements; that of staff conduct and discipline. You may recall in an earlier section I related how I nearly got into trouble when I refused to extend the contract of a local staff driver who after getting drunk, hijacked a UN vehicle and nearly ran over a security guard. The procedure I was supposed to follow was to order a full investigation of the matter, forward the case to the Office of Human

Resource Management in HQ for their review and decision, and put the man on fully paid leave while they considered the case. That is still the procedure and I can tell you it simply does not work. Never did and never will. It is as if the General Manager of a Giant Wall Mart store was unable to terminate a cleaner who had the habit of getting drunk, taking his mop and hitting colleagues over the head. All this with several witnesses looking on. The manager would of course be expected to follow proper procedure but not to have to send the case directly to Wall Mart World Headquarters and wait months to years for a decision while the staff member continued to draw full pay.

A more recent case from my last mission assignment concerned one of my staff whom I had suspected of many things but could never prove anything. Shortly after I left that particular mission he was finally caught selling jobs (taking bribes to be sure recruitment papers weren't lost), and when confronted with that grabbed his supervisor by the arm and with several witnesses present threatened to beat her, or worse. An investigation ensued during which he confessed to selling jobs. All the required paperwork was sent to the black hole in HQ. Two and one half years later I happened to be back in the same mission and who should greet me as if I were a long lost brother than he. Enraged that he was still there I followed up on his case. Indeed the investigation report and all necessary documentation, along with his confession had been properly sent in but never any response. Eventually the case was simply forgotten.

I have gone into such detail not to put anyone or the organization in a bad light. It should be clear that I have great respect for both and am very grateful for the opportunity to have the career I have had. I do this only because it is necessary, even vital to point out the failure of the organization to allow DPKO to respond in a meaningful way to what are essentially administrative issues. And again I might take a different view if over the past years one had seen some progress in this regard. However the actions taken have only had the effect of twisting tighter and tighter the knot of centralization through the addition of more layers of review, more committees and panels, and the creation of entire new units and sections to review the reviews of the other reviewers. It long ago reached the point that there is only painfully slow movement or simply no movement at all on many administrative matters, in all areas.

This in turn results in the inability of administrators and managers to make decisions and react in a timely manner to the many challenges they all face. As the situation drags on month after month, year after year, all the constant rearranging of the deck chairs on the sinking ship does nothing more than give people the false hope that something is being done.

This then is the biggest problem facing UN Peacekeeping. This is the thing that unless addressed will sooner rather than later grind it to a halt and render it unable to respond to the increasing demands placed on it; that will render it irrelevant. And when that happens, something or somebody always arises to fill the void. Ask General Motors, the giant that many said could never fail. The real question is then, like General Motors, will UN Peacekeeping be allowed to reinvent itself. Will it manage to take control of its own administration and remain a relevant organization? If it continues on its current path, which if one takes a historical view is most likely to occur, it seems unlikely. In that case the world will either loose a valuable organization, or if it does continue it will be as an inefficient one that is never allowed to make the full contribution it is capable of making.

After serving with the Peace Corps in South America, the author completed a graduate degree in Social Anthropology and taught university for more than a decade before changing careers to study Administration. Based on his international background and experience in labor relations and administration he was recruited by the United Nations in 1993. With short breaks to serve in the Middle East as the Country Director of an NGO and with USAID, he went on to serve with the U.N. in high profile and hazardous peacekeeping missions in Somalia, Iraq, Afghanistan and Sudan until 2010.

The author lives on the Chesapeake Bay near Annapolis with his wife, whose career also includes international appointments in the Persian Gulf and in Washington DC.